A Dance with Death

A Dance with Death

Canadian Women
On the Gallows
1754–1954

Frank W. Anderson

FIFTH
HOUSE
PUBLISHERS

SASKATOON
& CALGARY

Cover photograph of Florence Lassandro reproduced courtesy estate of Carmen Picariello
Cover design by NEXT Communications Inc.

The publisher gratefully acknowledges the support received from The Canada Council and the Department of Canadian Heritage.

Printed in Canada by Webcom Limited, Toronto
96 97 98 99 00 / 5 4 3 2 1

Editor's note: This book differs from our usual house style and reflects the author's preference in retaining much of the uppercase usage found in the original documents upon which he based his research.

Canadian Cataloguing in Publication Data
Anderson, Frank W., 1919–

A dance with death
ISBN 1-895618-82-7

1. Female offenders – Canada – Biography.
2. Hanging – Canada – History. I. Title.

HV6805.A52 1996   364.6'6'092271   C96–920076–5

FIFTH HOUSE LTD.
#201 – 165 – 3rd Avenue S
Saskatoon SK Canada S7K 1L8

#9 – 6125 – 11th Street SE
Calgary AB Canada T2H 2L6

Contents

The Poisoners

Murder for Profit

The Strange Ones

Love Triangles

Death by Gunshot

Child Victims

Pot-Pourri

Preface

S OMEWHERE IN THE CROWDED ARCHIVES of a European library is recorded the name of the first woman to be hanged in Canada. It is probably noted in the report of a long forgotten governor of New France as an interesting footnote to colonial life, or included in a letter home from a resident of Newfoundland, New France, or the Maritimes, where settlers first established a toe-hold in the New World. Perhaps a Canadian historian will eventually come across that notation and include it in a yet-to-be-written account of early Canadian society, but it is doubtful that there will be a story to go with it. Life was cheap in those days, and the fate of some poor wretch who strangled to death on a short rope attached to a rough wooden beam was of little importance.

Throughout the sad history of capital punishment in Canada, more than a hundred women have heard the sombre sentence of death passed against them. Their crimes have ranged from simple theft in colonial times to murder in the present century. In selecting these cases, which span the period from 1754 to 1954, I have used two major criteria.

The first is the nature of the offence. While at one time more than 150 crimes called for the noose, the only ones that are consistent throughout the two-hundred-year span are murder and treason. Since no woman has ever been convicted of treason in Canada, the focus is therefore upon murder, but even the definition of murder has undergone modification over the years; until 1948 it included a category of homicide known as *infanticide,* the killing of a newborn child by its mother. While our legal system now deals separately with this, it was classed as murder for many years. Likewise, some early murders were classed as *petit treason* or the slaying of a husband by his wife.

The second criterion arises from the nature of our appeal system. Previous to 1891, when a woman was found guilty of murder at her first trial and had the original conviction set aside, no new trial was ordered but a pardon was granted. After the Criminal Code was revised in 1891, new trials were ordered, as in the instance of Olive Sternaman. Having been convicted of the August 1896 arsenic poisoning of her husand, George, Sternaman was sentenced to be executed at Cayuga, Ontario, on January 20, 1898. Three days before she was to walk up the gallows' steps, David Mills, Minister of Justice, ordered a new trial. It was the first time this provision in the new Criminal Code was used. Since she was subsequently acquitted at a second trial, her case and those of other women who underwent the same ordeal, have been screened out.

The forty-nine cases included here constitute 95 percent of all women from colonial times to the present who fall into these categories. They are those who have exhausted all avenues of legal appeal and whose ultimate fate has depended upon the decision of a colonial governor or a modern governor-general acting for the Crown upon the advice of the cabinet. In thirty-one instances, the Royal Prerogative of Mercy was exercised and the death sentences were commuted to life imprisonment or a lesser term. In eighteen others the verdict of the court was not interfered with and the women expiated their crimes on the gallows.

While many of the colonial records have been destroyed by fire, flood, and neglect, an effort has been made wherever possible to seek out primary sources such as trial records. Capital Case Files were established in Canada in 1867 and from the records contained therein civil servants made recommendations to the Canadian government regarding the fate of convicted persons. These are invaluable to the modern researcher and have been studied extensively in the preparation of this account.

Acknowledgements

*E*VERY RESEARCHER owes an enormous debt of gratitude to the many people who take time out to lend a helping hand. Much as one would like to proffer a grateful handshake and a smile of thanks in person, the written word is often the most effective method of expressing appreciation to a large number of people. In lieu of a more gracious gesture, therefore, we would like to say thanks to:

Don Morris, Provincial Archives, St. John's, Nfld.; Ian R. McIntosh, Cape Breton Regional Library, Sydney, N.S.; Lynne Cuthbert, Newfoundland Public Library Services, St. John's; Ellen Green, Reference Department, Sarnia Public Library, Ont.; Marie Baboyant, Montreal Public Library, P.Q.; W. Eisenbichler, Sault Ste. Marie Public Library, Ont.; Marilyn Bell, Public Archives, Charlottetown, P.E.I.; Margaret Hardie, Sudbury Public Library, Ont.; Ken Favrholdt, Kamloops Archives, B.C.; Jean-Claude Arcand, Edmundston Public Library, N.B.; Jeri Miltenberger, Mary Kaeser Library, Fort Smith, N.W.T.; Margaret Houghton, Special Collections, Hamilton Public Library, Ont.; A. Yetman, superintendent, H.M. Penitentiary, St. John's, Nfld.; George Caron, former warden, Prison for Women, Kingston, Ont.; Jack Fitzgerald, St. John's, Nfld.; and the staff of the Harriet Irving Library at Fredericton, N.B.

A special note of thanks to James M. Whalen, archivist, and to Sylvia McKenzie, Access Section, National Archives, Ottawa, for their patience and understanding during my hectic visits with them.

All quotes, unless otherwise noted, are from the trial transcripts of each individual case or from official notes and letters contained in the Capital Case files, National Archives, Ottawa.

Finally to my wife, Edna, who has patiently abided my selfish and total absorption with this project; and to Nora Russell of Fifth House, who has tolerantly and carefully corrected my mistakes, offered hundreds of valuable suggestions, and gently banged my knuckles when required, what can I say? How lucky can I get.

To our granddaughters Stephanie and Taylor

The Poisoners

The deliberate and premeditated murder of a human being by poison requires the shutting out of all moral principles for a long period of time. There are usually many places along the path where the potential murderer may step aside and abandon the deadly scheme. There are thus many elements of the serial killer to be found in the poisoner, for the latter must usually administer several doses to the victim, never knowing which will be the fatal potion. It is the killing of the same individual several times, rather than the slaughter of several people once. Thus it is always difficult to understand or accept. Of the forty-nine female killers whose deeds are outlined here, seven used this method.

Sophie Boisclair
Strychnine Cocktails

*T*HE FIRST WOMAN IN CANADA known to have used poison as her weapon was Sophie Boisclair, thirty-eight, of the parish of St. Zephirin in Quebec. She was married to François Joutras, but according to a common French-Canadian custom of the time she was known by her maiden name.

Lying about twenty kilometres (twelve miles) north of Drummondville, St. Zephirin was noted for its forests, ponds, and small lakes. Its chief industry in the 1860s was lumbering, and its sparse population was scattered in hamlets and small farms throughout the woodlands. Among the residents of the parish were Modiste

Villebrun (more commonly known as Modiste Provencher) and François Xavier Joutras. Both men were woodcutters, both were married, and both were childless. They had one other thing in common. Modiste Provencher and Sophie Boisclair, wife of François Joutras, were lovers.

The onset of the relationship is not known, for both partners were discreet, but their secret was out on October 31, 1866, when they were seen together at a hotel in Sorel. Events moved swiftly after that.

Two days later, on the evening of November 2, Modiste Provencher brought his wife to visit with François Joutras and Sophie Boisclair. The get-together proceeded pleasantly with no outward show of discord, and as the Provenchers prepared to leave, Sophie offered Mrs. Provencher a drink of whisky to fortify her against the chill of the cutter ride home. Three nights later, Mrs. Provencher died. Strangely, though she had always been in good health, no inquest was conducted and no autopsy performed. Her death was ascribed to natural causes and she was buried in the local cemetery.

François Joutras and Modiste Provencher had always been good friends, and when Sophie suggested that Modiste should move in with them after his wife's death—to save money—François readily agreed. Though tongues wagged in the district, he saw nothing unusual in the arrangement.

The trio soon settled into a regular routine. Both men were frequently away in the woods, cutting trees, but sometimes one of them remained at home to take care of the chores around the cabin and yard. Occasionally, one of them went to Sorel or Trois Rivières for groceries and supplies. On one of these trips, in mid-December, Modiste Provencher obtained strychnine from a Sorel doctor, explaining that he needed it to poison foxes, which were common pests in St. Zephirin parish.

On Saturday, December 22, Joutras and Provencher left the cabin around nine in the morning to cut trees a few kilometres distant. Before they left, Sophie prepared lunches for them and included a flask of home-made whisky. At noon, Provencher was careful to drink only tea while his companion tipped the flask. Joutras complained that the whisky had an odd taste but, being poor, he was accustomed to second-grade liquor. Immediately after dinner, Provencher excused himself to attend to some errand and left Joutras to finish the daily quota of logs.

A short time later, experiencing severe stomach pains and

spasms, Joutras made his way to the cabin of Michael Cajoulette, where he collapsed. Messengers were sent to St. Zephirin for Dr. Ladouceur and Sophie, who arrived around three in the afternoon.

Expressing the opinion that Joutras was suffering from strychnine poisoning, Dr. Ladouceur questioned Sophie, who told him that she had been using the poison to kill some foxes that were after her chickens. It was assumed that some of this had accidentally gotten into her husband's lunch. After cautioning her on the use of the toxin, Dr. Ladouceur gave her instructions on how to care for her sick spouse and helped carry the stricken man to a sleigh for transport home. He assured her that all would be well.

François's health did not improve under his wife's care, and on December 24 the parish priest was called to give the last rites. Christmas Eve was a sombre one at the cabin with death so imminent, but then, miraculously, François began to recover. By Christmas Day, he was on his feet again.

The murderous pair wasted little time resuming their attack. On December 30, Provencher drove to Trois Rivières and bought more strychnine from a Dr. Giroux. At the same time, Sophie obtained some morphine from Dr. Ladouceur to ease her husband's pain. The next day, New Year's Eve, François himself returned the morphine to the doctor, saying it was no longer needed. He explained that his wife was giving him whisky with some additives their friend Modiste had brought back from Trois Rivières.

Towards seven that evening a neighbour, making late New Year's Eve social calls, stopped by and found that Joutras had taken to his bed again. Joutras said that his wife had been giving him some special medicine in his whisky but that it was not helping. In fact, he claimed, he had been feeling quite well until he tried this mixture.

After the visitor left, Joutras's condition worsened and towards eleven o'clock he asked his wife to call a doctor. Instead of going for Dr. Ladouceur, however, Sophie went to the home of the neighbour who had been visiting earlier and brought him to the cabin. When François saw them, he seemed to suspect for the first time that he was being murdered. "You did not go for the doctor," he accused. She did not reply.

When the medical man finally arrived, he found that his patient was already dead. He was told that Joutras had been well until supper but had taken ill immediately afterwards. Later in the evening, his wife had fed him some soup, but that only seemed to aggravate the problem and he had died shortly after midnight.

When he again detected signs of strychnine poisoning, the doctor called for an inquest to be held the next day, New Year's.

An idea of the crude state in which forensic medicine was practised in the backwoods in those days can be obtained from noting the conditions under which the medical examination was carried out. Dr. Ladouceur returned to the Joutras home the next day to find a constant stream of neighbours passing through the kitchen to pay their last respects to the 120-pound man who was laid out on the table. Under these conditions, he proceeded as best he could.

A closer examination convinced him that the cause of death was strychnine poisining and he cut open the body under the curious stares of several visitors. Removing the stomach and intestines, he discovered he did not have any glass jars, so he borrowed some clean plates from Sophie and placed the organs on these. They sat in open view on the kitchen cupboard until he was ready to cover them with paper and carry them to his cutter. That completed, he sewed up the body and released it for burial.

An autopsy performed by Drs. Provost and Bruneau at Sorel on January 7 confirmed the presence of strychnine in the entrails, and the police were notified that murder had been committed. A canvas of doctors and pharmacists in Sorel and Trois Rivières indicated that both Sophie and Modiste had purchased this poison shortly before the deaths of Mrs. Provencher and François Joutras. On January 10, Narcisse Joutras, brother of the murdered man, found a white powder wrapped in paper in the attic of the Joutras home. When analysis showed it to be strychnine, the police moved. Both suspects were arrested on January 15, 1867.

Presented with the findings, the coroner's jury brought in a verdict of death by poison and accused both Sophie and Modiste of murdering Joutras. No action was taken on the suspicious death of Madame Provencher.

It was decided to try the accused separately, and on March 25 the trial of Modiste Provencher was opened before Mr. Justice Loranger. It lasted ten days, making it the longest in Sorel's history to that point, and most of the time was taken up with the examination and cross-examination of a series of medical experts for both sides. While those for the Crown contended that Joutras had been murdered by strychnine, those for the defence insisted that the symptoms described were not consistent with that poison, despite its proven presence in the man's stomach.

On April 6, Mr. Justice Loranger concluded a thirteen-hour charge to the jury, carefully sifting the mass of technical evidence. The jurors, who had sat patiently through days of medical wrangling, took a short five minutes to return a verdict of guilty. There was no recommendation to mercy. When asked to respond to the decision, he answered simply that he was not guilty. He was sentenced to be hanged on Friday, May 3.

With scarcely a pause in the proceedings, Judge Armstrong replaced his colleague on the bench and a new jury was empanelled. Sophie Joutras, née Boisclair, was put on trial for her life. Though greatly condensed at this hearing the medical evidence still extended over four days. When Judge Armstrong summed up on April 10, he left no doubt in the minds of the jurors that he considered the woman equally guilty, if not the instigator, of the foul plot that appeared to have taken two lives. The new jury quickly returned their verdict and like the first made no recommendation to mercy.

When asked to comment before sentence was passed, Sophie declared her innocence and added that she was pregnant. Court was immediately adjourned so that she might be examined and a probable date of birth estimated. Two days later, her condition was confirmed and her execution put ahead to November 20.

• • •

Sophie Boisclair was the last woman sentenced to death before Confederation, and though the country was in the final complex stages of passing from the old colonial regime to Confederation, the wheels of justice turned without a hitch. On May 3, 1867, Modiste Provencher was hanged at Sorel in view of an estimated ten thousand people who crowded onto the sloping lawn behind the prison. Sophie, whose death cell overlooked the scaffold, had to be dragged away from the window.

Following the birth of her child, which was later removed to an orphanage in Montreal, Sophie's case was reviewed by Mr. Cartier, Minister of Justice. "Considering that seven months would elapse since conviction," he wrote, "under the circumstances the death sentence should not be carried out." His recommendation was forwarded to Governor-General Viscount Monck and on November 12, 1867, His Excellency signed an Order in Council commuting her sentence to life. A few days later, the Royal Prerogative of Mercy was again exercised and her sentence altered to twenty years. Having served every day of that sentence, on April 11, 1887, she was released from Kingston Penitentiary. The warden concluded that she was then "of unsound mind but harmless and capable of attending to her own needs." She later died in poverty, thus ending Canada's first poison case.

. . .

Marie McGaugh
Poisoned Porridge

*T*HE SEVEN WOMEN who chose poison as their insidious method of murder accounted for at least twelve victims, and possibly thirteen. Of these, seven were children. The first child to die was Marie Clara De Villers, aged seven and a half months; her killer was twenty-nine-year-old Marie McGaugh.

Marie McGaugh was the daughter of John McGaugh of L'Isle Verte, a small village on the banks of the St. Lawrence River about twenty kilometres (twelve miles) northeast of Rivière-du-Loup, Quebec. She grew up with several strikes against her. She was not an attractive child and to this were added the burdens of deafness and limited mental ability. When she was about seven years old, her mother died and her father remarried. Her stepmother was a patient and understanding woman named Sophie Clarke. Sophie protected Marie as best she could, keeping her close to the family hearth, and although she managed to instil in her some ability to read simple words and phrases, writing was completely beyond Marie's capacity. In all, she struggled through a year and a half of schooling in her first twenty-two years of life.

In August 1870, Marie was taken as a maid by Charles De Villers and his wife, Marie Angele, who operated a small farm and trading store about halfway between L'Isle Verte and Rivière-du-Loup. Her main function was to babysit Marie Clara, their only child. Being a distant relative of the McGaughs, Mrs. De Villers knew well the limitations of her new maid and though from time to time the young woman pilfered small amounts of cash and trinkets from the store, she was otherwise well behaved and obedient. No one fussed over the minor items.

Although Marie had free run of the house and farm, there was one area of the store where she was forbidden to venture, a small alcove that contained a glass case in which were kept small amounts of rat poison such as phosphorus and arsenic. Strangely, this cupboard was never locked.

On Sunday, May 21, 1871, the baby, Marie Clara, took ill and had trouble keeping her pap down. She was also suffering from mild fits of convulsions, but Dr. Paul Granvois, the local physician, was not alarmed and prescribed some soothing medicine. As a precautionary measure, knowing that Marie McGaugh sometimes forgot things, Mrs. De Villers hired a neighbourhood girl, eleven-year-old Leopoldine Martin, to help her with the babysitting duties. Despite this additional assistance, however, Marie found that a good deal more of her time was taken up with caring for the sick child than she wished, and on the afternoon of May 25 she decided to do something about it.

While Mr. and Mrs. De Villers were preoccupied in the garden, Marie seized the opportunity to slip into the store and take a vial of phosphorus from the cabinet. Her companion, Leopoldine, was in and out of the kitchen a lot so Marie was able to break open the vial without discovery and secrete some in a kitchen drawer. She disposed of the rest by dropping it down the hole of the outdoor privy.

About six o'clock, she prepared the baby's formula as usual, but covered the bottom of the bowl with the granular phosphorus. As soon as the hot porridge was ladled in, it reacted with the phosphorus, giving off a vapour with the acrid smell of matches newly struck. Undaunted, she fed the baby several spoonfuls before it began to protest. At this moment, Leopoldine Martin came into the kitchen, and taking alarm at the child's screams, dashed into the garden and called Mrs. De Villers.

From the smell and look of the porridge, Mrs. De Villers immediately sensed what had happened and screamed: "It is you who have done this, you wretch!" Marie turned pale and retorted simply: "You ought not to say that." Claiming there was nothing wrong with the pap, she took a mouthful herself but quickly spat it out. She then went to her bedroom and remained there until the following morning.

Dr. Paul Granvois came and confirmed that the child had been poisoned with phosphorus. Though he drove at top speed in his horse and buggy into Rivière-du-Loup for an antidote, it was an hour and a half before he returned. The remedy was administered but it was too late; little Marie Clara died that night.

At the inquest held by Dr. Ludger Tetu on May 26, Marie McGaugh appeared calm and cool and continued to deny any involvement in the tragedy, maintaining that the mysterious illness that had struck the child the previous Sunday had resulted in her death. Nevertheless, the coroner's jury held her responsible.

The next day, Marie "told the truth" to Mrs. De Villers and a friend, Miss Helene Ely. She said she had been drinking that day. She cried frequently during the confession and lamented that "it was an evil idea which had occurred to her." She explained she had taken advantage of the time when the child was sick, hoping that everyone would believe it was the original illness that had caused her death.

The McGaugh trial was held before Mr. Justice Casault at Rivière-du-Loup from November 21 to 24, 1871. Most of the time was occupied with a series of witnesses for the defence to prove that the accused was very childlike and "did not converse like a reasonable person of her age." She was variously described as "silly" and "foolish," but of good conduct and reputation in the community. There was no hint of insanity.

His Lordship was unsatisfied with the evidence of the medical men for the Crown, who had concentrated entirely on the presence of phosphorus in the child's body and had neglected to ascertain the cause of the convulsions that had been going on for four days before the poison was administered. In his report to the Minister of Justice after the trial, he drew out this fact and expressed the opinion that the true cause of death was still in issue.

The jury found Marie McGaugh guilty on November 24, but added a strong recommendation to mercy. This sentiment was echoed by His Lordship as he sentenced her to be executed on January 9, 1872. A large petition calling attention to her limited abilities and previously good reputation in the community resulted in her sentence being commuted on January 1. Marie was taken to Kingston Penitentiary. After serving more than seven years, she was pardoned in September 1879 and placed in the custody of a married brother living near Rivière-du-Loup.

· · ·

Minnie McGee

And Then There Were None

*I*T IS DIFFICULT TO SAY whether the murders committed by diminutive Minnie McGee of St. Mary's Road in eastern Prince Edward Island should be listed under mass murders or serial killings.

Minnie was born in 1877, the first child of Thomas Cassidy, local constable and mailman of St. Mary's Road. Still little more than a child when her mother died, she found herself saddled with the upbringing of her brothers and sisters as well as all the household chores. She carried these duties cheerfully until her father remarried and another woman appeared on the scene.

At the age of twenty-one, Minnie married Patrick McGee, a gentle man four years her senior. Like many of his compatriots, he was unable to read or write and in some respects was more like a child than a dominant male. Having spent years mothering her own brothers and sisters, Marie had grown accustomed to being in command and took charge. Over the next fourteen years, nine children were born to them and all but one survived the rigours of childhood.

The McGees always tightroped along that imaginary line known as poverty, and while never in real want were never affluent. Patrick worked at various jobs in sawmills, on fishing boats, or in factories, which took him away from home most of the time, while Minnie looked after the home front. Although the children went to school sporadically, Minnie herself seldom ventured beyond the front gate of her property. She had the reputation of being fascinated with fire, and when a shed and then a haystack mysteriously burned in the district, mild suspicion fastened on her, though nothing was ever proven.

In late January 1912, an epidemic of whooping cough swept through St. Mary's Road and two of the McGee children died within a week. They were buried in the Sturgeon cemetery beside their sibling who had died in infancy. Minnie seemed greatly affected by their deaths. Normally a patient woman of even temper, she began to show bursts of unreasonable rage whenever thwarted or frustrated. Once when she tore a page out of a book to write a note, her husband remonstrated with her and she responded by flying into a frenzy and tearing the whole book to shreds. Always, however, she vented her fury on inanimate objects, never against her husband or children.

Over the next few months she became even more of a recluse, scarcely speaking to neighbours when they passed along the roadway. Unperturbed, they merely shrugged it off, commenting that "she wasn't herself after the children died." None, however, suspected what dark thoughts were going through her mind.

In early April 1912, Patrick McGee took a job in a factory some distance from home and left his wife alone with the six children. Minnie's terrible plot began to mature shortly after his departure. On Tuesday, April 9, she sent her oldest boy, Johnny, to a store for some candy and penny matches, the latter being the old-fashioned kind with phosphorus tips. A penny bought two boxes of fifty each.

That night, she cut off the phosphorus tips and soaked them in water, carefully burning the useless wooden stems in the pot-bellied stove. The deadly brew was ready the following day, and she disguised the smell and taste by mixing it with sugar, honey, and syrup.

Minnie had planned to administer the poison to all six children at supper that evening, but her scheme was disrupted when her brother, Ambroise Cassidy, borrowed her son Johnny, ten, to help around his farm. Thus, only five little people partook of the deadly mixture. By Thursday morning, all five were complaining of drowsiness and abdominal pains, but were still able to walk and move about the yard. Certain that her potion was working, Minnie sent her oldest daughter, Pansy, to the store for more matches. At the same time, she sent a message to her brother's farm, telling Johnny to come home. He, however, was still needed for chores and could not return. Undaunted, she administered another dose to the remaining five children.

Dr. J.D. McIntyre, one of two physicians in the district, was not called until Friday, and by the time he arrived three of the children had already died. Patrick McGee got home late that evening and he and another medical man, Dr. Roy Fraser, tried to save the remaining two children, but there was nothing they could do. The little ones died that night.

Judging from the symptoms displayed by all five children, Dr. Fraser was positive that they had been poisoned, but he did not suspect anything but an accident. It was well known that Minnie

McGee was a loving and careful mother. His investigation revealed that all five had eaten some fish and oatmeal. When he discovered that Mrs. McGee had eaten neither of these foods, he assumed that the source of the poison lay in one of these. Arrangements were made to bury the children and a next-door neighbour, Bernard McGuigan, began fashioning coffins for them.

On Saturday, while the funerals were being planned, Mrs. McGee went to her brother's farm and insisted that ten-year-old Johnny return with her.

The first to suspect anything was Thomas McCarron, a policeman who lived three kilometres (two miles) from the McGee farm. While attending the wake after the funerals, he observed Minnie looking at Johnny in a very peculiar way. "I knew then that she had killed them," he claimed later, "and I knew that she was going to kill Johnny next."

Engaging her in conversation, he said nothing of his suspicions but reported later that she talked vaguely of suicide and at times was irrational in her statements. Dr. Roy Fraser, who was present, noted Minnie's strange behaviour but ascribed it to the terrible shock she had just undergone. One moment she would claim that it was some candy that had poisoned her children, and a few moments later she would blame the fish or oatmeal.

Convinced that Minnie was a murderess, Constable McCarron conveyed his fears to Dr. Fraser, who, while reluctant to believe she could harm her brood, nevertheless contacted the Attorney General in Charlottetown and arranged to have one of the children exhumed. Recalling that two children had died in January, apparently from whooping cough, he also got permission to have them disinterred and examined.

Constable McCarron then paid a visit to Ambroise Cassidy, Minnie's brother, requesting that he take the last child, Johnny, and keep him away. Ambroise, however, was not convinced that the lad was in any danger and refused. He would hear no evil against his sister. Failing there, McCarron then appealed to a neighbour, Bernard McGuigan, to make some excuse to keep the boy away from his mother. While McGuigan could not bring himself to go that far, he did nevertheless agree to keep a close watch on the youngster.

By Monday, April 15, while McCarron was still trying to gain support for his theory, things seemed to be returning to normal at the McGee household. Minnie assured her husband that she could carry on despite her grief—Johnny would be home to assist her—and she insisted that he return to his job at the factory. He reluctantly left that morning.

. . .

There were only two stores in the vicinity of the McGee farm. One was the Mahar establishment from which Minnie had already obtained an unusual quantity of matches, and the other was that of the Hicken sisters. On Tuesday morning, Minnie sent Johnny to the latter to purchase eight boxes of matches and some candy. When he returned, she lost little time preparing a lethal dose of phosphorus poison.

By Thursday, Johnny was so ill that his mother went next door to ask Bernard McGuigan for help, claiming that she and Johnny had eaten some candy and both were sick. By the time Dr. Fraser arrived, the boy had improved and seemed to be out of danger.

Aware of the policeman's suspicions, Dr. Fraser left some medicine and also arranged for several of the district men to stop by and keep a watch on the lad's progress.

During that evening, a number of these men thought that Minnie's behaviour was stranger than usual. Her conversation was seldom logical and she often lapsed into profound silences. They benevolently ascribed this to the terrible emotional strain of the past week.

Though it seemed incredible that Minnie would poison her own children, Dr. Fraser was hesitantly beginning to place some credence in Constable McCarron's suspicions. When he called the next day and found that Johnny was no better, he sent for his colleague, Dr. McIntyre. While waiting, he gave strict instructions that the boy was to be given nothing to eat or drink, but the moment his attention was diverted, Minnie gave her son a drink of sweet, warm milk.

With the arrival of Dr. McIntyre, the two men conferred and agreed that the boy's symptoms were identical to those of the other five children, and consistent with phosphorus poisoning. Over the protests of his mother, they bundled Johnny into a wagon and took him to the home of his grandfather, Thomas Cassidy.

Johnny seemed to hold his own until around two o'clock in the morning, but then slipped dramatically. With phosphorus poisoning, the end comes suddenly when the toxin reaches the heart, and this was the case with the boy. Johnny died quickly and in considerable pain.

An inquest conducted by Dr. Archibald Allen revealed that the McGee children had purchased nearly fifteen boxes of matches during the ten days immediately preceding the deaths. Where were they? Minnie claimed that the unusual number of visitors to her house during her son's illness had used them or taken them away. Each of the visitors, however, vowed that they had used their own matches.

In her disjointed fashion, Minnie alternately laid the blame on bad fish, candy, and oatmeal. Her husband, who had again been called home, could add nothing to what was known.

At the conclusion of the inquest, the jurors stated: "We believe from the evidence before us that death was due to poisoning in some form." Faced with the uncontested fact that Minnie was known to be a good mother, they ascribed no blame.

The bodies of the two McGee children who had died in January were exhumed and examined, but these autopsies merely confirmed the original cause of death—whooping cough. Since the deaths of the other five children were identical with that of Johnny's, there seemed no need to hold an autopsy on one of these earlier cases.

The lad's vital organs were removed and taken to Montreal on April 23 by Dr. W.J. McMillan. Toxicological studies performed by Professor Robert Ruttan and Dr. Gruner performed revealed that while there was no free phosphorus in the organs, there were, in fact, tissue changes consistent with that type of poison.

On April 26, Constable Thomas McCarron arrested Minnie McGee for the murder of her son Johnny. She went to jail protesting her innocence and apparently undisturbed by her detention. She was indicted by a Grand Jury on July 16.

When trial opened the following day before Mr. Justice Fitzgerald and jury, a court-appointed lawyer, A.J. Fraser, pleaded her not guilty.

In his opening statement, Crown Prosecutor J.A. Mathieson raised the question of insanity, saying that while the Crown would make no move to disprove this, the jurors should keep the possibility in mind. It seemed to supply the only motive. His presentation of evidence went to indicate that following the death of her two children in January 1912, Mrs. McGee's behaviour had deteriorated, and that by the time the five children took ill in April, many of her words and actions appeared to friends and relatives to be abnormal.

Taking the stand on her own behalf, Minnie gave quite a lucid account of her actions and a logical theory for the death of her children—accidental poisoning. To sustain this position, she had to deny the statements of nearly every Crown witness, but she did this without the slightest change of expression.

In pleading her case, defence lawyer Fraser pointed out that there was no motive for the crime and that she had an excellent reputation as a mother. No normal mother would kill her own children. For the Crown, Mr. Mathieson stressed that she was the only adult in the house and that no logical explanation had been given for the purchase of such a large number of matches and their subsequent disappearance. He again stressed the option of insanity as a verdict.

Likewise, in his charge to the jury, His Lordship left three avenues open: guilty, not guilty and not guilty by reason of insanity.

The jury left the courtroom at 1:15 PM Friday, July 19, but after only ten minutes of deliberation returned with a verdict of guilty. Though they thus rejected the insanity plea, they tempered their decision with a recommendation to mercy. His Lordship reserved sentence to the following Monday.

Minnie McGee was confined to the county jail at Georgetown with a twenty-four-hour deathwatch mounted by jailer William Yoston and Constable Thomas McCarron. The day after her trial, she wrote a short, three-sentence confession and gave it to Dr. Duncan A. Stewart, the jail physician. While she admitted the murders of her six children, she gave no explanation other than to claim that she was not feeling well.

On Monday, July 22, when she was sentenced to be hanged on October 10, Minnie McGee made an impassioned statement in which she did not deny her guilt but claimed that she was the victim of her husband's abuse and that he was responsible for the deaths because he knew she was sick and did not take the children away from her. On hearing the sentence, she burst out with an appeal to be hanged right there in court and as she was led from the room, she flew into a frenzy in which she babbled senselessly and tore her clothing. Only the gentle treatment of her escort calmed her sufficiently that she could be taken away.

Though both the Crown and defence would have been satisfied with a verdict of insanity, the jurors had rejected this. The only avenue of clemency left open was the Royal Prerogative of Mercy. The Minister of Justice took insanity into account in rendering his decision on September 10, 1912, and an Order in Council commuted the sentence to life imprisonment at Kingston Penitentiary.

Mrs. McGee's mental problems continued in prison and her conduct deteriorated over the years. On October 1, 1928, she was transferred to the Falconwood Insane Asylum at Charlottetown, Prince Edward Island, where her behaviour seemed to improve. Eventually she was able to function quite adequately in the open atmosphere of the hospital.

During her sixth year there, word came that her father had fallen mentally ill. Since there was no one at home to look after him, the medical superintendent of the hospital took the unusual step of releasing her on February 12, 1934, to take care of him. Her conduct was so good that he decided to discharge her completely. Technically, he had no authority to do so, but faced with this *fait accompli,* the Department of Justice did not return her to prison but closed its file on her.

. . .

Catherine Tratch
The Childlike Killer

*I*N THE DETACHED WORLD of the fictional detective, the killer always resorts to some sophisticated poison such as curare or the milk of the Japanese poison fish, but in the real world of Canada's murderesses the fatal potions were simple things such as arsenic or strychnine. Unlike the suave poisoners of fiction, these women were poor, uneducated, and basic. A prime example was Catherine Tratch.

A sweet, simple, elemental woman, Catherine Tratch translated the world around her into black and white. Unable to comprehend delicate shades of meaning or to understand subtle nuances of language, she interpreted everything in the extreme. "Like" easily became "undying passion" and a friendly arm around the shoulders was equivalent to a declaration of eternal love. Such a primitive approach to life was bound to create problems and when a forty-six-year-old widower, Theodor Oleskiw, began "to be nice to her," his actions unwittingly set the stage for murder.

Born in Russia in 1885 to Ruthenian parents, Catherine Wawryk at the age of fourteen married Yakin Tracz, or Tratch, a man thirteen years her senior. Along with many others from her village, her family migrated to Canada around the turn of the century and settled at Fish Creek, about fifty-five kilometres (thirty-four miles) north of Saskatoon, Saskatchewan. Originally famous as the site of a battle during the Riel Rebellion, Fish Creek had been founded by French Metis from Manitoba, but these early settlers gladly sold their river lots to the Ukrainians who moved to the district on the east side of the South Saskatchewan River. Eight children were born to Yakin and Catherine over the next few years.

About 1903, Theodor Oleskiw, a tall, handsome, and well-built Ukrainian arrived at Fish Creek with his wife and children. Outgoing and friendly, he soon made his mark in the community and over the years was elected to several municipal offices. When his wife died, he became one of the most eligible bachelors in the district. In the friendly frontier manner of the times, many of the local women pitched in to help him raise his eight children. Among these was Catherine Tratch.

The Tratch family, by their own account and by all outside reports, were a happy group, despite the fact that they farmed marginal land and were sometimes in want. They mixed freely in community religious and cultural activities and their home was a friendly place to visit. Theodor Oleskiw was a frequent visitor there. At harvest time Catherine, often assisted by her oldest daughter, Teenie, cooked for the threshing crews at the Oleskiw farm. Theodor was grateful for her generous assistance and solicitous towards her.

On the evening of Saturday, October 6, 1923, Theodor Oleskiw drove Catherine home from his farm. Teenie, the twenty-two-year-old daughter, saw them drive into the yard and saw that as her mother got out of the buggy, Oleskiw handed her a small white package and talked earnestly with her for a few moments. Then he drove off and Catherine came into the house.

There was nothing subtle or complicated about the murder of Yakin Tratch. On Tuesday afternoon, October 9, he drove to Rosthern on business and on his return partook of a hearty supper. He also liked a nip of home-brew after his meals but on this occasion the drink his faithful wife brought him was laced with strychnine.

Though he complained that the liquor was not up to its usual standard, he drank it and went to chat with Theodor Oleskiw, who was visiting in the front room. A few minutes later, he fell to the floor, clutching his stomach in agony.

Theodor excused himself and left for home.

In emergencies, the farmers turned to the only educated people in the district, schoolteacher William Hopper and his wife, who always seemed to know what to do. William Tratch, sixteen, was dispatched to bring them. When Hopper and his wife arrived, Yakin told him that he was burning up inside. Suspecting food poisoning, Mrs. Hopper prepared a draught of water and ginger and when this failed to bring up the stomach contents, she tried some mustard. This also failed.

In the meantime, young William had been sent on horseback to bring Dr. E. Penner from Rosthern. Illustrating the difficulty of frontier life, this involved a ride sixteen kilometres (ten miles) north to Dumont's Ferry (now called Gabriel's Bridge) across the South Saskatchewan River and another twenty kilometres (twelve miles) across the prairie.

Although Mr. Tratch was still conscious when Dr. Penner arrived and able to describe his symptoms, his condition worsened rapidly and he died before the physician was able to counteract the deadly substance. From the evidence, Dr. Penner had no difficulty ascribing his death to strychnine, but the thought of murder never crossed his mind. Rat poison was commonly found on prairie farms and more than one death had resulted from its accidental ingestion. When he returned to Rosthern, however, the doctor notified Constable Yorke of the Saskatchewan Provincial Police as a matter of routine.

Constable Yorke, accepting the accident theory, did not place the matter high on his agenda, and it was nearly eleven-thirty the next night before he was able to call at the Tratch farm. Finding several women gathered in the kitchen—among them Mrs. Annie Wawryk, Catherine's mother—he was presented with an entirely different and dramatic situation. Mrs. Wawryk said Catherine had told her she had given Yakin poison. She claimed Catherine was quite anxious to talk about the matter, and that "there was another involved."

Constable Yorke spoke no Ukrainian and Catherine Tratch knew little English, so the circumstances in which he took down her "confession" were probably among the most unusual in Canadian jurisprudence. Seating himself at the kitchen table, he informed her through the women that she did not have to speak but could make a voluntary statement if she wished. She said she wanted to tell him about it.

There were at least five women present, all participating as translators. Sometimes they agreed on the wording of a phrase and other times they were not sure. Nevertheless, the constable managed to write down a reasonable story in English.

The tale was simple enough. She said Theodor Oleskiw had told her to poison her husband so they could be married. He had obtained strychnine for her and told her how to prepare it; she had simply followed instructions and her husband had died after she gave him the poison in his liquor. When her story was complete, she dutifully signed the English translation with an X.

When an autopsy performed by Dr. A. Stewart, of Rosthern, confirmed strychnine poisoning, Constable Yorke arrested both Mrs. Tratch and Theodor Oleskiw and charged them with murder. Questioned at his farm, Oleskiw admitted giving poison to Catherine, explaining that he believed that she had wanted it for rats. He had been at the Tratch farm the evening Yakin fell ill and immediately suspected something was wrong. When he got up to leave, Catherine had tried to detain him by saying: "You are a part of this." He had ignored her and gone home. When friends told him that Tratch had died, he had remained on his farm waiting for the police.

In Catherine Tratch's two-day trial, which concluded at Prince Albert on February 6, 1924, the bulk of testimony given before Mr. Justice J.F.L. Embury and jury was rendered by family members. While her confession was admitted, His Lordship cautioned the jurors to pay little attention to it because it had been interpreted from Ukrainian by friends and written down in English. More telling was the evidence of her mother, Annie Wawryk, who related how her daughter had confessed to her the day following her husband's death, telling her that "there was someone else in on it." Catherine did not take the stand in her own defence.

Despite the clear-cut combination of motive, opportunity, and malice, the jury still took four hours to reach a decision. It was difficult to believe that the friendly, open-faced woman they had watched in the prisoner's box could have carried forward so dastardly a plot with such open recklessness and abandon. In the end, however, the weight of evidence overawed them and they found her guilty. She was sentenced to be executed at Prince Albert on May 20, 1924.

Theodor Oleskiw went on trial the next day, February 7, with J.H. Lindsay for the prosecution and J.E. Lussier for the defence. After proving the murder through medical testimony, Mr. Lindsay placed Teenie Tratch, the daughter, on the stand to detail the relationship between her mother and the accused. He emphasized her story that she had seen the accused give her mother a small package on the Saturday before the crime, and he followed this with the testimony of Mrs. Tratch herself. Speaking through an interpreter, Catherine told a simple story of being enticed with a promise of marriage, of receiving the poison from her "lover" with instructions on how to prepare it, and of giving it to her husband in his home-brew.

Taking the stand in his own defence, Theodor made an excellent impression on the jury, admitting that he had "been friendly towards Catherine" for some time and was grateful for the help she had given him, but denying that they had ever engaged in sex. He also admitted giving her the poison, but said his instructions on its use had been confined to the proper dosage for rats and mice. It was only when he saw Yakin collapse on the floor that he realized the true purpose for the strychnine. Nevertheless, as he stepped down from the witness stand, the weight of evidence was against him, and seasoned courtroom observers were betting five to one for his conviction.

The outcome of murder trials often hinges on very small points, and this was clearly demonstrated in Oleskiw's case. Since there was no known animosity between Yakin and Theodor, the matter appeared to rest on the existence of a love triangle. Defence attorney Lussier next introduced a special piece of information. Far from being romantically involved with Catherine, he contended, Theodor was engaged to another woman in the district and they would have been married after harvest had not his arrest and incarceration prevented it.

Most juries today are reluctant to convict if there is an avenue of doubt open, and this was even more patent when the death penalty was in vogue. True to form, the Oleskiw jurors after a short deliberation returned a finding of not guilty and he was released from custody.

. . .

While awaiting execution in the death cell at Prince Albert provincial prison, Catherine Tratch was examined by a panel of medical experts, who found that the thirty-eight-year-old woman had the mentality of a child of eight and was easily influenced. As such, it was highly unlikely that she would know how much poison to put in the home-brew unless she had been carefully coached and the instructions repeated to her several times. At the same time, the medical men cautioned that their findings might be distorted by the language barrier and that Catherine might be more capable than their tests indicated.

Accepting the psychiatric panel's detailed report, Department of Justice officials suggested to the Minister that her sentence be commuted to life imprisonment. Acting on this recommendation, on May 18, 1924, just two days before she was scheduled to be hanged, the Governor-General altered her sentence to life. Catherine remained in the Kingston penitentiary for fourteen years before it was felt that she could function on her own and in June 1938, at the age of fifty-two, she was released and taken by family members to the West Coast, where she later died.

. . .

Marie Viau

Too Much Haste

THE MURDER OF ZEPHER VIAU, a simple French-Canadian backwoodsman from Montelier, Quebec, had nothing to recommend it to either students of criminology or to the mercy of man or God. It was the cold-blooded slaying of a middle-aged man who had known nothing but poverty all his life and who showed his love for his family by working at miserable jobs to provide them with the necessities of life. His only fault was that he overlooked the true nature of his wife, Marie Beaulne, and his good friend, Philibert Lefebvre.

Marie was a stern, resolute woman who ruled her brood and husband with a dominant hand. Twenty years younger than her spouse, she had the reputation of being "a hard character" who would stop at little to gain her ends. It was an ill-kept secret in the isolated community seventy kilometres (forty-four miles) northeast of Hull in the Gatineau Hills that when her husband was away she often entertained Philibert Lefebvre, a trapper and friend of her husband. He was thirty-two, single, a war veteran and a tall, hardy, good-looking man.

Zepher Viau died on Sunday, January 27, 1929, after a short, mysterious illness. Administering the last rites, Father Lucien Major's suspicions were aroused by the nature of the illness, and further strengthened when Marie insisted upon an immediate burial. He passed along his thoughts to the nearest detachment of the Quebec Provincial Police. When detectives from Hull arrived to look into the situation, they felt that an investigation was warranted and ordered the body exhumed and an autopsy performed.

When deadly amounts of strychnine were found in the corpse, a fuller investigation was undertaken and this quickly brought to light the illicit romance between Marie and her thirty-two-year-old lover. They were both arrested on suspicion. Philibert Lefebvre was not made of the same stern stuff as his mistress and quickly broke down under questioning, admitting he had purchased the poison and that Marie had given it to her husband. It was Marie's idea; she had planned the killing for some time.

For her part, Marie scornfully denied having any part in Zepher's death, claiming that if he had been poisoned it was by accident. Faced with her lover's confession and his attempt to place all the blame on her, however, she told a different story, one that implicated him to a marked degree.

The pair were tried in early June at Hull before Mr. Justice L.J. Loranger. Defence attorneys Jean D'Aoust and Paul Ste. Marie offered no testimony to refute the strong case advanced by the Crown. In his summation to the jury, His Lordship gave strong direction, giving as his opinion that the confessions indicated the murder had been planned for months and that Lefebvre had supplied the strychnine, knowing for what purpose it was intended. The trial ended on June 12 with a verdict of guilty in both instances. Neither was recommended to mercy.

In speaking to sentence, both Marie and Philibert responded

that they were innocent and asked that they be recommended to the mercy of the court. His Lordship refused to grant this, remarking that their crime was most despicable. He ordered that they be hanged at Hull prison on August 23, 1929.

Mr. Justice Loranger's words seemed to sum up the feeling of officialdom, for there was no interference with the sentence. Marie Viau was the first poisoner to pay for her crime with her life. As the days sped by, she maintained her icy calm, but her lover collapsed emotionally and spent his last days protesting his innocence and pleading for an exercise of clemency that did not come. While she expressed a wish to see him before her execution, he made no such request and continued to shower the blame upon her. Marie wrote to each of her children towards the end, but there was no response from any of them.

The morning of Friday, August 23, dawned with ill omen; a violent thunderstorm broke over the city and lightning flashed in the early morning hours. It had been planned to hang the pair separately just at dawn, but the storm delayed the executions, and it was not until eight that Philibert Lefebvre was taken from his death cell. He had collapsed completely and had to be carried across the rain-soaked lawn to the crimson scaffold. As he was supported on the trap, the bells in the Parliament buildings directly across the Ottawa River began to toll. Hangman Arthur Ellis did his job well and death was instantaneous for the backwoods trapper.

Once his body was removed, Maria Viau was brought out. Scorning the ministrations of a priest, she marched steadfastly through the drizzle to mount the red death machine without assistance from her escort. Composed to the end, she kept her eyes fixed on the distant parliament buildings until the white hood was lowered. She dropped through the trap at exactly 8:21 and death was pronounced minutes later.

That afternoon, Philibert's aged father came with a horse and buggy to claim his son's body for burial, but no one appeared to collect Marie. She was later buried in an unmarked grave.

· · ·

Elizabeth Tilford

She'll Kill No More

*A*CCORDING TO THE SCANTY RECORDS AVAILABLE, Elizabeth Ann Tilford was born in England in 1885. When she was fifteen, she married Frank Yaxley. It is said that some older women dared her to marry him and that she did it to win a bet. Yaxley is alleged to have died under mysterious circumstances shortly after marriage. Elizabeth Ann was a Sunday School teacher with the Salvation Army and active in other church work. She was also involved in the Girl Guides and rose to the rank of captain. In 1911, she married William Walker, thirty-two, who was a sergeant major in the Salvation Army Corps.

The couple came to Canada in 1928 and settled in Woodstock, Ontario, where he continued his work with the Salvation Army. Unknown to them, he was suffering from a brain tumour that was slowly robbing him of sight and life. On February 19, 1929, he died and was subsequently buried in the Baptist cemetery at Woodstock.

Elizabeth Ann was then forty-five years of age, a stout woman with four grown children, but she had an air about her that drew men. One of these was Tyrell Tilford, a man fifteen years her junior, who worked as a local teamster. Meeting at church, they were soon romantically entangled and they were married at Woodstock on November 10, 1930.

After about four years of marriage, Elizabeth Ann became restless again and her name was linked with that of William Percy Blake, forty-two. Tyrell Tilford apparently objected to this entente, but beyond complaining to his numerous relatives, did nothing about it. Whatever was left of the marriage deteriorated quickly under these circumstances, but despite the growing mutual antagonism, they continued to live together.

The matriarch of the Tilford family in Woodstock was Mrs. Mary Tilford, and little went on in the lives of her children of which she was not aware. She was later to testify that as early as February 1935, her son Tyrell was complaining of a burning sensation in his stomach after meals. His wife scoffed at the idea and accused him of imagining things.

The first clear hint of poisoning came on March 20, 1935, when Elizabeth Tilford phoned a local druggist and ordered two ounces of arsenic with which to poison rats. When the delivery boy, Victor King, delivered them to the house, she was absent on church work but her daughter from a previous marriage, Isabella, accepted the package and signed for it. Later, checking the delivery slip, the druggist noted that the girl had signed for the arsenic and he altered the order form to read Isabella Tilford.

When Tyrell Tilford arrived home that evening before his wife, the girl turned the parcel over to him. He opened it and found the arsenic. This was apparently the first intimation he had of his wife's plan to murder him and he cautioned the girl not to tell her mother that the poison had arrived.

Over the next few weeks, he told several members of his family that Elizabeth was poisoning him. "Elizabeth is giving it to me," he was reported to have told his mother. "She has killed two husbands and I am to be the third. I'm sure she'll kill more." Edward Tilford, his brother, later claimed that Tyrell had told him that his persistent stomach trouble arose from arsenic. These statements were all made under oath.

If the evidence given by these people was the truth, one wonders why Tyrell Tilford remained in the house and why he continued to eat the meals his wife prepared for him. Annie Tilford, Tyrell's sister, was also to testify that her brother had once accused his wife in her presence of giving him poison. Still, he stayed at home! For her part, Elizabeth Tilford protested that the family was conspiring against her.

Through the last week of March, Tyrell became quite ill and though he was attended by Dr. Hugh Lindsay, his illness became more severe, and he died on April 1, 1935. Dr. Lindsay consulted with the local coroner, but neither man felt that any of the circumstances warranted further investigation, and no autopsy was ordered. Tyrell was buried in the Woodstock cemetery.

Unsatisfied with "death from natural causes," Mrs. Mary Tilford and her brood began to press the police for an official investigation. The local office of the Ontario Provincial Police received so many calls that they finally referred the matter to headquarters in Toronto, where Inspector Edward D. Hammond was assigned to look into the complaints.

A troubleshooter for the department, Hammond had joined the force at an early age and risen through the ranks by virtue of a special aptitude for investigation. He was known as a sound officer and a bulldog once he had a theory on a case. He was perhaps most famous for his work in the prolonged probe into the puzzling disappearance of Ambrose Small, millionaire Toronto theatre owner, in 1919.

After hearing about Tyrell's complaints that he was being poisoned, Inspector Hammond began a canvas of local and district druggists to determine whether Mrs. Tilford had purchased any poison. Discovering that an Isabella Tilford had ordered and taken delivery of two ounces of arsenic on March 20, he questioned the girl. The druggist later confirmed that Elizabeth Tilford had originally placed the order and that he had changed the name on the order sheet to coincide with that on the delivery chit. No other arsenic could be traced to the Tilford home.

There was, of course, one major problem. Isabella had given the package to her stepfather, not her mother. When questioned, Elizabeth Ann denied ordering the arsenic and declared that she had never received any, intimating that her husband might have ordered it in her name.

Inspector Hammond was a persuasive man, however, and with only the suspicions of the Tilford family to support him, he managed to obtain an order for exhumation and had the body of Tyrell Tilford examined. Although the results were inconclusive, the Tilford family continued to press its case, now claiming that the medical examination had not ruled out the possibility of murder. While he was reasonably sure by this time that Tyrell Tilford had died of natural causes, Inspector Hammond decided to clear the issue once and for all. Ordering a second medical examination, he had the remains sent to Dr. E.R. Frankish, a renowned forensic expert on poisons. After a protracted study, Dr. Frankish was able to determine the presence of arsenic in the hair and fingernails and concluded that the toxin had been ingested over a long period of time. On this, Mrs. Tilford was arrested and charged with the murder of her husband.

The preliminary hearing held by Magistrate E.S. Livermore at Woodstock on June 24 demonstrated the tenuous nature of the

Crown's case. Beyond Dr. Frankish's opinion that Tilford had died of arsenic poison, the only thing that tied his wife to murder was that she habitually prepared his meals. No purchase of poison was directly connected with her and the other witnesses consisted primarily of members of the Tilford family, who merely repeated the accusations made by the victim. The possibility of a romantic link between Mrs. Tilford and William Blake provided the only hint of a motive. In the end, feeling that Tilford had probably been murdered and that his wife was the logical suspect, Magistrate Livermore committed Elizabeth Ann to trial before a higher court.

At her trial, which opened in Woodstock on September 24, 1935, Crown Prosecutor C.L. Snyder contended that Tyrell had died slowly of arsenic poisoning and that Mrs. Tilford was the only one who had the opportunity to administer the poison on a continuing basis. He suggested that the motive was the love affair between Mrs. Tilford and William Blake. Twenty-four Crown witnesses took the stand to support his theory.

In contrast, defence counsel C.W. Bell called no witnesses, nor did he allow Elizabeth to take the stand. Instead, he reserved his most telling arguments for his address to the jury. Pointing out that the only arsenic traced to the Tilford home was that delivered on March 20 and that this had ended up in the hands of the victim, he suggested that the man's hatred for his wife was so intense that he had committed suicide by taking this poison himself. His statements to other family members were merely to fasten suspicion upon his wife. If he suspected that he was being poisoned, why did he remain in the home unless it was to commit suicide in such a manner that she would be blamed?

The case was handed to the jurors shortly after lunch on Wednesday, October 2, and they took eight hours of deliberation before reaching their verdict. There was no question that Tilford had died of arsenic poison administered over a long period of time—beginning before the delivery of the parcel on March 20—and the moot question was whether he had also obtained poison before the misdirected delivery, or whether Elizabeth had obtained some before and after it. In the end, they found her guilty and saw no reason to recommend her to the mercy of the Crown. Mr. Justice A.C. Kingstone immediately passed sentence, ordering that she should be hanged on December 17.

Upon hearing the sentence, Elizabeth Ann shouted: "Lordship, it's not fair. If I only had a chance to give my evidence. Framed. Absolutely framed. May God have mercy on the Tilfords!"

Convinced that the Crown's case was weak, defence counsel C.W. Bell carried the question to the Ontario Court of Appeal, but with unusual speed that tribunal heard the issue in November and rejected the appeal. The original sentence of the lower court was allowed to stand.

Unlike most cases in which a woman was involved, the Tilford affair did not evoke a mass of petitions. A few were circulated asking for executive clemency but these had little impact; it was evident that Ottawa did not intend to intervene. While some cabinet members doubted her guilt or felt that the case had not been proven, the majority believed that the crime merited the punishment. The male-dominated society of that era frowned upon wives disposing of husbands and the officials recommended to the Governor-General that there be no interference with the sentence.

Normally, veteran hangman Arthur Ellis would have been called upon to officiate, but the memory of his bungled hanging of Mrs. Tomasina Sarao at Montreal earlier in the year[*] was still fresh in the minds of officialdom, and another experienced executioner, Samuel Edwards, was asked to perform.

Because the prison yard at Woodstock Jail was open to public view, a scaffold was erected inside a large coal-shed in the compound. Mrs. Tilford, as befitted a church-going member of the Salvation Army, passed her last hours in quiet prayer, resigned to her fate but still protesting her innocence.

A light snow was falling as she was led from her cell shortly after midnight and escorted across the prison yard. With the exception of the coroner's jury and a few officials who huddled in the snow, the site was clear. Outside, about a hundred people waited silently. The hanging was clean, swift, and efficient, and after remaining on the rope for twenty minutes she was cut down and carried into the prison, where she was viewed by the coroner's jury, placed in a coffin, and removed. Elizabeth Tilford was buried quietly by her family beside her second husband, William Walker, at two-thirty in the morning in the Baptist cemetery.

· · ·

---

[*] See "The Blue Bonnet Murder," page 49.

Marie Cloutier

A First-Class Embalming

*T*HE TRIAL OF MARIE GRONDIN, née Cloutier,
for the murder of her husband, Vilmond Brochu,
was probably more remarkable for the evidence that Mr. Justice
Noel Belleau refused to allow than for the testimony that eventually
found its way into the records. There were whispered tales of
witch-craft, of malevolent curses and counter-curses, and all the dark
paraphernalia of black magic mixed with a goodly dash of old-fashioned sex. It was even said that witnesses were willing to affix their
oaths to these stories but they were never called. Alluring as these
tales may have been were, the bare facts are intriguing enough to
arouse the interest of Canadian crime aficionados.

At the time of her trial, Marie Louise Cloutier was a short,
dark-eyed, vivacious woman of thirty-nine. Men found her enchant-
ing and their fascination seems to have been rewarded. She was a
dark-eyed little enchantress who loved men and who was loved by
them. At age seventeen, she married Vilmond Brochu, a twenty-year-
old lad from St. Methode de Frontenac, a small village southeast of
Thetford Mines in the south of Quebec. Within a few years, they had
built up a small farm and appeared to be well matched. Over the next
twenty years, their marriage underwent the usual stresses and strains,
but serious trouble did not develop until late 1935.

By that time the Brochu farm had prospered to the point where
Vilmond decided to purchase a taxi-cab. Thereafter, he began to
spend a lot of time away from home. When Marie Louise complained that she was stuck with all the farm work while he enjoyed
cruising around the countryside, he solved the problem in February
1936 by taking on a hired hand, forty-three-year-old Achille Grondin.
Within a year, however, Vilmond began to suspect that his wife was
carrying on with the hired man and he fired him. Marie Louise
countered this move by packing her things and disappearing.

Marie turned up at Magog, not far from Sherbrooke, where she
stayed with friends until she could obtain a job. She gave as her

excuse for leaving home that her husband was unnecessarily jealous of men, and that he himself was using his taxi business to cloak his affairs with other women.

Devastated by his wife's departure, Vilmond Brochu launched a civil suit charging Achille Grondin with alienating her affections. When he finally located her at Magog and pleaded with her to come home, Marie laid down some pretty strict ground rules for resumption of the marriage. First, Vilmond was to give up either his taxi business or his farm so he could devote more time to her. Second, he was to drop his lawsuit against Achille Grondin and not interfere with their "innocent relationship" in the future. Vilmond was so eager to have his exciting woman return that he promptly sold his farm and purchased her a cottage in St. Methode. Complying with all her demands, he made no objection to her continued relationship with Grondin, and dropped the civil suit as well.

Among Marie's friends at Magog was an undertaker, who was to recall later that Marie took a special interest in the effect embalming had on various poisons in the body. At the time, he merely ascribed her curiosity to her high level of intelligence. He might have thought otherwise had he known that on returning to her husband, Marie developed a sudden interest in growing tomato plants and purchased some arsenic to stimulate their growth. A few weeks later, Achille Grondin also took up gardening and bought a small quantity of arsenic to encourage his vegetation.

With the dawn of 1937, St. Methode de Frontenac was in for a strange year. First, Vilmond Brochu took ill on New Year's Day following a few drinks with his wife and Grondin; he recovered after a short but severe attack of stomach cramps. Next, a rumour spread that Grondin had hired a gypsy to place a curse on the taxi driver. Brochu, engaging another gypsy, had retaliated with a curse of his own. Gossip also began to link Marie's name with several other men in the community, and the old stories of her husband's infidelities were resurrected and women named.

On July 16, following six months of rumour and innuendo, Vilmond was again taken ill with stomach pains. The doctor at St. Ephrem, where Marie drove him, was unable to diagnose the problem but gave her a reassuring prognosis when Vilmond seemed to recover after taking some soothing medication. Five days later, however, he suffered another attack; this time she took him to Dr. LeLage at Thetford Mines. Once again, Vilmond responded to medication and the illness was ascribed to indigestion.

On August 16, Brochu was seized by another of his mysterious illnesses, but this time he did not recover and died three days later. In view of his recent troubles, no suspicion attached to his death, and he was buried quickly at the local cemetery. To show her concern, Marie Louise insisted on a "first-class embalming" for her beloved spouse.

• • •

Achille Grondin was not the only local man who had enjoyed Marie Louise's bedroom charm, both before and after her husband's death, and while most of these were a mere afternoon's dalliance, there was one other serious contender for her affections. To settle the matter, Grondin met with his rival over some whisky to discuss which of them should marry the widow. Grondin emerged the victor and he and Marie were married within six weeks of Vilmond's death.

Mathilda Brochu, Vilmond's sister, had never been entirely satisfied with the ascribed cause of his death, and the quick marriage reawakened all her latent suspicions. Not wishing to alert them to her intentions, she waited until they went on their honeymoon before she took the train to Montreal and confided her concerns to Jacques Piuze, chief of the Quebec Provincial Police, who agreed that there might be some basis for her fears and obtained an exhumation order. Three nights later, he had the body secretly unearthed and taken to Montreal for examination by specialists. Dr. J.M. Roussel, one of Canada's top forensic scientists, conducted the post-mortem and confirmed that Brochu had died from arsenic poison administered over a period of months.

Marie Louise and Achille were arrested on their honeymoon and an intensive investigation ensued. By November, sufficient evidence was amassed for a preliminary hearing, following which they were committed to stand trial before a superior court.

Madame Cloutier went on trial at St. Joseph de Beauce on September 20, 1938, defended by the brilliant Rosaire Beaudoin. Crown Prosecutor Noel Dorion presented a hundred witnesses, tracing her matrimonial history, her involvement with Achille Grondin and numerous other men, and her flight to Magog. He outlined the conditions of her return to her husband, his subsequent illness, and his burial following the meticulous embalming upon which Marie had insisted. An effort was made on September 22 to introduce the tangled web of curses said to have been evoked, but His Lordship refused to hear such evidence. There was also an attempt to put Achille Grondin on the stand, but this was thwarted when it was ruled that he could not testify against his wife.

The chief Crown witness was Dr. Roussel, pathologist, who testified that arsenic had been given to the victim over a period of at least eight months. Having been given samples found in the Brochu home after the murder, he was able to state that these were the same as those found in the body. Others testified that both Marie and Achille had purchased this type of toxin. Although Roussel was cross-examined at great length by the defence, his testimony remained unshaken.

Tension rose to a high pitch in the small courtroom on Friday, September 30, when Marie Louise took the stand and stoutly denied that she had ever given poison to her husband. Intensely cross-examined by Noel Dorion, she spent nearly four days on the witness stand, maintaining to the end that her husband had died of acute indigestion.

By Friday, October 7, all the evidence was in and both the defence and prosecution had concluded their addresses to the weary jurors. Once His Lordship had given his summation the following morning, the jurors requested permission to attend the local church to pray for guidance in their deliberations. On their return, they were closeted together for just over an hour before they reached their conclusion: she was guilty.

There had been some hesitation about trying Achille Grondin, since the only evidence against him was that Vilmond had taken ill the day after Achille had purchased some arsenic. There had been some hope that he might turn King's evidence. When it was ruled that he could not testify against his wife, however, it was decided to proceed against him, and he was brought to trial at St. Joseph de Beauce in mid-November. Once again the two protagonists, Noel Dorion and Rosaire Beaudoin, battled each other in the courtroom through endless hours of complicated evidence, but on November 26, 1938, the Crown emerged victorious.

Marie Louise Cloutier had not been sentenced pending the outcome of Grondin's trial, but when he was found guilty she was returned to the courtroom and both were sentenced to be hanged at St. Joseph de Beauce on March 3, 1939.

When news of this reached local parishioners, it created such a wave of protest that the site of the proposed hangings was transferred to Montreal, and both prisoners were taken to Quebec City to await the outcome of their appeals.

The case dragged on through all of 1939, with both judgements being taken to the Quebec Court of Appeal. Both were rejected. The cause of Marie Louise was then carried to the Supreme Court, but it was dismissed. The lower court then set the new date of execution for February 23, 1940.

The Remission Service of the Department of Justice was responsible for clemency reviews. When its exhaustive study of the evidence failed to reveal any reason to grant mercy in either case, a recommendation went first to the Minister of Justice, then to Cabinet for endorsement, and then to the Governor-General, who issued the warrants of execution.

Achille Grondin was removed from Quebec City to Bordeaux Jail in Montreal on February 15. A week later, Marie Louise was brought to Montreal and held at the Fulham Street Women's Prison.

Almost all executions in Quebec at that time were carried out by Camile Branchaud, a former prison guard in the provincial service. A big man with a penchant for liquor, he was such an efficient workman that his services were also in demand in other areas of Canada. Robert M. Deildahl, former deputy warden at Oakalla Prison Farm in British Columbia, described one of the tricks of his trade: "He had a trick. Just before he pulled the lever . . . you can imagine the tenseness in the witnesses who had to be present . . . he would make a slight gesture with his hand or suddenly look off to the side. Everybody would look away to see where he was pointing or what had caught his eye and when they looked back all they would see was the open trap with the rope taut . . . "

Shortly after midnight on February 23, Branchaud hanged Marie Louise Cloutier and Achille Grondin for the murder of Vilmond Brochu. Hanged separately in flawless executions, they were later buried in unmarked graves, marking a grim finale to their own particular tale of horror.

It is interesting to note that of the seven women convicted of murder by poison, the first four—Sophie Boisclair, Marie McGaugh, Minnie McGee, and Catherine Tratch—all had their sentences commuted to life while the remainder—Marie Viau, Elizabeth Tilford, and Marie Louise Cloutier—all suffered the supreme penalty.

• • •

Murder for Profit

Murder for profit in Canada is primarily a male domain. Its roots are fixed in the Old World cultures that our forefathers brought to this continent, and probably extend back into the dawn of history when man first began to slay his brother in order to gain his possessions. It may well be linked to the predatory instincts that group together to form the masculine role of the hunter and the provider. Of all the motives for homicide it is the one most deeply fixed in the economic differences that exist between one person and another. Of the seven female cases presented here only one–Jessie Taylor–actually carried out the murder by herself. The other six women were either willing accomplices or in some instances the ones who handed their man the weapon.

Eleanor Power

The First One

C ANADA'S FIRST CASE was the murder of Magistrate William Keen at his home in St. John's, Newfoundland, on the night of September 29, 1754. A servant discovered the body the next morning and fled screaming from the house on the shore of Lake Quidi Vidi to spread the alarm. Though there were no newspapers at the time, the details were soon known and an investigation was launched. The old man had been stabbed by a wide-bladed instrument and his head bore a terrible bruise. The deed appeared to be the work of robbers, for the rooms showed signs of hasty searching.

Then in his sixties, William Keen was a well-known figure in the community, and his involvement with law and order dated back to 1723, when he had headed a vigilante group of merchants. He had been one of the first magistrates appointed by Governor Osborne in 1729. A harsh and vindictive man, he bore a special malice towards soldiers and sailors, and his name was a curse among them.

Lacking police, the governor called upon the military for assistance in tracking down the murderers, and a force of soldiers from the barracks took to the streets to interrogate likely suspects. This was not a difficult task, for the total population of St. John's and district was less than three thousand, and the criminal element was concentrated in the saloons along the harbour. Special attention was paid to all men with naval or army backgrounds who might have run afoul of the magistrate in his official capacity.

When the first drag-net failed to produce results, the scope was widened, and at a little cluster of shacks on Freshwater Bay the posse struck pay dirt. A man named Richard Power admitted that he had knowledge of the crime, and in return for immunity from prosecution told a tale that resulted in the arrest of eight men and one woman.

The woman was Eleanor Power, about twenty-five years of age, of Irish descent, and a former maid of William Keen. She had left his employ to marry a fisherman, Robert Power, and had gone to reside in a shanty on the shore of Freshwater Bay. According to the police informant, it was she who had instigated the chain of events that resulted in Keen's death.

Little time was wasted and the trial of the nine conspirators began in early October, a scant week after the discovery of the body. The case was heard before Magistrate Michael Gill, a man with a reputation as formidable as that of the murdered man. Richard Power's evidence wove a powerful net around the gang. A frequent visitor at his brother Robert's, Richard revealed that on more than one occasion Eleanor had talked about a mysterious oaken chest she had seen in Keen's basement. Since the old man kept it locked and was very secretive about it, she was sure that it contained a fortune, for her employer was reputed to have amassed vast wealth as a trader, fishing fleet owner, and magistrate. According to her brother-in-law, she repeatedly suggested that the others help her steal it.

Another visitor at the Power home was Edmund McGuire, a soldier at the barracks who bore a grudge against Magistrate Keen. On learning of the plot, he recruited three other men—John

Munhall, Dennis Hawkins, and John Moody—who had also received harsh treatment in the magistrate's court.

There were apparently few secrets at Freshwater Bay and within a short span of time three other men were involved in the scheme. These were Mathew Halluran, a quick-tempered brawling Irishman, and two of his cronies—Paul McDonald and Lawrence Lamley.

Plans were finalized in the middle of August at a secret meeting of all ten conspirators at the home of Robert and Eleanor Power. The six people from Freshwater Bay were to row across to St. John's, rendezvous with the four soldiers from the barracks, raid the Keen house under cover of darkness, and secure the treasure chest. The rooms would be upset to make it look like the work of random burglars. There being no Bible, they swore secrecy on a prayer book.

Richard Power told a hushed courtroom that the first two attempts were abandoned when the gang arrived at the house and found visitors present. Their third try, on the night of September 29, was more successful. Dressed in men's clothing, Eleanor Power assembled the Freshwater men—her husband, Robert, her brother-in-law, Richard, Paul McDonald, Lawrence Lamley, and Mathew Halluran—and rowed across to a small cove near St. John's where they were joined by Edmund McGuire, John Munhall, Dennis Hawkins, and John Moody.

Arriving at William Keen's wharf on Lake Quidi Vidi (now within the limits of St. John's itself), they found the two-storey house in darkness. Leaving some men on guard at the wharf and in the yard, Eleanor led the others to the rear entrance. The lock was easily forced; once inside she guided them by torch to the cellar, where the chest was stored. While they carried it out, two of the others went silently through the downstairs rooms, carefully tipping chairs and opening drawers.

Their work completed, the gang gathered on the pier and snapped off the lock on the chest. To their dismay, it contained only whisky and other liquors. There was no hint of gold or treasure.

By this time, some of the conspirators were becoming uneasy and voted to give up the idea and return home. Edmund McGuire, however, would have none of this. Their crime had already placed them in the shadow of the noose, for robbery was a capital offence, and they had nothing to lose by going back and robbing the old man himself. Threatening the others with death if they deserted him, he took Mathew Halluran and returned to the house. He had come for revenge rather than profit and he did not want to leave without some satisfaction for his risk.

Making their way undetected to the upper floor, the two men located Keen's bedroom with little difficulty, but the noise of their entry awakened the old man and he sat up in bed. McGuire snatched a blanket to wrap around his head, but he still managed to struggle and scream. In a panic, Halluran stabbed him twice with an old scythe blade that he carried, and McGuire finished the job with a blow from the butt of his rifle.

That was the substance of Richard Power's testimony, and it was confirmed by confessions from two of the other gang members. The evidence concluded on October 8 and the jury took but thirty short minutes to find all nine people guilty. Magistrate Gill sentenced them to be hanged on October 10, two days hence.

Prior to 1750, reports of all murder trials had to be sent to England for review before an execution could be carried out, but in that year Governor Drake applied for permission to have the local governor make that decision. This was vital since it could take as long as a year to receive a reply, and it was difficult to keep prisoners in the crude local jails for that long. The power was granted to Newfoundland governors in 1751 and as a consequence, Governor Drake was able to review the Keen murder case with dispatch.

For the two men who actually committed the murder—Edmund McGuire and Mathew Halluran—there was no mercy. With a grim touch of humour, Governor Drake ordered that they be hanged on a special gallows erected on William Keen's wharf on Quidi Vidi. This sentence was carried out on the morning of October 10.

Deeming that Eleanor Power and her husband were responsible for the plot, Drake ordered that they be executed on the regular gallows at St. John's Market Place the same afternoon. After being on display there for twenty-four hours, their bodies were to be taken to Freshwater Bay and suspended in public view with the body of Mathew Halluran as a warning to other malefactors.

The remaining five conspirators—John Munhall, Dennis Hawkins, John Moody, Paul McDonald, and Lawrence Lamley—had their sentences commuted to banishment and they were to be held in the local prison in the basement of the courthouse until they could be put aboard the first ship bound for the Caribbean. If they returned to Newfoundland, they would be hanged.

On the morning of October 9, word was brought to Magistrate

Gill that Eleanor Power was pregnant. Since it was repugnant to British justice to execute a woman who was with child, Gill communicated with Governor Drake and a respite was ordered. A panel of married women was convened to examine the condemned woman and report to the court. While awaiting their decision, Eleanor was permitted to bid farewell to her husband before he was led to the gibbet on the afternoon of October 10.

When the matrons reported that Eleanor was not pregnant after all, a new date of execution was set within the week, and once again Governor Drake refused to intercede. She was executed on the same gallows that had earlier claimed the life of her husband. On October 13, she was taken from her cell in the old Market House to a scaffold built out from a second-storey window. A large crowd was in attendance at the spectacle.

Thus died the first woman in Newfoundland to suffer the supreme penalty for murder. It would be fifty years before another woman paid with her life.

. . .

Geneviève Lafleur
The Murder of Dan Narbonne

*T*HE CASE OF GENEVIÈVE LAFLEUR, the oldest woman in Canada to face the gallows, was one of the strangest on record. Even today, more than 115 years later, the malevolence of her character and the terror of the crime that she inspired are still as vivid as the day the story unfolded in the little courtroom of St. Scholastique, Quebec, just north of Montreal. Though the case came to its climax on January 14, 1881, when his Lordship Judge Johnson sentenced Jean Baptiste Narbonne, twenty-one, François Narbonne, seventy-nine, and Geneviève Lafleur, sixty-five, to be hanged by the neck until dead, it had its origin years before.

François Narbonne was born in 1801 at the little village of St. Benoit, about thirty kilometres (nineteen miles) west of Montreal. By all accounts he was a difficult boy to understand, and after trying patience and kindness to curb his unruliness, his parents resorted to violence and beatings. Spurred by these unpleasant conditions, he escaped from this home as soon as possible, and after several scrapes with the law seemed to settle down at age twenty-seven, when he married Louise Laroque and proceeded to have a number of children. Daniel arrived in 1829 and thereafter followed two girls. By the time the fourth and last child—Jean Baptiste—arrived in 1859, they had moved to Île au Chats in St. André Parish, where Louise Laroque unfortunately died the same year.

François Narbonne lost little time replacing Louise. The same year she died, he met Geneviève Lafleur and took her into his home as a maidservant. If he anticipated another thirty years of marital bliss such as he had enjoyed with his first wife, he was quickly disillusioned. She not only moved into her master's bed, but took control of the household and soon had them all under her domination.

Geneviève Lafeur was also born at St. Benoit and was at this time a woman of forty-three. Toughened by life at an early age, she left home and embarked upon a number of escapades that brought her close to the law, though eventually she reformed and took up the profession of a live-in maid. Along the way, she married a journalist named Charles Rochon, but she did not let marriage stand in the way of her pleasures and began entertaining his friends. He disappeared from the scene early on, whether by death or disgust is not known, and Geneviève returned to her career as a live-in maid. Then, in 1859, she met François Narbonne and moved in with him.

Friction soon developed between the three eldest Narbonne children and their new mother and they left home. Mary Pane Pilon in her book *Une Famille d'Assassins* suggests that the two girls went to the United States and there met unfortunate deaths. Dan obtained a position in one of Montreal's shipyards and worked his way up the economic ladder. The fourth child, Jean Baptiste, remained with his father.

François Narbonne had always been an argumentative man and under the manipulative tutelage of Geneviève he grew worse. A year after his "marriage" to her, he got into some unfortunate litigation over his property and lost everything. Gathering together what few resources remained, he disappeared into the north woods, taking with him his youngest child, Jean Baptiste, and Geneviève.

He next turned up at Arundel, about fifty kilometres (thirty-one miles) westsouthwest of Sainte Agathe des Monts. Mountainous and heavily wooded, the area offered the ideal spot for anyone wanting to escape the worries of civilization. François built a crude, one-roomed shack, added a pole barn and granary, and settled down to hew a new life from the forest.

Over the next fifteen years the Narbonnes fought loneliness and poverty on their farm, making few friends and avoiding any contact with the religious or cultural activities of the community. As time passed, they re-established contact with their prodigal son, Daniel, and he began to visit them from time to time.

Then, in July 1875, Dan arrived for his annual visit with the news that he had forsaken shipbuilding and had saved enough money to start his own farm. He had already selected a plot of land not far from theirs and would need only to stay with them long enough to clear a patch on which to erect a small shelter. Over the years, he had managed to save more than three hundred dollars, which he carried with him, and this would serve to get him started.

With the lure of three hundred dollars dangling before her, Geneviève Lafleur immediately began to plot murder. She had long ago established dominance over her vicious but docile husband, and now turned her attentions to sixteen-year-old Jean Baptiste, whose main weakness was an unquestioned admiration for his father. Playing upon this, she reminded him frequently that a good son always carried out the wishes of his father. Following upon this, it was easy enough to plant the idea in his mind that Dan, who had left home, was therefore not a good son.

Geneviève's first scheme was to employ strangers to murder Dan on his homestead, but she had to abandon this when she realized they had no money to pay assassins. It was then that she hit upon the idea of poison.

On August 2, 1875, she prepared a brew of milk and rat poison (arsenic), sweetening it with honey. She poured the deadly mixture into a glass and left on the table, hoping that Dan, returning from work hot and thirsty, would see it and drink it. But the macabre plot went awry when Dan came home that evening and ignored the milk, slaking his thirst instead with water from the well. The next day, Jean Baptiste threw the poison out.

By now completely involved in the diabolical murder conspiracy fostered by his elders, Jean Baptiste implicitly obeyed all instructions from his father. Assisting with a new plot, he went to the home of a neighbour, Pierre Proulx, and borrowed a single-shot rifle under the pretext of using it to shoot a troublesome bear. When he brought the gun home, François Narbonne loaded it and hid it in the granary.

Wednesday, August 5, dawned dull and cloudy, and by noon a light drizzle had begun to fall. The two older people spent the day coaching Jean Baptiste on their latest murder stratagem. When Dan was asleep, Jean Baptiste was to shoot him in the heart. They warned him that he must make the single shot count, for if he missed his brother would awake and surely kill them all. To give him added motive, Geneviève told him a pitiful story that Dan had tried to rape her one day when they were alone in the cabin.

The rain that had been falling lightly all morning intensified in the afternoon, and by supper-time it was pouring, with wind, thunder, and lightning adding to the devastation. When Dan returned, all four were kept busy combatting the ravages of the storm that threatened to destroy the crude, one-roomed shack. It was two o'clock in the morning before the downpour ceased and they were able to breathe more easily. Though Dan stretched out on his blankets in one corner of the room and was soon asleep, the three conspirators kept silent vigil, waiting for the dawn to cast enough light for their evil purpose.

François had brought the rifle from the granary the evening before, and when the time came he handed it to the boy. Holding the muzzle close to his brother's heart, the young man pulled the trigger. There was a deafening roar.

Medical evidence later indicated that Dan Narbonne had died instantly, but nervous reflexes in his body caused him to sit bolt upright. Fearing that he was not dead and remembering his parents' warning, Jean Baptiste began battering at his brother's head with the rifle until he fell back onto the blankets. The force of these blows broke the butt.

Scarcely had Dan fallen back to his deathbed when François leaped across the room and scooped up the dead man's pants. In the grey dawn light, he and Geneviève began counting out the money on the table. Completely unnerved by what he had done, Jean Baptiste huddled on the floor and sobbed, ignored by those who had used him as the instrument to satisfy their murderous greed.

The family spent the rest of the day cleaning up. They tied a rope to Dan's foot and dragged his body out behind the shack, where it was covered with the bloodstained blankets. While Geneviève scrubbed the floor, François went out and dug a grave in the mud behind the stable. The next day, August 7, father and son dragged the body to the grave and covered it.

Jean Baptiste returned the rifle to Pierre Proulx, explaining that the butt had been broken when his shot only wounded the bear and he'd had to finish it off by beating it on the head.

Unlike his parents, Dan Narbonne had been a friendly, outgoing man whose industry and cheery attitude during the few weeks of his residence at Arundel had brought him to the favourable attention of the neighbours. Nevertheless, because of the isolation of the district and the small number of people, it was some weeks before he was missed. When casual inquiries were made, the Narbonnes were able to allay suspicions by saying that Dan had gone back to Montreal to earn more money for his farm.

· · ·

The following year, at age seventeen, Jean Baptiste left home and took employment at Ste. Agathe des Monts. For the first time, he came into contact with the church and was gathered into its fold. Baptized in 1876, he went on to marry a local girl, Marceline Gibras, and after a few months they settled in the parish of St. Faustine.

With the departure of Jean Baptiste, François and Geneviève found that the upkeep on the farm was too much for them. Geneviève had begun to go blind and François was losing his hearing with advancing age. When the money from the robbery was gone, they sold their property to Martin Samson. As part of the sale, Samson allowed them to live in a small house on one of his other properties near Lachute, Quebec.

With more time on their hands the old couple found themselves drawn into the local religious circle and commenced attending church. Whether it was because their new-found religious beliefs awakened their consciences or not, they decided to make a clean breast of their crime. Geneviève was later to confess that she had been suffering from dreadful nightmares since the murder, and that the pressure had finally become too much. In any event, during the first part of October 1880, she told her story to Madame Samson, wife of their benefactor.

When Mrs. Samson became convinced that her horror story was not just the rambling of a senile old woman, she sought confirmation from François, who gave it readily. She then went to magistrates

Barron and Simpson at Lachute and swore out a deposition. The Narbonnes were arrested at Lachute and Jean Baptiste, now twenty-one, was taken into custody at St. Faustine.

Jean Baptiste showed no reluctance in confessing to his brother's murder five years earlier, and willingly accompanied the coroner and police to the farm. Under his direction, they located the grave behind the stable, which, when excavated, yielded up the remains of the victim in a remarkable state of preservation. Upon seeing the mutilated body, the young man broke down, and it was some hours before he was able to regain his composure. A coroner's jury named him as the killer and indicted François and Geneviève as accessories before the fact. All three were removed to the district prison at St. Scholastique to await trial.

The two oldsters accepted their imprisonment without rancour and seemed pleased that the tragic affair was at last nearing its end. Jean Baptiste, however, convinced that he would be hanged for his part, plotted to escape. Apparently using the visits of his young wife to smuggle hacksaws into his cell, he tried to cut the bars, but his guards soon discovered the plot and moved him to more secure quarters. Next, he attempted to murder his jailer, Mr. Drouin, and make his getaway, but this plan, too, was also detected and he was clamped into irons. Making one last bid to escape the gallows, he turned King's evidence against his father and Geneviève.

The trial opened at St. Scholastique on January 11, 1881, before Mr. Justice Johnson. Using Jean Baptiste as his chief witness, prosecutor J.H. Filion quickly built up an ironclad case. Though François Narbonne neither took the stand nor made any confession, Geneviève Lafleur was very vocal. Trying to minimize her participation, she claimed she had been asleep that night and knew nothing of the murder until she was awakened by the shot. Maintaining that her only crime was to clean the cabin and keep her silence, she insisted that the real culprit was Jean Baptiste, and denied that there was any plot to have Dan killed by strangers, or that she had tried to kill him with rat poison. For his part, François Narbonne seemed completely detached from the proceedings, at times even appearing to be asleep.

Jean Baptiste's gamble to escape the noose through his testimony came to naught when after four days of hearings the jury returned verdicts of guilty against all three—Jean Baptiste for the murder and François and Geneviève as accessories before the fact.

When the time came for sentence, an enormous crowd fought its way into the courtroom and the hallways. Pointing out that all were equally guilty before the law, His Lordship sentenced them to be hanged on Friday, February 25, 1881.

It was anticipated that in view of the advanced ages of two of the condemned their sentences would quickly be commuted, but when Monday, February 21, arrived and no word had been received from Ottawa, the sheriff ordered the erection of the scaffold in the jail yard. Since it was planned that all three would be executed together for their common crime, the structure was rather large and complicated. Jean Baptiste's cell window looked out on the grim death machine, but he refused an offer to move him to a more remote part of the prison where the sound of the hammer blows would not disturb him.

Two days before the scheduled command performance, a meeting of the condemned was arranged by the parish priest, and all three gathered in Geneviève's cell. Realizing that no mercy might be expected at this late date, the three spent their visit in prayer and repentance. As he returned to his own cell, Jean Baptiste noted that three coffins had been placed beside the gibbet in preparation to receive them.

Last-minute respites had not been a feature of Canadian justice to this point, the final cabinet decision usually being taken ten to fifteen days before the date established by the court. In this case, word did not reach the prison until thirty-six hours before the deadline. Minister of Justice Campbell announced that a commutation had been granted to Jean Baptiste because he had turned King's evidence. With respect to the older pair, mercy was being extended because they themselves had brought the crime to light. Thus, on Friday, February 25, instead of walking to the gallows, the two men were transported to the federal penitentiary at St. Vincent de Paul near Montreal, while Geneviève Lafleur was whisked away to Kingston to serve her term in the women's quarters on the second floor of the men's cell block.

· · ·

Doris McDonald

A Tough Little Cookie

M R. AND MRS. GEORGE MCDONALD, of Portland, Maine, appeared to be just the kind of
guests who were welcome at Montreal's Mount Royal Hotel for the
1927 season. George McDonald listed himself as a United States
naval officer, and his strikingly beautiful wife, Doris, let it be known
that she had starred in several movies in California. This was their
first trip to Quebec—part of a belated honeymoon—and they did not
know how long they would be staying. As it turned out, their stay was
much longer than either anticipated.

George "Cross Eyes" McDonald was known to the police of
several eastern Canadian and American cities as a con artist of long
standing. Despite the fact that he was not yet twenty-five years old,
his criminal record for forgery and false pretences stretched back
ten years. Born in the Maritimes, he had moved with his family to
Portland, Maine, and by the time he was fifteen had already come to
the attention of the law.

His wife, Doris, was American-born but had been orphaned at
an early age and reared as a foster child by a family in Providence,
Rhode Island. She had married George McDonald in April of 1927.
Though only twenty years of age, she was known as "a tough little
cookie," who had starred in some lurid, back-room movies. She
always carried a .25-calibre revolver on her person.

The McDonalds made quite an impression on the staff and
clientele of the Mount Royal Hotel, and were frequently seen in the
company of another man known only as Mr. Palmer. They were
friendly and approachable, and good tippers. After a short stay they
announced that they were looking for a limousine and driver to take
them to Syracuse, New York. They were willing to pay $150 for the
service.

Adelard Bouchard, forty, taxi-driver from Lachine, just south of
Montreal, took up their offer and arrived at the hotel on the evening
of June 16, 1927. Before departing, George McDonald cashed a

cheque for $200 at the hotel. The doorman recalled that when they left, George McDonald was on the front seat with Mr. Bouchard, while Mrs. McDonald and the man known as Palmer were in the rear compartment.

They followed the Malone Highway (now Highway 138) to a point near Huntingdon, a short distance north of the American border, where they attacked Mr. Bouchard, striking him over the head with a blunt instrument, possibly a bottle, and then shooting him twice with a .38-calibre revolver. One bullet entered his neck, causing a fatal wound, while the other hit him in the arm. Although several other shots were fired, none of these struck him. He was then taken, still barely alive, and thrown into a roadside ditch filled with water and tall grass, where the combination of bullets and water in his lungs brought death in a few minutes.

Following the murder, George McDonald donned Adelard Bouchard's chauffeur's cap and drove on to the customs station at Trout River. Doris McDonald and Palmer remained in the back seat.

Presenting the taxi-driver's stolen identification, McDonald tried to pass himself off as Bouchard, and said that he was driving the couple in the back to Syracuse, for which he was to be paid $150. His passengers, he reported, were married.

William C. Robie, the customs official at the crossing, first became suspicious when he discovered that McDonald did not have a French accent. Deciding to investigate further, he asked Palmer to step into the office and there asked him some questions about his marriage. Then, interviewing Doris McDonald separately, he asked her the same questions about her marriage. When the answers did not jibe, he refused them entry.

The trio then retraced their steps to Montreal, arriving in the early morning hours. Leaving the automobile on a side-street near the Mount Royal Hotel, they disappeared. But it was a distinctive-looking machine, and when they were seen abandoning it and walking away without locking it, a witness remembered the incident.

· · ·

The body of Adelard Bouchard was discovered about one o'clock on the afternoon of June 18 by Charles Helm, a young lad delivering meat by horse and wagon near Huntingdon. His elevated seat enabled him to see the taxi-driver lying in the long grass, which hid the body from pedestrian or car traffic. When the police arrived, they found that Bouchard's wallet and other identification were missing, but they did locate a woman's hat, some stockings, and other feminine apparel near the body, which were later identified as articles worn by Doris McDonald.

Bouchard's vehicle was soon discovered in Montreal, and on examination disclosed a .38-calibre bullet lodged in the roof. There were two other slugs in the car, both fired from a .25-calibre gun. One was embedded in the floor and the other in the roof.

It was not difficult to trace the movements of the Bouchard limousine from Lachine to the Mount Royal Hotel, where detectives obtained complete descriptions of the three passengers. These matched those of the three people seen leaving the car on a side-street. Later, police were able to place the trio at the Trout River customs post where they were turned back by William C. Robie. At this point, a reward of one thousand dollars was posted for their capture.

In the meantime, the manager of the Mount Royal Hotel discovered that the cheques issued by the affable George McDonald as well as his credentials from the United States Navy were fraudulent, and this information was added to an all-points bulletin issued by the Quebec Provincial Police to Canadian and American forces.

A trail of worthless cheques later established that the McDonalds had moved westward across Canada to the vicinity of Winnipeg and from there had ducked down into the United States. By this time they were alone; the man known as Palmer was no longer with them.

The McDonalds next surfaced in Denver, Colorado, where they marked their stay by a cheque-cashing spree. Once again they were travelling with a male companion, but it was apparently not Palmer, as the description did not match. Wanted bulletins posted by Denver police throughout the West were eventually successful. On the morning of August 11, 1927, a car stopped on one of the highways leading into Butte, Montana, proved to have been purchased by a fraudulent cheque. The occupants identified themselves as Mr. and Mrs. Harry Carter. They had a male passenger, but since he was simply a hitchhiker, he was sent on his way.

The American police had as yet made no connection with the Montreal murder, and thus had no indication of the couple's true character. They were soon to find out.

Escorting them to the police station, Constable Rowe left them standing in the reception area while he reported to his superior officer. As they were waiting to be questioned, Doris McDonald asked one of the officers if he would go to their car and bring in her little dog. When his absence left them alone in the waiting area, George and Doris hastily hid their guns—the .25 and the .38—on top of a filing cabinet and covered them with papers. They were not completely concealed, however, and during the questioning that followed, one of the officers caught sight of a revolver butt. Confronted, the McDonalds admitted they had placed them there.

This suspicious act triggered a more intensive interrogation and within an hour they had been matched against the QPP wanted posters. Later, the guns were identified as those used in the murder of Adelard Bouchard. Since there were no charges against them in Montana and a strong possibility that extradition hearings would be commenced, the Butte police turned the pair over to the Denver boys.

Extradition proceedings were initiated by the Canadian government and were successful. In due course, Dan Lorrain, head of the QPP, arrived in Denver to escort the suspects back to Montreal.

In the trial that began in Valleyfield, Quebec, on December 6, 1927, Prosecutor Phillipe Brais presented sixty Crown witnesses who placed the McDonalds at the hotel, in the car with Bouchard, at the customs post without him, and finally abandoning the vehicle in Montreal. Mr. R.L. Calder, who with J.A. Legault represented the couple, advanced the interesting theory that the missing man Palmer had fired the fatal .38 shots and that the woman's .25 had only been discharged by George McDonald in a vain attempt to prevent him from killing the driver. He also suggested that Doris was completely under her husband's domination and was therefore even less responsible.

His Lordship Judge Walsh summed up heavily against the accused, and in his address to the jurors sought to link both the McDonalds to the deadly sequence of events. He was quite precise in pointing out that the .25 belonged to the woman and that she carried it habitually. There was no evidence to suggest that anyone but she had fired it inside the limousine.

Because the jury was composed of both French and English jurors, everything had to be presented in both languages and this lengthened the proceedings. Nevertheless, by December 17, the case was in the hands of the jury.

The jury agreed with His Lordship and the Crown, taking only twenty-five minutes to find both guilty of murder. They did agree with the defence on one point, however, for they added a recommendation to mercy for the woman based on their belief that she was merely a pawn. Mr. Justice Walsh sentenced them to be hanged at Valleyfield on March 23, 1928. By coincidence, this would be George McDonald's twenty-fifth birthday.

Despite the fact that Mr. Justice Walsh had made several grievous errors in his charge to the jury, the defence team decided that the weight of evidence was so clearly against them there was little to gain by following the usual appeal route. His Lordship had, for example, stated that there was no evidence that she had not fired the smaller gun. Since the only persons who could have refuted this were the accused, his comments highlighted the fact that neither had taken the stand. This type of error has always been grounds for appeal. However, Calder and Legault pooled their efforts to persuade the Minister of Justice to intervene.

On Sunday, March 18, George McDonald issued a statement absolving his wife from all blame but still claiming that the murder had been committed by the elusive Mr. Palmer. What effect this had on the Minister's final recommendation to Cabinet is not known. The Cabinet's subsequent suggestion to the Governor-General was based on her youth—twenty—and their belief that "she was absolutely under the influence of her husband." On March 20, the Governor-General issued Orders in Council confirming McDonald's execution and commuting Doris's sentence to life imprisonment.

Her last communication with her spouse was to send a telegram of love the day before his execution. He was hanged at Valleyfield by Arthur Ellis at 5:37 AM on March 23. Doris served ten years of her sentence before being paroled on March 28, 1938. Like her husband, she remained silent about the actual sequence of events in the slaying of the taxi-driver, though she did support her husband's assertion that Palmer was the chief actor. She was deported to Rhode Island to the care of her foster parents. The mysterious Mr. Palmer was never located, though the Quebec Provincial Police kept the file open for years. His part in the slaying remains unsolved to this day.

· · ·

Tomasina Sarao

The Blue Bonnet Murder

*B*Y COINCIDENCE, the next murder for profit took place in Quebec just seven years later. The slaying of Nicholas Sarao, fifty-nine, was planned around the kitchen table at the Sarao residence, 1513 Barre Street, Montreal. The ringleader was his wife, Tomasina, thirty-five, and her associates were Leone Gagliardi, twenty-nine, and his friend, Angelo Donafrio, twenty. From time to time, Mrs. Giovannia Teolis, Mrs. Sarao's sixty-eight-year-old mother, sat at the table with them, but her contributions to the cause were minimal. Indeed, her senility was so advanced that it is questionable whether she even knew what they were talking about.

The motive behind the proposed killing was based on ten, thousand-dollar life insurance policies on the life of Nicholas Sarao; his wife, needless to say, was the beneficiary. Once he had been dispensed with and the insurance collected, the plotters intended to turn their attention to the oldest Sarao son, who also carried insurance payable to his mother. The only delay in initiating their fiscal program was their inability to decide upon a safe method of committing the first murder. By the third week of June 1934, however, the last detail had been worked out and the three conspirators were ready to take the first step.

The success of the scheme hinged upon the ability of Leone Gagliardi and Angelo Donafrio to lure Nicholas Sarao to some deserted spot and there murder him. This accomplished, Tomasina Sarao would then go to the police with a story that she had been walking with her husband, who had left her for a few minutes but had not returned. She would carefully establish the time of this event as having taken place after the actual killing, in order to allow the men to set up alibis. The date was set for Saturday, June 23, 1934. Leone Gagliardi would earn seventeen hundred dollars for his part and Angelo Donafrio would pocket five hundred once Tomasino had received the insurance money.

On the appointed day, Gagliardi lured Mr. Sarao to the vicinity of the Blue Bonnet Race Track with a story that a rich Montreal businessman wanted them to work on his garden. They were joined, by prearrangement, by Angelo Donafrio, but it soon became apparent there was a problem. Conferring out of earshot, the two men discovered that neither of them had brought a weapon, each having thought that the other would bring the instrument of death. They covered their blunder by explaining to Sarao that they had mistaken the day on which their prospective employer wanted them to come.

Undaunted, they resurrected their murderous scheme the following Thursday, June 29. Leading Nicholas Sarao to the Blue Bonnet Race Track, Gagliardo waited with him on a railway spur that ran beside the stables. Young Donafrio soon appeared, carrying a wooden leg torn from a baby crib. In an unguarded moment, Gagliardi struck the victim from behind with the wooden club. To finish the job, he used a large rock and then left Sarao lying with his neck across a rail. Having reported to Mrs. Sarao that their part of the bargain had been carried out, the killers then proceeded to establish alibis for themselves.

The next morning, Tomasina Sarao went to the police station with her report, which was dutifully noted. She was advised that the police would keep watch for him.

The body was first discovered about eleven o'clock that morning by Olivier Deschamps, a private detective. While he was absent notifying the police, a second man, Steven Brassen, also came upon the battered corpse and contacted the authorities. Once the cadaver had been identified as that of Nicholas Sarao, an Italian labourer employed by the Montreal Roads Department, the murder investigation was placed in the hands of Detective Sergeant Ernest Francoeur.

Quickly linking Tomasina Sarao's missing-person report to the victim, Detective Francoeur sent a team of men to the courtyard where Mrs. Sarao claimed her husband had disappeared. The occupants reported unanimously that no one had entered the area at the time in question. Confronted with this contradiction, Mrs. Sarao nevertheless maintained her position.

After ruling out robbery and a gangland slaying as motive, the sergeant examined possibility of a love triangle. Noting that Sarao was much older than his wife, he turned his attention to male visitors at the couple's home, and brought Leone Gagliardi in for questioning after learning that he was frequently seen at 1513 Barre Street during the husband's absence.

The police announced shortly that Gagliardi had confessed to the murder and had implicated both Donafrio and Mrs. Sarao. Gagliardi claimed under questioning that Mrs. Sarao had been after him for nearly three years to kill her husband for the insurance and further that her mother, Mrs. Giovannia Teolis, had also been present during many of these discussions around the kitchen table.

As a result of this alleged confession, the police arrested the other three and all four were held for the coroner's inquest. Under intense questioning, Donafrio broke down and added his voice to the canary song.

At the inquest conducted by veteran Deputy Coroner Pierre Hebert on Tuesday, July 3, all four were found criminally responsible for the death of Nicholas Sarao. Tomasina continued to maintain her story that she had last seen her husband alive on the evening of Thursday, June 29, and vigorously denied any "murder plot."

Commonly referred to as the Blue Bonnet Murder, the case attracted a great deal of attention from local media, who covered it from every angle. As a result, the details were public knowledge before it came to trial and it was extremely difficult to find unbiased jurors. One hundred and fourteen people had to be called on October 1 before a panel could be assembled to hear the evidence along with Mr. Justice Loranger.

Crown Prosecutor Gerald Fauteau decided to try the three main conspirators at the same time and to delay the prosecution of Giovannia Teolis, whom he believed was incapable of forming any intent and had been only an innocent, uncomprehending bystander. Eventually, he dropped all charges and released her.

The only real evidence linking the trio to the murder were Gagliardi's and Donafrio's confessions, and on the third day of the trial prosecutor Fauteau made an attempt to introduce the one attributed to Gagliardi. When the defence objected, the jury was excused while both sides debated the issue. Gagliardi took the stand and stated that the confession had been beaten out of him by the police who assured him, he claimed, that if he signed a confession, he would receive only a short sentence. Several police officers then testified that the statement had been made voluntarily and that neither force nor inducement had been used. At the conclusion, Mr. Justice Loranger decided that the confession was admissible and allowed the whole *voir dire* to be repeated with the jury present.

The following afternoon, young Angelo Donafrio took the stand

and the jury was excused once again while the court discussed his confession. Guided by his lawyer, Donafrio claimed that Detective Sergeant Prysky had dictated a copy of Gagliardi's confession and then forced him to sign it. The confession said that Gagliardi was the killer and that he, Donafrio, had merely been a witness. Once again, police officials denied the allegations, and once again His Lordship decided to admit the document and arguments to the jurors.

At the conclusion of the Crown's case, Mrs. Sarao's lawyer, Mario Latroni, announced that he would not call her or any defence witnesses to the stand.

Despite the dramatic nature of the case, the jury took only thirty-five minutes to return guilty verdicts against all three. There was no recommendation to mercy. In ordering them to be hanged at Montreal's Bordeaux jail on January 18, 1935, His Lordship was most harsh in sentencing the woman, remarking that not only was she the instigator, but that she had kept the murderous plot alive for months while carrying on the facade of being a loving wife.

The controversial admission of the two confessions stimulated the appeal process, and the execution date was set back to March 29. When the appeals failed, the new date was confirmed.

Mrs. Sarao was housed in the Fulham Street Women's Prison but was moved to Bordeaux the evening before the command performance. There, in addition to Leone Gagliardi and Angelo Donafrio, a fourth person shared death row. Joseph Alisaro had been sentenced to hang in the early morning hours of March 29 for the murder of his girlfriend, Miss Graziella Viens. Thus, when seventy-one-year-old hangman Arthur Ellis arrived at the prison on March 28 to test the scaffold and interview his victims, he expected to perform one double and two single hangings. However, Alisaro was granted a last-minute respite while his conviction was being appealed, and a new date of May 3 was set for him.

There were two scaffolds in place that night, situated on opposite sides of the junction between the cell block and the administration wing. Ellis planned to execute the two men together on one scaffold and then cross the building and hang Tomasina Sarao from the other. His normal procedure was to interview his clients and weigh them before calculating the drop for each one, and he did this for both Donafrio and Gagliardi. However, he was refused permission to examine Mrs. Sarao at the women's prison and was handed a slip of paper with a number on it that he was told was her weight.

On the eve of the executions, the two men were moved from their death cells to waiting-rooms opposite the gallows, and Mrs. Sarao was housed in a cell on the other side of the administration block. At eight the next morning, Ellis went for his first two victims, secured their arms, and escorted them to the infernal machine. Strangely, it was the young man, Donafrio, who walked steadily to his fate. Gagliardi staggered a few times before reaching the trap.

Arthur Ellis was an old-fashioned hangman who scorned such innovations as the Marwood Noose, a rope with a steel eye-bolt at one end through which the other end was passed to form a loop. This form of noose slid easily and freely, and there were rarely any bungled hangings in which the victim strangled to death rather than dying instantly from a broken neck and ruptured spinal cord. A man with theories and techniques of his own, Ellis preferred to make a series of knots in his ropes, this cluster of knots then supposedly striking the condemned person behind the left ear and breaking the neck. Because the knotted rope was stiff, however, it had a tendency to slip from its position and fail to perform the function properly. Victims in these fouled-up executions died from strangulation.

The deaths of Donafrio and Gagliardi were not "clean," and both men strangled to death before being cut down by the prison doctor. As he left the platform and went to the room where Mrs. Sarao waited, Arthur Ellis was disturbed and agitated by his failure with the first two hangings. It was perhaps this state of mind that accounted for the incredible blunder that followed.

On entering the Women's Prison, Tomasina Sarao had weighed 145 pounds. This was the weight recorded on the slip given to Arthur Ellis. He calculated her drop based on this figure. However, she had gained 42 pounds in jail and now weighed 187. Ellis's degree of distraction must have been considerable for him not to have noticed the discrepancy between the large woman before him and the comparatively small figure on the slip of paper.

Quickly pinioning her arms, Ellis led Tomasina out onto the second metal scaffold, where she stood calm and motionless during the brief ceremonies that took place there. Ellis invariably asked his clients to confess on the scaffold—it made his job easier—but in response to his question, Tomasina Sarao merely smiled at him grimly. The hangman then lowered the black County Kerchief (the hood) and pulled the trapdoor lever. As a result of his miscalculation, Tomasina's head was snapped from her body when she reached the end of the fall, both parts falling into the room below. Blood spurted from her corpse, drenching the walls and both convicts who waited beneath the trap to place her body in the coffin.

Mrs. Sarao's decapitation posed special problems for the authorities. Her family had petitioned for and received permission to take her body away for burial. In addition, the press had followed the case intently and reporters were waiting for the final announcement. In a gruesome compromise, the body was released to the family only when they promised not to capitalize on its sad, headless state. Further, no photographs were to be taken. The coroner's jury under Dr. Pierre Hebert duly noted that Tomasina had come to her death by decapitation and assigned no blame for the "judicial error."

Such a *faux pas* could not be concealed, however—too many people knew about it—and the press had a name-calling field-day. The macabre mismanagement of Mrs. Sarao's death ended Arthus Ellis's professional career. He had, by his own estimates, hanged or assisted at the executions of more than six hundred people in England, Canada, the Caribbean, and the Middle East. Fearing another blunder, sheriffs across the country placed a virtual boycott on his services. When requests came from other countries for the loan of an experienced executioner, they were passed on to other practitioners of the deadly art. Writing to the Minister of Justice, Mario Latroni, Tomasina's lawyer, complained bitterly: "Justice should take its course, but carelessness in inflicting the death penalty is inexcusable."

. . .

Jessie Taylor
The Body in the Road

O F ALL THE MOTIVES FOR MURDER, the classic murder for profit is the simplest to demonstrate for a jury but the most difficult for the average person to understand or accept. Rage, lust, fear, and hatred are emotions that well up within each of us at some time during our lifespan and are thus closely associated with the act of being human, and we are therefore better able to comprehend them and, perhaps, even lean towards a greater acceptance. Murder for gain evokes the least amount of sympathy and its presence sets the perpetrator aside as having an inhuman quality that presents a greater risk to society than mere emotional instability. Crown prosecutors love it, for it ensures a greater conviction rate. In the case of Jessie Taylor, the only one of these seven women who actually committed the crime herself, the prosecution presented profit as the motive, but the jurors based their final decision upon another cause.

The Crown's case seemed clear-cut. George and Jessie Taylor, both fifty-two, lived in a run-down house on Pall Mall Street in London, Ontario. During their marriage, they had brought fourteen children into the world, of whom eleven had survived to adulthood. Since neither George nor Jessie was skilled or trained, their modest abode had few of the amenities of gracious living. In short, they were dirt poor.

Annie Templeton, sixty-seven, a widow from Stratford, Ontario, was a frequent visitor at their home. Like them, she had experienced a difficult early life, and with the passage of the years, death had taken her friends and relatives. Never having been blessed with children, she was alone in the world, and at this point the Taylors were the only people who might qualify as friends. In February 1939, they invited her to come and live with them on Pall Mall Street.

Around March 1, the two women went to see lawyer Harrison G. Fraser for the purpose of drawing up a will for Mrs. Templeton. Although it was understood that Templeton wished to leave everything she possessed to Mrs. Taylor, Mr. Fraser suggested that because of her advanced age it might be wise to obtain a certificate of health from her doctor before he drafted the document.

Back the following day with the doctor's certificate, Mrs. Templeton went in to see the lawyer alone while Jessie Taylor waited in the anteroom. She had changed her mind. Instead of leaving her modest estate of nineteen hundred dollars to her friend, she decided to make the Continuing Presbyterian Church her beneficiary, and she asked Harrison Fraser to say nothing of this change.

The Crown was to contend that Jessie Taylor believed herself to be the sole beneficiary and killed Annie Templeton for this reason. There was, however, another issue.

Jessie Taylor and Annie Templeton were both women with set patterns and strongly held views. From time to time there were spats over the rearing and care of the Taylor children, about the preparation of meals and the sharing of common household chores, but none of these appeared to be of a serious nature.

On the evening of March 27, which was a Monday, the two women attended services at the Continuing Presbyterian Church and returned in good humour. Both in their own ways were religious, though the older woman seemed to take her beliefs more earnestly. As they entered the kitchen, they found George Taylor playing cards with three children while a fourth looked on.

Annie Templeton undertook to warn George Taylor that this was sinful, that cards were the tools of the Devil and that he was corrupting the lives of his children. A weak man, George wilted under her attack, but his wife leaped to his defence and the argument was on. Like most family squabbles, it quickly abandoned the original cause of conflict and branched out to include other sore spots. According to George's later testimony, it was no different from any previous argument, though it did persist for longer than usual.

Around nine-thirty, he and the children retired to their bedrooms on the second floor, leaving the two women muttering at each other in the kitchen. A short while later, when the voices stopped, he assumed that both women had gone to bed in a room they shared on the ground floor.

About ten minutes to four the next morning, Tuesday, a truck-driver named Henry Whitworth was driving past the Taylor home on his way to work when he saw a dark object lying in the roadway. With his headlights illuminating the spot, he got out to check and discovered an elderly woman, fully clothed, lying on her back with both hands folded across her chest. Beyond assuring himself that she was dead, he did not touch her but contacted the London police.

Detectives Walter McCullough and Earl Knight answered the call, expecting to find that the woman had been the victim of a hit-and-run accident, but the discovery of several jagged wounds on her head, coupled with no corresponding cuts in her hat, quickly disposed of that theory. In addition, her shoes were scuffed in such a way as to suggest that she had been dragged into the middle of the road. A medical examiner later confirmed that she had been killed elsewhere and left in the road. The blows, he said, had been inflicted with a blunt instrument, possibly wooden. The wounds had been partially cleaned and since there was no blood on her undergarments and blouse, she had clearly been dressed after the attack.

When the woman was identified as Mrs. Annie Templeton, the police turned their attention to the Taylor household. George could tell them little except that he had turned in for the night with his children around nine-thirty and that he had heard nothing unusual during the night. The children confirmed this. Jessie Taylor added that she and Annie had retired around eleven, and that when she awoke in the morning the older woman was gone. She assumed that her friend had gone for an early morning walk and she knew nothing more until she heard the commotion outside her house and learned that Annie had been struck by a truck or something.

Noting that the kitchen floor showed signs of having been freshly scrubbed, the detectives believed she knew much more than she was admitting and took her down to headquarters for further questioning. Faced with a growing mass of medical and other information that the police had gathered, Jessie Taylor made a fuller statement.

She admitted that they had been arguing in the kitchen but contended that Templeton had lost her head and struck her. Since Templeton was a bigger woman and stronger despite her years, Jessie had grabbed a piece of wood from the woodbox and struck her with it, upon which Annie had fallen backwards and hit her head on the side of the stove. When water failed to revive her, Jessie had dragged her outside in the hope that the fresh air would restore her to consciousness. When this did not help, she had taken her to the middle of the road and left her there, hoping that the death would be attributed to a hit-and-run driver. She placed the time of this last act at shortly after midnight.

On the basis of this statement, she was charged with murder.

At her preliminary hearing in April 1939, Jessie Taylor stuck to this version, but the weight of physical and circumstantial evidence punched two major holes in her statement. First, tests showed that Annie Templeton had been attacked in the bedroom, probably while she was sleeping. Her body had then been moved to the kitchen, where it was cleaned and dressed in outdoor clothing before being dragged outside to the roadway. The kitchen floor had probably been cleansed of blood after this. Second, Jessie had claimed that she had left the body in the street around midnight but the Crown unearthed several witnesses who had driven along Pall Mall between midnight and three o'clock in the morning. None had seen anything in the roadway.

Defended by A.B. Sudkind, Jessie Taylor made her appearance

before Mr. Justice Makins and jury on September 26, 1939, and after a three-day trial was found guilty. The Crown contended that she had killed Mrs. Templeton in bed with a piece of kindling, and that the motive was to profit from the will supposedly drawn up in her favour. Taking the stand in her own behalf, Jessie maintained that the death was the result of the prolonged quarrel that had arisen over the card-playing and that she had acted in self-defence.

While the jurors clearly believed that her account of the sequence of events was not completely accurate, they also felt that she had acted with belated anger and rage in striking the older woman in bed, and that she had been driven by emotion rather than by any sordid profit-based motive. So, although they found her guilty of murder, they strongly recommended her to mercy on this basis.

Sentenced to be hanged at London, Ontario, on December 14, Jessie's sentence was commuted to life imprisonment on December 9, 1939. She was confined in the Women's Penitentiary at Kingston, and after serving twelve years to the day she was paroled in 1951 and returned to her family.

. . .

Elizabeth Popovich
The Death of Louis Nato

*T*HE CASE OF ELIZABETH POPOVICH is typical of the murder-for-profit profile of Canada's female killers. She had been associated with the victim at one time; she was an accomplice rather than the actual murderer; and she was reckless of the consequences of her behaviour.

Some time around one o'clock in the early morning of Monday, June 17, 1946, Elizabeth Popovich and her husband, George, appeared at the home of Louis Nato, storekeeper in the village of Thorold South, a few kilometres from Welland, Ontario. A fifty-year-old Yugoslavian, Louis had operated his store for some years and was known as a friendly, happy-go-lucky character with an eye for the ladies.

The Popovichs remained at Louis's home only a short time before the three of them left in the Nato car. He was driving and they were sitting in the back seat. They were seen at about one-thirty by Charles Manning, an employee of the Ontario Paper Mill, who recognized Nato but was unable to identify the couple in the rear.

Two hours later, Louis Nato showed up at the home of Mrs. Helen Weiser, his face was bruised and his head bleeding. He was having difficulty walking and was clad only in shoes, socks, underwear and a sweater. His pants were missing. He asked Mrs. Weiser to phone for a taxi, but as she had no phone, all she could do was wipe some of the blood from his face and give him a drink of water before he disappeared into the night.

A few minutes later, Louis appeared on the doorstep of John Tychynski, another storekeeper in the village, and again asked that a taxi be called. Noting his battered condition, however, Tychynski made him lie down and contacted the local chief of police, Dennis Harold.

When Chief Harold arrived, Nato would give no information about the beating he had received, but left the chief with the impression that it was a personal matter that he preferred to deal with himself. Dennis Harold then drove the injured man to Nick Bougay's house, where he was given first-aid treatment. When dawn broke, Harold took him to the Maplehurst Hospital, a nursing home operated by Dr. William H. McMillan and Mrs. Florence Stevenson.

When Louis did not respond to medical treatment and his condition worsened over the next two days, Dr. McMillan finally advised him that he was dying. He had bandaged his wounds and treated him for broken ribs, but the injuries were far more serious than at first expected. Nato then made a death-bed statement in the presence of Dr. McMillan and the matron, Florence Stevenson, saying that a man named George Popovich and his wife, Elizabeth, had visited him early Monday morning and asked him to drive them to an unknown destination in his car. Following their directions, he had chauffeured them to a deserted stretch of back road, where they had attacked him, kicking and beating him. He had managed to get out of the car but was struck on the back of the head and lost consciousness. When he awakened, his car and the assailants had gone and he was lying in the ditch beside the lane. His pants had been torn off and were lying some distance away and $283 had been taken from his wallet. He had managed to make his way to Mrs.

Helen Weiser's home and from there to John Tychynski's place. The rest they knew.

Shortly after making this death-bed statement, Louis lapsed into a coma and was taken by ambulance to St. Catharines General Hospital, but efforts there to assist him also failed and he died on Friday, June 21.

Inexperienced in murder investigations, Chief Harold enlisted the assistance of Inspector George MacKay of the Ontario Provincial Police, and acting on Louis's death-bed statement, questioned George and Elizabeth Popovich. He knew them both well. George Popovich was of Polish descent, forty-five years of age, and had lived in Welland for fifteen years before moving to Thorold South in 1944. His thirty-eight-year-old wife, Elizabeth, was originally from Regina, Saskatchewan, where she had been married to a man named Johnson, who had died, leaving her with three daughters. She had lived in and around Thorold for the past ten years.

There had been a problem over Elizabeth's marriage to George Popovich. She had been housekeeper for Louis Nato in 1943–44 but had left him and a year later married George. At that time, 1945, Louis Nato had gone to the police chief and asked him to prevent the marriage. "I delivered Nato's message twice," Chief Harold recalled, "but she said that she would marry George because Nato had treated her bad."

On being questioned, the couple produced an alibi that placed them in Welland at the time of the attack on Louis Nato, which was presumed to have taken place around two o'clock in the morning. The alibi was strengthened by their oldest girl, Florence, who said she had heard her parents' car drive into the yard well before this time and that they had not gone out again. George also stated that he had no need for Nato's car since he had one of his own and had driven it to Welland and back that night.

Louis Nato's car did not surface for some time, but when it was finally found abandoned on a side-street, its discovery proved to be a turning point in the case against the Popovichs. Lying on the floorboards of the car, Inspector MacKay and Chief Harold found a button from a woman's coat, which had apparently been torn from its mooring during a struggle as threads and cloth still adhered to it. The button matched those on one of Elizabeth Popovich's coats from which a button was missing. While not conclusive in itself, it suggested they were on the right track.

The Popovichs were arrested in early July and committed to stand trial before the Fall Assizes at Welland. Their trial opened before Mr. Justice W. Schroeder on September 10, 1946, with Mr. Hopp for the prosecution and Mr. Musgrove for the defence. The strongest evidence against them was the victim's death-bed statement and the button found in the rear of his car. The weakest link was the apparent alibi that the couple were in Welland that night and had returned before the murder and had not left their home afterwards.

Florence, eighteen, Elizabeth's daughter from her former marriage, had earlier given a statement to OPP Inspector George MacKay that supported her mother's alibi, but under vigorous cross-examination she admitted that she had lied earlier and in fact did not know when her parents returned home that night.

On the second day of the trial, both George and Elizabeth took the stand in their own defence, continuing to maintain that they had been in Welland that evening. The testimony of other defence witnesses was so vague and their reputations in the community so questionable that they made somewhat unfavourable impressions on the jurors.

A verdict of guilty was returned against both defendants after only three days of trial, and they were sentenced to be hanged on November 12. There was no recommendation to mercy for either.

A respite was granted in order to take the case to the Ontario Court of Appeal, but the action was based upon an entirely new explanation for the death of Louis Nato. It contended that George Popovich had returned home on the night in question to find the victim in bed with his wife. In a fit of rage, George had attacked him and had beaten him. Later, he and Elizabeth had taken the unconscious man to a lonely road and dumped him there "to teach him a lesson." They had not expected him to die.

This story might have been plausible had it not been for the evidence of Charles Manning, who had identified Louis Nato as the man driving away from the Nato home on the fatal night. The appeal was dismissed and a new date of execution fixed for December 5, 1940.

Normally, the gallows would have been built well in advance of the official date, but during the week just prior to it Rev. Dr. Harvey Forester sought a last-minute respite from the Minister of Justice, The Hon. Louis St. Laurent. Because of this, the Welland County sheriff delayed construction.

When reached for comment, Mr. St. Laurent was attending a United Nations conference in New York and he refused to intervene further in the case and word was sent to Welland at the last moment. On December 4, the day before the execution, the hammers of local carpenters reverberated throughout the prison as the grim structure swiftly took shape. The couple's last-minute request to spend a few quiet moments together was refused and Popovich was hanged on schedule at 12:45 AM in the prison yard. His clean, efficient execution meant that there was scarcely any delay before the woman was taken from her cell.

Calling out "God bless you all," Elizabeth Popovich plunged to her death at 1:00 AM to become the only woman ever executed in Welland County. After the dire rites, relatives spirited the bodies away for secret burial.

· · ·

Marguerite Pitre

The Woman in Black

*T*HE FORTY-NINE WOMEN who were sentenced to death between 1754 and 1954 took the lives of seventy-nine known victims; there were three or four other possibilities, but authorities were never able to clearly establish the manner of death as homicide. This figure is distorted by the inclusion of Mrs. Marguerite Pitre's case, in which twenty-three persons died, although there was only one intended victim. Had she not employed such a diabolical method of murder, the statistic would have read forty-nine killers and fifty-seven dead.

Simply put, the crime of Mrs. Pitre, J. Albert Guay, and Genereux Ruest, who perpetrated Canada's worst mass murder, was the personalized killing of one human being and the incidental destruction of twenty-two other "things." Had they shot Mrs. Rita Guay and the bullet in passing through her body had shattered a window-pane, that sheet of glass would have had the same significance for them as the lives of the other twenty-two passengers and crew aboard the bombed-out aircraft. In this, their crime was unique in Canada and has only one other parallel in the Canadian scene—the tragic Air India disaster of 1985.

The crime itself was simple enough. On the afternoon of September 9, 1949, a Quebec Airlines DC-3 took off from Ancienne Airport in Quebec City and headed for Baie-Comeau and Sept-Îles; it was a regular triweekly flight from Montreal via Quebec City and promised to be uneventful, but the plane crashed on Cap Tormente on the north bank of the St. Lawrence River. It was some hours before rescue teams could reach the remote site, and when they arrived they found all twenty-three persons aboard dead. Fortunately, the plane had not caught fire on impact and there was plenty of wreckage to examine for clues.

Because of the magnitude of the disaster—it was Canada's worst plane crash to that point—a special inquiry was launched. An investigative team headed by RCMP Inspector René Belac, assisted by Corporal Gerald Houle, and composed of members of both the RCMP and Quebec Provincial Police, went to the scene. Under the supervision of air-crash specialists, they collected and examined all parts of the DC-3 and after two days of exhaustive work, they reached the horrifying conclusion that an explosion in the baggage area had caused the crash. This finding was made public on September 12.

The resulting murder investigation concentrated on two areas of interest. The first centred on the baggage on the aircraft. This task was simplified by the fact that all luggage had been removed from the airplane at Ancienne Airport in Quebec City, and that only new baggage consigned for Baie-Comeau and Sept-Îles was on board at take-off. By tracing the sender and consignee of each piece, the police eliminated all articles except one, a twenty-eight-pound (thirteen-kilogram), paper-wrapped parcel addressed to a fictitious name and number at Baie-Comeau. The sender's name and address were spurious as well.

Willie Lamonde, freight-handler at the airport, was able to recall this specific parcel because of the way it arrived at his desk. Brought by a stout woman in a taxi, it had been too heavy and awkward for her to carry, and the taxi-driver had toted it to his counter. Except that the woman was dressed entirely in black, he could not recall any other distinguishing features.

It did not take the police long to locate the cab-driver, but he could add little to the description of the woman the police were to dub "The Raven" because of her black costume. And since there was no requirement for taxi companies to keep a record of fares in those early days, he could not tell them where he had picked up this passenger. With no further leads, that line of investigation seemed to have stalled.

The second investigative approach centred on the personal lives of the crew and passengers. None of these, it turned out, had recently had large insurance policies taken out on their lives, and none had large estates from which a murderer might benefit. A scrutiny of ex-employees of the airline failed to unearth any disgruntled people or "weird ones" with a possible motive for terrible revenge. The only unusual item that turned up was that the husband of one of the passengers had been fined the previous June for threatening a sixteen-year-old waitress with a revolver. His name was J. Albert Guay and he was a Quebec City jeweller.

It was a slender lead indeed, but since it was 'the only game in town,' the police pursued it. Contacted at the Monte Carlo Cafe in downtown Quebec City, the waitress, Marie Ange Robitaille, admitted that she knew Guay and explained that their earlier spat had been reconciled and they were still friends. The police were to discover that the word "friends" concealed a much more intense relationship. When asked if she knew any stout woman connected with J. Albert Guay, she replied that a Mrs. Marguerite Pitre might fit the bill. Mrs. Pitre lived at 49 Monseigneur Gauvreau Street, Quebec City.

Picking up the cab-driver, the police staked out this address. When Mrs. Pitre came out, the chauffeur identified her as the woman he had taken to the airport and whose parcel he had carried to the counter. Convinced that they were closing in on their prey, the police began an intensive investigation into Mr. Guay and his associates.

Albert Guay was thirty-two years of age and had married Rita during the war, when they both worked in the same munitions factory. He sold jewellery on a part-time basis and after the war opened a store on St. Sauveur Street in a quiet district of Quebec City. He employed fifty-two-year-old Genereux Ruest, a crippled watchmaker. Ruest was Marguerite Pitre's brother.

The association between Guay and Mrs. Pitre was even closer than that; the two had worked together in munitions factories and after the war Guay had loaned her money on several occasions. Although she had not been able to repay these loans, their relationship appeared to continue on an even keel.

Despite the fact that Rita Guay was a strikingly beautiful young French-Canadian woman, the jeweller's eyes had strayed to Miss Marie Robitaille and his interest had been returned. With the assistance of Mrs. Pitre, he had set up a love-nest to which he could bring his young mistress without fear of detection.

The bomb that destroyed the Quebec Airlines DC-3 had been triggered by a clock mechanism of intricate design. The police were sure that Guay, more of a salesman than an engineer, did not have the expertise to construct such a device. Of all his associates, the only one sufficiently skilled would be the watchmaker, Genereux Ruest. As they reconstructed the crime: Guay had masterminded the plot; Ruest had made the bomb; and Pitre had carried it to the airport.

Having the strongest case against the woman, the police arrested her first. Faced with the evidence against her, The Raven sang. She agreed that Guay had the motive to kill his wife and that her brother possessed the skill to manufacture the instrument of death, but vowed he would never willingly create such a mechanism and she denied any knowledge about the contents of the package she had delivered; the jeweller had asked her to take a parcel to the airport and she had done so.

J. Albert Guay was brought to trial in Quebec City in late February 1950, and after seventeen days of testimony and argument was found guilty on March 15. The principal witnesses against him were Marguerite Pitre and her brother, Genereux Ruest. Accepting his statement that he had made several pieces of equipment for the jeweller "which might have formed parts of a bomb," but that he had never manufactured the death machine itself, the police dropped all charges against Ruest and his sister.

Probably the most incredible thing about Guay's trial was that the jury recommended clemency. Though they did not give a reason, it was thought they believed him to be mentally ill. While the method conceived to kill Mrs. Guay might have been spawned in a moment of madness, that decision had to be followed by a pattern of deliberate moves that were truly psychopathic, each designed to carry the diabolical plot one step closer to the final insane act of placing the device on the plane.

In his death cell at Bordeaux, J. Albert Guay seemed despondent and made no effort to appeal his conviction, apparently resigned to his fate. A month after the trial, however, he called the Crown prosecutor to his cell and dictated a 114-page confession in which he implicated both Pitre and her brother. They were both aware of the bomb's intent, he asserted. Ruest had put the thing together and timed it to explode while the plane was in the air; Pitre had taken it to the airport knowing what it was and what it was supposed to achieve. As a reward for their services, Pitre was to have her loans written off and the watchmaker was to receive a handsome sum of money.

On the basis of this accusation, Mrs. Pitre and Genereux Ruest were re-arrested and placed on trial. Guay's execution was postponed in order that he might give testimony at their preliminary hearings. Once he had done this, his usefulness was over and he was executed at Bordeaux Jail on January 12, 1951.

The other two conspirators fared no better. Despite his plea that he knew nothing beyond the fact that he had "made some parts for his employer," Ruest was convicted on December 13, 1950. After his case had been carried to the Supreme Court of Canada and rejected, executive clemency was refused and he was brought to the scaffold in his wheelchair on July 25, 1952.

While her brother's appeals were still pending, Mrs. Marguerite Pitre was tried and convicted on March 19, 1951. She likewise launched a series of appeals that went to the Supreme Court before she had exhausted all regular avenues of redress.

Of the three, Marguerite Pitre endured the long ordeal of trial and appeal with the greatest amount of calm. Her icy demeanour contrasted sharply with the weakness of the two males, suggesting to some observers that she might have been the prime instigator of the crime. The Department of Justice's official position, however, was that she was "the dupe of J. Albert Guay, who engineered the whole plot." Despite this primary clemency feature, the Royal Prerogative of Mercy was not exercised on her behalf, and on the night of Thursday, July 8, 1953, she was brought from the Fulham Street Woman's Prison to a cell in death row on the second floor of Bordeaux Jail. Her wait was a short one. After a few quiet moments with the two nuns who escorted her, Marguerite Pitre was led to the metal scaffold overlooking the prison yard. At 12:35 on the morning of July 9, she became the last woman to be executed in Canada. Hangman Camile Branchaud performed his task efficiently and with what humanity he could muster.

· · ·

The Strange Ones

The incidence of insanity in Canadian murderers, though this is often invoked as a measure of defence, is no higher than in the population in general, that is, about 1 percent. The incidence in the female killers selected here is six out of forty-nine. There was about each of them an aura of madness that raised their crimes above the ordinary.

Susan Kennedy

The Head in the Pail

*T*HE THREE-STOREY HOUSE at 242 William Street in Montreal was a dilapidated structure whose outside walls had long forgotten what paint was and whose dingy rooms were resplendent in cracked ceilings and falling plaster. Its occupants were no less down on their luck, but they all had one thing in common: they took care not to cross the foul-mouthed woman who lived on the second floor—Susan Kennedy.

Susan was a tall, well-built young woman of twenty-three who had arrived from Leeds, England, around 1874 and married an Irishman named Jacob Mears. After three years of marriage, they moved into 242 William Street to pursue their vocations. Jacob was a jack-of-all-trades and Susan was a prostitute. Then thirty years of age, Jacob was completely under the domination of his ill-tempered wife. They had no children.

Police frequently visited the second floor of the house, but they always came in pairs. Susan Kennedy had the habit of sitting at her front window and shouting down at passers-by in the street. Sometimes she invited the men to visit her, but more often she was just amusing herself by calling down insults to neighbours and strangers alike. When the police arrived, she was always contrite, promising to stop her outrageous conduct, but a few days later she would be at it again.

Friday, June 27, 1879, was a typical day on William Street. About seven in the morning Mary Gallagher, thirty-five, arrived, bringing with her Michael Flanagan, a customer with whom she had spent the previous evening. A stout, healthy woman, Mary had been married to James Connolly, maltster, for some six years, but had left him to pursue her calling as a whore. Michael Flanagan had brought along a bottle of whisky, but after a few drinks with the two women he stretched out on Susan Kennedy's bed and fell asleep.

Susan appeared several times at the second-floor window that morning to shout out bawdy invitations to passing males, and once she got into a screaming match with a woman across the street. At one point, Mary Gallagher came to the window to drag the cursing shrew back into the room. The street was relatively quiet after that.

Jacob Mears was in and out of the house several times that morning, and once, spotting the whisky bottle on the table, remonstrated with his wife. There were few rules he attempted to enforce, but one was *no whisky in the house*. When told that Michael Flanagan had brought it, he told her that Flanagan had to go. She merely laughed at him.

Around noon, Helen Burke, who lived in the rooms above the Mears apartment, heard a loud thump, followed by a series of noises like someone striking flesh. This went on for about ten minutes with an interval between each sound, and then, all was quiet. Towards two o'clock she heard Susan Kennedy at the window again, shouting something that sounded like: "I have been looking for revenge and I have got it at last."

When Jacob Mears returned to his home shortly after this, he stepped into a scene of horror. Mary Gallagher's body lay on the kitchen floor in a pool of blood. Beside it was a pail, and inside the pail rested a severed hand and the woman's head. When he recovered his senses, he went into a bedroom and found his wife asleep beside Michael Flanagan. Rousing her, he told her to get rid of her guest and at the same time scolded her for having allowed a murder to take place in his home. Susan, who was quite drunk, scarcely listened to him.

Needing time to think, Jacob Mears walked to the nearest grocery and bought some food. When he returned to the flat, Michael Flanagan had left, but his wife was still passed out on the bed. Jacob took his lunch into the other bedroom and ate it while he considered what was to be done about the corpse in the kitchen.

After some heavy thinking, Jacob decided that he should tell someone about the dead woman and made his way to the ground-floor apartment occupied by Helen and John Troy. Though John was absent, he told Helen about the "killed woman in the kitchen." She told him to get lost. He then went outside and stopped several passers-by but no one wanted to meddle in the affair. Rebuffed, he went back to the murder scene and sat down in the spare bedroom to await developments.

About nine o'clock in the evening, having heard no sounds from the apartment above, Helen Troy discussed the situation with her husband. Though neither wanted to risk meeting the erratic Susan Kennedy, they decided that something had to be done and compromised by sending their eight-year-old son up to investigate. He returned within seconds, white-faced and stuttering, to announce that there was a dead woman on the floor and her head was in a pail. Shocked, the couple climbed the stairs to confirm for themselves that the scene was as their son had described it. They also found Jacob Mears sitting on a chair in the kitchen and his wife asleep in the bedroom.

They called the police.

Neil McKinnon was the first officer on the scene and he was followed shortly by others. Having taken a statement from Jacob Mears, he went into the rear bedroom to rouse and question the sleeping woman. According to her, Michael Flanagan and Mary Gallagher had arrived that morning, and after an altercation, he had killed her and run away. When the policeman noticed some blood on Susan's outer clothing, he called several women into the room and asked her to remove her dress. Observing that her underclothing was saturated with blood, he promptly arrested her.

Officer Thomas McCormack arrested Flanagan on the banks of a canal the next morning. Brought to the police station, he readily gave an account of his movements. He admitted going to the Mears apartment, but said that after a few drinks he had gone to sleep, leaving Susan Kennedy and Mary Gallagher in the kitchen. When he awoke around four in the afternoon and discovered the body on the kitchen floor, he had panicked and run and then spent the night wandering the streets wondering what to do.

Although Susan Kennedy positively identified Flanagan in a police lineup, she changed her story, saying that Flanagan had indeed arrived with Mary but had gone to bed. While he was sleeping, she said, another man had come to the apartment and killed Mary.

The coroner's inquest opened on June 28, 1879, and continued with several adjournments until July 7. Besides stories from Susan Kennedy, Michael Flanagan, and Jacob Mears, the jurors heard medical testimony indicating that Mary had been severely beaten and struck repeatedly on the head. There were fourteen gashes on her skull caused by a small meat axe that was identified as the property of Jacob Mears. The woman's head had been neatly severed from her body and placed in a small tub, or pail, and later, a dismembered hand had been laid on top of it. It appeared that the murderer's original intention had been to dismember the corpse and dispose of the pieces, but the grisly task had not been completed.

Mears testified that the axe was normally kept in a trunk in his bedroom. The police found that it had been returned to the trunk with blood still clinging to it.

At the close of the inquest conducted by Dr. Joseph Jones, the jurors returned a verdict against Susan Kennedy, Michael Flanagan, and the husband, Jacob Mears, all of whom were detained for the Grand Jury. After hearing the evidence, however, it refused to indict Jacob Mears, and held him only as a material witness in the trial of the other two.

The case that became known as the Griffintown Murder began before Mr. Justice Monk on September 30, 1879. P.G. Coyle, representing Flanagan, requested that his client be tried separately, and when the prosecutor made no objection, only Susan Kennedy stood before the bench. The evidence against her was overwhelming, the only unresolved question on the minds of the jurors was the state of her mental health. When they found her guilty, they appended a recommendation to mercy on the grounds that she might have been insane. Mr. Justice Monk was not of the same opinion, however, and bound her over for sentence after the completion of the second trial.

The trial of Michael Flanagan opened on October 4 with Crown Prosecutor B. Devlin contending that both Susan Kennedy and Flanagan had murdered the unfortunate Mary Gallagher and afterwards had gone to bed together. The chief witness, Jacob Mears, gave such a confused account of the events of the fateful afternoon that his testimony was difficult to follow. Parts of it seemed to suggest that Flanagan had gone to sleep after the slaying, while other statements indicated that he had not awakened all day until after two o'clock, when Mears found the body. The poor husband had told his story so many times that the sequence had become blurred in his mind.

The jury retired at six o'clock that evening but was unable to reach a verdict. Requesting a conference with Judge Monk, they returned to the courtroom at 9:45 to ask if they could ignore the evidence given by Jacob Mears. When Mr. Justice Monk said that they could not, a heated argument ensued between judge and jurors. Finally, His Lordship announced that they might not believe Mears's testimony, but they could not ignore it. In that case, said the foreman, they had their verdict. They found Michael Flanagan not guilty.

At the conclusion of Flanagan's trial, Susan Kennedy was returned to the courtroom to hear her sentence. In her voluble remarks, she reaffirmed that her husband had not been in the house when the murder was committed. As for Flanagan, she said he had slept through the whole thing. On awakening, he had seen the corpse and cried out: "My God, the woman's head is cut off!" and with that had run from the place. Maintaining her own innocence, she still claimed that an unknown man had committed the murder. Holding out no hope that mercy would be shown, His Lordship sentenced her to be executed on Friday, December 5.

The state was not finished with Michael Flanagan, however. On Monday, October 6, the tall, slender Irishman was brought to trial for being an accessory to the murder of Mary Gallagher. Prosecutor Devlin presented a condensed statement to show that murder had been committed, and then, just before calling his first witness, suddenly decided to drop the case. Approaching the bench, he moved to dismiss the charge.

Mr. Justice Monk agreed wholeheartedly with this move. Addressing the jury, he told them that in his opinion, while Flanagan's actions were unusual, there was no evidence to show that he had participated in the murder or even tried to conceal it. He had simply run from the house in panic and kept his mouth shut, behaviour almost identical to that of other witnesses who possessed knowledge of the crime but had been reluctant to call the police. His Lordship instructed the jurors to acquit the prisoner, which they did without leaving the box.

Though there was a strong suggestion that Susan Kennedy had been of unsound mind when the terrible murder was committed, the jury had found her guilty and the case now wound its way through the usual governmental channels until it reached the office of the Secretary of State, which at that time handled all clemency cases. Officials eventually decided that the suspicion of insanity was strong enough to cloud the issue of premeditation, and on November 4 her sentence was altered to life imprisonment. She was taken to the federal penitentiary at Kingston, Ontario, where, after two years of incarceration in which her mental health deteriorated rapidly, she died of a social disease and the case of the Griffintown Murder was closed.

. . .

Hope Young

Haunted by Witches

THE TRAGIC TALE of Hope Young rocked the Maritimes in 1905 and for days the readers of every newspaper in Nova Scotia and New Brunswick were kept abreast of every minute detail. It is unlikely that any other case up to that time commanded as many column inches of front-page coverage. This of itself was unusual since the incident occurred in a sparsely settled area on the southwest coast of Nova Scotia overlooking a body of water known as St. Mary's Bay. The town, Plympton, was situated about thirty-two kilometres (twenty miles) south of Digby and was unremarkable in those early days except for the fact that it lay on the road to Yarmouth. Likewise, none of the characters who flitted through the story were either famous or particularly distinctive. The only outstanding feature was that the murder revolved around children.

The first suggestion that anything was wrong came on the afternoon of Friday, June 16, 1905. Hope Young, an extremely attractive woman of thirty, arrived at the home of a Mr. Comeau and announced that her two children were missing. She had been visiting with a neighbour, Mr. Boudrat, around four o'clock—having left the children playing in the yard—and when she returned home had discovered the two girls gone. Someone had also broken into their cabin and stolen $10.25 and a revolver before making off with the youngsters.

With most of the able-bodied men in the district out fishing on St. Mary's Bay, the search-parties consisted mainly of young boys and the women of the village, but though they searched the woods until darkness fell at ten o'clock, they found no trace of the children or their abductor.

The villagers knew little about Hope Young. She had arrived in the district only three months before with two small girls, and had taken a position as housekeeper with Kingsley Melanson, a fisherman. It was believed that she came from Boston, Massachusetts. The oldest girl was Minnie Ward, aged seven, a sickly child, very frail and underweight for her age. The younger was Elma Young, eighteen months old and rumoured to be an illegitimate child. Kingsley Melanson had lived in the district for years and was known as a kindly, industrious man. He was about forty years of age.

The following morning, a new search party consisting of about twenty-five men, women, and youths congregated at the Melanson home with the intention of fanning out from there. It was then that Hope Young made a strange statement; she said that she thought the children would be found in the woods tied and gagged. Immediately suspicious, her listeners began to question her closely but she became very vague at that point, saying evasively that she had had a vision of her children in which they were bound and had their heads wrapped. She had last seen them playing together at the woodpile, she said, and was sure their kidnapper would leave them to be found close by. Suspicion turned to anger and although several of the posse threatened her with a beating if she did not reveal all she knew, she merely repeated that her information had come to her in a dream the previous night.

The search was fruitless until about four that afternoon, when Fred O'Neil, seventeen, came upon a clump of loose branches about a mile from the Melanson cabin. Brushing these aside, he found the baby, Elma Young, her wrists and ankles bound with cloth strips and her hood tied around her head. Though bitten by mosquitoes and badly frightened, she was still alive.

The second child was found about a quarter-mile away by

Fred's brother, Clifford. This time the search-party was not so fortunate; Minnie Ward was dead. Like her sister, her hands and feet had been tied with cloth and the hood of her coat bound around her head, but where the infant's bonds had been loose, those of Minnie had been so tightly secured that she appeared to have died from suffocation.

At the inquest, which opened on Monday, June 19, the first clear picture of the tragedy began to emerge. Kingsley Melanson testified that he had left for fishing around five o'clock Friday morning and knew nothing of the affair until he returned that evening and found that a search had already been organized. A doctor gave evidence that Minnie Ward had died of suffocation, probably about twenty-four hours before he examined the remains, which placed her death some time on Friday afternoon.

Problems began to surface as further witnesses took the stand. Mr. Boudrat placed the time of Hope Young's visit to his home at four o'clock. She had stayed only a few minutes, he said, before excusing herself by saying that she had left the children playing in the woodpile. She had left about four-fifteen with a fifteen-minute walk ahead of her. A young lad testified that he had been passing the Melanson place around four-thirty and while he had not seen the children, he had heard them laughing and playing in the backyard. When Mr. Comeau set the time of her arrival at his home at a few minutes after five, it became apparent that she could not have returned home, carried the two children a mile into the woods, placed them a quarter-mile apart, tied them and then arrived at Comeau's to announce their disappearance in so short a span of time. Further complicating the time frame, the Boudrat and Comeau houses were in opposite directions from the Melanson home and equidistant from the spot where the children were located.

In her own testimony, Hope Young was quick to fasten on this time discrepancy, contending that it supported her theory that the crime had been perpetrated by some stranger during her absence.

The manner in which juries arrive at their decisions has always been, and probably will always be, a mystery to prosecutors and defence lawyers, and the Hope Young jury was no exception. Faced with irrefutable evidence that Hope Young could not have put the children in the woods in the time frame allotted, the jurors reasoned that two people could have accomplished the crime. Though Melanson claimed that he had been out fishing, they found that

Minnie Ward had been murdered by Hope Young and her employer, Melanson.

Undoubtedly, Hope Young's vision that the children would be found tied and gagged in the woods figured largely in this reasoning. The most tenable theory was that the woman had come up with this story in order to inspire the search-party to find the eighteen-month-old child before it died of exposure. The tightness of Minnie Ward's bonds and the loose manner in which those of the younger child had been fashioned lent credence to this belief. Acting on this, authorities arrested both Young and Melanson. The baby was placed in a foster home.

. . .

Two days after the coroner's jury returned their strange verdict, the case took another unusual turn. A man named Elmer E. Young arrived at Digby, Nova Scotia, announcing that he was a notary and private investigator from Boston, and that he was the father of both the children in the case. The murdered child's mother, Marie Ward, he explained, had come to live with him as his housekeeper when she was seventeen. Minnie had been born to them on September 20, 1898, and later a second child, a boy, had been born but had died at the age of nine months. He and Marie Ward had separated in 1903 and he had kept the child, Minnie.

A short time later, Hope Young moved in with him as a housekeeper and Elma was born to them soon afterwards. In 1905, Hope had expressed a desire to return to her home in Digby. Elmer had agreed and promised to send her money if she would care for both children.

The day after his arrival in Digby, Elmer Young made an attempt to take his daughter from the temporary foster home in which she had been placed. He was arrested by Sheriff H.A.P. Smith and placed in jail overnight. On his release, he hired the law firm of Frank Nichols to represent the accused woman.

Both the women named by Elmer Young told quite different stories. Hope said that she had been born at New Tusket, Digby County, one of a large family. After working in the district as a maid for a number of years, she had gone to Boston, where on May 12, 1902, she had married a man named Fred Young, Elmer's brother. He had died on September 20, 1903, leaving her pregnant. Elmer Young had taken care of her over the next few months and an arrangement had been made for her to take her child and his—Minnie—to Nova Scotia. She had never been his housekeeper or his mistress.

Scarcely had the ink dried on Hope Young's story than denials came. Her own sister, Kate Brodie, declared that Hope had never married anyone named Fred Young and that the infant Elma really was her daughter by Elmer Young. In addition, Fred Young—very much alive—stated that he had never married her and that the child was not his.

For her part, Marie Ward announced that she had never been Elmer Young's mistress/housekeeper; she had been his wife. He had apparently shown her a marriage notice with the date October 20, 1897, and while there had been no ceremony, she trusted him and believed that she was his legal wife. The rest of her story tallied with that told by her "husband."

While the good folk of the Maritimes were still trying to figure out who was lying and who was married to whom, the murder case was progressing. Hope Young and Kingsley Melanson were brought before a magistrate at Digby on June 27 and committed to stand trial. The one significant development was that the youth who claimed to have heard the children playing in the backyard on Friday, June 16, now conceded that it might have been the day before.

Reviewing the case, the local deputy attorney general decided that the only weak link lay in the fact that Hope Young's story of strangers in the neighbourhood on the day of the murder had not been thoroughly investigated. Accordingly, he dispatched two policemen—Power and Dennison—to question her at Digby prison. Frank Nichols, her lawyer, was in attendance.

The interview was held on June 30 but scarcely had the questioning begun when Hope Young announced that she wanted to make a statement. In her "confession" she said that Minnie Ward had died in her arms that morning of natural causes. Afraid that she would be accused of maltreating the sickly youngster, she had panicked and carried the body into the woods and hid it under some brush. Later, she had carried her own child out and bound it lightly. Then she had concocted her alibi. When the search-party was organized, she tried to steer searchers to where the children were located, hoping they would arrive before some ill befell her baby. She absolved Kingsley Melanson from any knowledge of her actions.

When this information was later laid before a Grand Jury, they found no case against the forty-year-old fisherman and refused to indict him. Hope Young, however, was placed in the prisoner's box on August 22.

Hope Young's confession claimed that Minnie Ward had died of natural causes and that her only crime had been to conceal this fact. But medical evidence clearly established that the child had died from suffocation. Despite ample testimony that she had always "been good to the children," psychological testimony indicated that she was of "an irresponsible character." No motive for the murder was advanced beyond the suggestion that she had become tired of caring for a sickly child. Although he had doubts that her "confession" had been voluntary, His Lordship decided nevertheless to admit it after pointing out that if he was in error, the mistake could be rectified by a superior court. The next day, taking only minutes to reach their verdict, the jury found her guilty of murder but appended a heartfelt recommendation to mercy. In sentencing her, His Lordship intentionally set the date of execution—December 20—well into the future to allow time for an appeal court to rule on the confession. Hope Young received the sentence with no expression of any kind on her pretty face. It was almost as if she did not hear the dreaded words.

The conduct of Hope Young's lawyer throughout the whole affair, and especially around the rendering of the confession, was open to some question. The most charitable view expressed was that he was too unskilled to conduct a case of such complexity. In any event, when the appeal was argued before the Supreme Court of Nova Scotia on November 19, Frank Nichols had been replaced by a Mr. R.G. Munroe. The issue argued before the five-man panel was whether the confession had been voluntary and after reserving their judgement for some days they returned an opinion that it was questionable and ordered a new trial.

As the days passed, Hope Young became increasingly distressed in her prison cell and began to suffer from fits of explosive rage in which she set fire to her cell and broke the furniture and windows. Finally, she had to be restrained in a straightjacket. By Christmas Day, her condition had become pitiful. Raving that she was beset by witches who were trying to murder her, she boasted she had bested them all and hanged every last one of them except Marie Ward, mother of the murdered child. Marie remained her only tormenter, but she was certain she would catch her and hang her, too.

A court-appointed panel of medical experts concluded that Hope Young was mentally ill and would probably never recover.

The sensations were not over yet, however, for her lawyer, R.G. Munroe, openly accused Sheriff H.A.P. Smith of abusing her in prison and thus bringing on the insanity. He made this claim on New Year's Day and followed it up a day later by alleging that county officials had taken money raised for Hope's defence and used it for other purposes. Those accused of course denied all charges, but whatever the truth, the subject around whom they revolved had long lost interest in reality.

On January 9, 1906, Hope Young was brought under heavy escort from Digby prison to the train station. Before her keepers were able to get her into a private compartment, she broke loose and began to tear her clothing from her body, alternately whimpering and screaming all the while that the witches were haunting her, trying to kill her. Eventually, she was subdued and calmed sufficiently to be taken aboard and a few minutes later left for the mental hospital at Dartmouth, Nova Scotia, where she ended her days in terrible torment.

· · ·

Angelina Napolitano
The Sharpened Axe

*I*T REQUIRES A CERTAIN FRAME OF MIND to decide to murder someone and then to seize a weapon and carry out the deed. The time that elapses between the decision and the act is often of vital importance in determining which homicide is murder and which is manslaughter. However, to decide to slay someone with an axe and then to lovingly and carefully whet that weapon to a sharpness that will ensure death seems to border on a pattern of thinking that goes well beyond ordinary murder and touches on madness itself.

The spectacle of a woman sharpening a hatchet was not an unusual sight in the Little Italy section of Sault Ste. Marie, Ontario, and no one took special interest in the activities of Angelina

Napolitano in the days immediately preceding Easter, 1911. Most of the inhabitants of Little Italy had arrived in the area directly from Italy and brought with them all the mores and customs of their native land. One of these was the belief that the husband owned his wife and that she did all the heavy work around the home. When on Easter morning, April 16, it was reported that Peter Napolitano had been found in bed with his head cut off, people remembered how industrious Angelina had been with her axe-whetting chore. They recalled other things as well.

The Napolitanos had arrived in Canada directly from Italy around the turn of the century. After several years in Montreal and Toronto, where he had been moderately successful, Peter had moved his family of wife and four children to Sault Ste. Marie. Here his fortunes changed. He was unable to find work and had no friends upon whom he could fall back in time of need. He then hit upon the idea of using his wife to mend the family fortunes, but when she refused to go into prostitution for him, he became moody and morose and substituted fists for words in his efforts to convince her. When these failed, he deserted his family in the fall of 1910 and returned to Toronto to find employment.

Left without money and with four children to support, Angelina moved in with a man named Nish, who was willing to supply the necessities of life in return for her favours. This economic union lasted only a week. After an unsuccessful search for work in Toronto, Peter came back to the "Soo" and almost immediately found employment on the night shift at the steel mill.

Angelina came home.

When he learned what his wife had done during his absence, Peter Napolitano became enraged and attacked her with a knife. At first it was thought that she would not survive the murderous assault, but after several weeks in the hospital she was discharged. With nowhere else to go, she returned to her husband.

Peter was charged with deadly assault and Mr. Uriah McFadden, one of the town's two prosecutors, conducted the case against him. To his surprise, Mr. McFadden found that public sympathy in Little Italy was all on the side of the husband. Most felt that he should never have taken her back. In the face of this, McFadden did not push the case too hard. The police magistrate, "believing that there had been considerable provocation," put Peter on probation. Mr. McFadden tried to impress upon him that stabbing wives was frowned upon in Canada but Peter insisted that in Italy these matters were settled within the family circle.

As his wife's health improved, Peter began to renew his requests for her to supplement the family income by prostitution, but she refused. Conscious of a prison sentence hanging over him if he resorted to physical violence again, Peter confined his pressure to words and veiled threats. Unable to see her way out of an intolerable situation—and with his probation drawing to a close—she decided upon murder and began to sharpen her axe.

On Easter morning, when Peter had returned from his night shift at the plant and gone to bed, she waited until he was asleep before she took the axe from its place beside the chopping block. Delivering several well-aimed blows, which severed his head from his body, she laid down the weapon and went to inform her neighbours of what she had done.

When Mrs. Napolitano came before Mr. Justice Britton and jury on May 8, 1911, she attempted to plead guilty, but His Lordship would not accept this plea and entered a not-guilty response on her behalf. He appointed Uriah McFadden to represent her. McFadden, of course, was well acquainted with the tangled circumstances of the case, having prosecuted her husband the year before. He had since gone into private practice. With no possibility of acquittal, Mr. McFadden concentrated on bringing out the sordid details of her husband's attempt to force her into prostitution. Canadian newspapers picked up this "white slavery" angle, as did the American journals, and almost before the trial was under way it had gained international repute. After a short, two-day hearing, she was found guilty. The evidence that she had first carefully sharpened the axe told heavily against her, removing any doubt about premeditation on her part. Learning that she was about six months pregnant, His Lordship ignored the usual six-week interval between sentence and execution and delayed the date to August 9, suggesting to her that because of the brutality of her crime, she should not expect leniency.

· · ·

Under normal circumstances, the Napolitano case would scarcely have attracted notice beyond the bounds of Sault Ste. Marie, but 1911 was a slack year for news and the Ontario papers picked it up and began to bombard their readers with editorials. The central theme was that Angelina was a virtuous woman driven to murder to keep from becoming a white slave. This aspect was seized upon by American journals, and several papers sent reporters to Sault Ste. Marie for additional material. They were solidly behind an exercise of clemency and published only the most favorable aspects of the issue. One paper even printed up two hundred extra copies of a petition begging for mercy and offered to supply them free of charge to any who wished a copy. It was reported that when this petition was circulated in The Soo's Little Italy it did not receive one signature.

Though the Canadian editors, seemingly confident that a commutation would be granted to Mrs. Napolitana, soon dropped the editorial pressure, the American press maintained its interest throughout the summer. One Canadian editorial suggested that the story was ideal for the American market because it combined elements of white slavery and the chance to slam a foreign government. Petitions poured in from all across the United States—even one from as remote as New Orleans—and at one point Sir Allen Aylesworth, Minister of Justice, had seven sacks of mail sitting in his office.

It seems evident that the Canadian government had no intentions of allowing Angelina Napolitano to be executed. Her sentence was commuted on July 15, 1911, long before the birth of her child. After the welfare of her children had been settled, she was removed to the federal penitentiary at Kingston. She served eleven and a half years before a Ticket of Leave, or parole, was granted to her on December 22, 1922. Her fate after that remains a mystery.

. . .

Marie Anne Houde

I'd Be Happier If You Were Dead

*T*WELVE OF THE WOMEN who were sentenced to death stood in jeopardy for their lives for the murder of children. Of these, Marie Anne Houde came the closest to paying the supreme penalty. She was indeed one of the strangest of all the female killers. The heart-wrenching murder of ten-year-old Aurore Gagnon, of St. Philomene, Quebec, was one of the most pitiable cases to come before the Quebec courts during the first quarter of this century. Indeed, so horrible and graphic was the uncontested evidence of some of the witnesses that the defence, halfway through the trial, begged to be allowed to change the original plea of not guilty to one of insanity. Also charged with the crime was the child's natural father, Telesphore Gagnon.

Marie Anne Houde had been born in 1890 in an isolated section of southeast Quebec reached only by trails leading from Montmagny on the St. Lawrence River. She was married at age thirteen and bore her young husband six children before his death. Members of her family testified that she tended to be hard on her children, rearing them strictly, but that they had never known her to abuse them. Her favourite weapons of punishment were her hands or a small whip.

After the death of her first husband, she married Telesphore Gagnon, a neighbour. Since he had three children by his first wife, Marie Anne left her own children with relatives and went to live with him. The Gagnon children were Marie, fourteen; Aurore, ten; and a boy of nine. For some reason, the chemistry between Aurore and Marie formed a powerful, explosive force and almost from the first days of their relationship she mounted a campaign of violence against the child. The father, Telesphore, instead of protecting his daughter, found himself caught up in the dreadful dynamics of the insanity and he added his abuse to that of his wife.

Because of the isolation of their small farm, the children did not go to school or church. Thus there was little chance that the marks of abuse would be picked up by the authorities. It was not until a serious injury to the child's left foot was remarked upon by neighbours that the deadly couple agreed to have her examined by a doctor. She was taken to the Hotel Dieu in Quebec City on September 16, 1919, where her injuries were cared for by Dr. Simard. Though he was suspicious about some of the bruises found on other parts of the child's body, he accepted the explanation of her stepmother that she was an awkward youngster, always falling or bumping into something.

Aurore was returned to her parents in October, only to be subjected to new horror. On several occasions Marie Anne announced in the presence of others that she "would be happier if she (Aurore) were dead." Over the next three months, the child was systematically beaten, her body burned with a red hot poker, and her arms and legs twisted painfully. Open wounds were left to fester and old ones reopened by further maltreatment. When neighbours visited, Marie Anne and Telespohore hid the poor victim from sight and enforced silence from the other two children by threats to wreak the same kind of punishment upon them.

The frail child could not long endure this kind of merciless treatment and on February 12, 1920, she died. Her body was hidden in a shed while the two murderers debated what evasive action to take. They would have preferred to bury her in secret but they feared that she would be missed.

Their problem was solved for them, however. In some manner word of the child's death spread through the community and with it the ugly rumour that something was very wrong at the Gagnon residence. The following day, Constable Laureat Couture of the Quebec Provincial Police, accompanied by Dr. A. Marois and two other physicians, arrived at the home. When they asked to see the child, they were told that she had died of natural causes and that her body was being held in a shed pending burial.

After retrieving the now-frozen corpse, the doctors made a careful examination of the other two children but found nothing amiss; both appeared to be frightened but in good health.

The autopsy performed by Dr. A. Marois on February 14 revealed fifty-four separate wounds, bruises, and fractures on the tiny remains. The oldest of these dated back several months and it was estimated that Aurore must have been in constant pain during the last ninety days of her life. Some of the wounds were as recent as twenty-four hours before death. She had literally been tortured to death. That same evening, a coroner's jury returned a verdict that she had been murdered by her father and stepmother. The pair were arrested and taken to the provincial prison at Montmagny.

When first questioned, the remaining two Gagnon children were reluctant to say other than that they had seen Marie Anne strike their sister on one or two occasions. However, with the removal of the adults from the house, the atmosphere of terror they had established lessened and the children began to reveal more and more details. By the time the trial opened before Mr. Justice Pelletier, both children had overcome their fear of talking and had gained sufficient confidence to testify in court.

Had the circumstances of Aurore's death not been so barbaric, Marie Anne Gagnon—or Marie Houde as she was more commonly known—would have been tried at Montmagny, but the emotional climate of that town was so supercharged with hostility against the pair that the hearing had to be transferred to Quebec City in the hope of obtaining a reasonably impartial jury. The woman was tried first and her trial opened on April 12, 1920.

A jury was selected with difficulty as defence counsel Francoeur challenged each panel member stiffly. During the long-drawn-out process, none of the spectators who had almost fought for seats departed from the room even to eat. The case promised to be spectacular.

The first witness was Dr. A. Marois, and his quiet presentation did not disappoint those who had hoped for sensationalism. He was followed by other medical men whose testimony was much more pragmatic but still devastating. On Thursday, April 15, young Marie Gagnon, fifteen, was led to the stand. In a clear though halting voice, she described how she had seen her stepmother beat Aurore with whips and clubs. When she narrated how the woman had burned her sister with a red-hot poker, even His Lordship had difficulty controlling his tears.

On Friday, with the young girl's matter-of-fact recitation of horror and torture completed, defence counsel Francoeur rose for cross-examination. Treating her with gentleness, he led her back through much of her testimony, hoping that it was a fabrication of an over-active imagination, but beyond a few discrepancies in small details, her evidence remained the same.

Aurore's nine-year-old brother was then placed on the stand and his story was carefully coaxed from him. In testimony that lasted into the next day, he confirmed much of what his sister had already told the court and added some incidents that had not yet been made public. Long before his testimony was completed, Mr. Francoeur had risen to his feet: "Your Lordship, before further testimony is heard the defence would like to change its plea from not guilty to not guilty by reason of insanity."

Mr. Justice Pelletier ordered that a panel of medical men be chosen—four for the Crown and four for the prisoner—and that the accused be examined over the weekend. Court was adjourned to the Monday.

When court reconvened on Monday morning, a spokesman for the medical team reported that there was no evidence of insanity in Marie Anne. While their examination had been as detailed as possible, given the time frame, they had reached a consensus that she was totally irresponsible but in no way mad. Her responses were typical of a psychiatric classification then known as "moral imbecile." The modern equivalent would be a psychopath or sociopath. There was little disagreement on this conclusion.

His Lordship accordingly dismissed the defence request to change the plea and ordered the trial to continue. He advised members of the jury that they could consider this as an alternative verdict if they wished, but he clearly leaned to the belief that she was not mad but bad. As her stepson's testimony continued, Marie Anne sat and listened with an air of almost complete detachment. At times she scarcely seemed to be aware of her surroundings or the peril that faced her. For the most part, she stared blankly ahead of her.

The lad's testimony concluded the Crown case and the balance of the day was taken up with defence efforts to lessen the terrible impact of evidence to date. Marie's father and brother strove to show that she was as gentle with her children as any normal mother would be, and that they had never seen her abuse one.

The case was turned over to the jury on Tuesday, April 20, and they were absent from their box a scant eighteen minutes before they filed back with sober faces. Completely rejecting the defence contention that "only a mad woman could carry out the things attributed to this woman," they brought in a verdict of guilty.

Before sentence was passed, Mr. Francoeur brought to the attention of the bench that Marie Anne was well advanced in pregnancy and asked that this be taken into consideration. His Lordship responded by setting the normal execution date, which would have been in June, ahead to October 1.

The trial had been emotionally devastating for everyone in the court, and it was not therefore surprising that with this final painful duty completed, Mr. Justice Pelletier broke down and cried. Strangely, Marie Anne showed the first sign of emotion at this point. Seeing the eminent jurist sobbing quietly on his bench, she lowered her head and wept. Whether it was a psychopathic ploy to gain belated sympathy, or whether some realization of her terrible crime had finally penetrated the hard shell around her, is not known.

· · ·

Telesphore Gagnon went on trial on April 23 before Mr. Justice Desy, charged as an accomplice in the murder of his daughter. A condensed version of the evidence was presented, featuring the disquieting testimony of his two children. On April 28 the jurors found him guilty of manslaughter. Public repugnance at his behaviour found its expression in the sentence meted out when he was ordered to serve a life term.

Marie Anne Houde was to have been hanged at Quebec City on Friday, October 1, 1920, and a good deal of public sentiment favoured the execution. The original date had been delayed because of her pregnancy, but after the birth of twins in late July there seemed no reason to stay the penalty. An appeal was launched to the Supreme Court of Quebec but this was refused. The issue was then clearly up to Cabinet and the Governor-General.

There was a good deal of indecision in the Department of Justice as to what kind of recommendation should go forward from the staff to the Minister. Though the case was reviewed several times, officials found no personal grounds on which to grant clemency. As the days slipped away and the time of execution drew near, it seemed that Marie Anne would be the first child-killer to pay the penalty ordered by the court. Final preparations were made at the prison and the woman seemed resigned to her fate. She received the last rites of the church and was moved from the common cells to a room near the gallows erected on the second floor.

On September 30, less than twenty-four hours before the execution, it was announced that her sentence had been commuted to life. The only reason given was that she was indispensable to the lives of her twins, whom she was still nursing. It was ironic that having taken the life of one child, and having a sentence of death read out on the basis of the testimony of two other children, her own life was spared by her latest two children.

When her child-care services were no longer required, the twins were removed from her custody and taken by a charitable organization. Marie was transferred to the penitentiary, where she remained for fifteen years before another exercise of executive clemency granted her freedom in the form of a Ticket of Leave, or parole. She was released shortly after June 29, 1935, to rejoin her husband, who had been freed earlier.

· · ·

Dina Dranchuk

The Unfriendly Neighbours

*T*HE POLISH AND UKRAINIAN PEOPLE of Flat Lake, Alberta, north of St. Paul, were by nature of their cultural and historical backgrounds suspicious of officialdom and whenever possible avoided being caught up in "government business." Among themselves they were a friendly and generous group, and more than one newcomer to their district owed much to the helping hands extended to support them through the rough initial periods of homesteading. When Mike and Dina Dranchuk moved into the area in 1930 they were welcomed and neighbours were quick to help. As time passed, however, the constant quarrelling between the two drove even friends away, and by the summer of 1934 they were living in practical isolation from the other families. They became the community outcasts. Part of the ostracism stemmed from the feeling of many that Dina was "not quite right." This was a well-established sentiment even before "The Trouble."

The Dranchuks made no secret of their discontent with each other and could often be heard screaming in the farmyard. Dina, a solidly built woman of thirty-five, would complain that she was sick and needed money for medicine and other household necessities. Her middle-aged husband could be heard loudly retorting that she was not sick and that she had all she needed. These arguments would go on for hours and recur day after day; it is little wonder that no one wished to visit. Then suddenly, on the morning of August 20, 1934, the quarrelling stopped.

Mike Dranchuk had been absent most of Sunday, August 19, and did not return home until after four-thirty Monday morning. As he walked past the outside bake-oven towards the kitchen door, his wife ran from behind the oven with a small wood hatchet, and before he realized what was happening, she struck him on the head. She slashed him again. Though stunned, he managed to run towards the door but was hit several more times before he reached it and stumbled inside. She did not pursue him.

Their shack had only two rooms, the inner one of which served as a bedroom. Mike staggered into it and roused his thirteen-year-old son William. Telling him what had happened, he asked him to go for help and then collapsed on the bed.

William ran outside and found his mother standing beside the bake-oven with a bloody hatchet in her hand. When she did not react to him, he raced across the field to the shack of their nearest neighbour, Mike Kurtyshin.

Mr. Kurtyshin had no phone in his house, but after listening to the distraught youngster he dressed and went to the home of another farmer to call the police. William had gone by the time he got back, and after a few moments of indecision Kurtyshin decided to investigate. He approached the Dranchuk shack with caution, though all was quiet and Mrs. Dranchuk nowhere in sight.

Kurtyshin was met at the door by young William, who told him that his father was dead and his mother had disappeared. With the aid of a kitchen lamp, they went into the bedroom where Dranchuk was lying across the bed with a coat over his head. Pulling it back, they saw that his skull bore numerous ugly slashes that had bled profusely. Someone, presumably Dina, had placed the garment over his face. There was only one other member of the family, a lad named Peter, six, who occupied the second bed with his mother. He had slept through the whole affair. Awakening him carefully, Kurtyshin shielded him from the sight of his father's bloodstained body as he guided him outside.

With the arrival of a medical man and the Royal Canadian Mounted Police, the body was examined and removed for autopsy. A posse was organized to search for the missing woman, while statements were taken from the two boys. William's was vital to the case, but Peter could only verify that his parents were quarrelling all the time.

Dina Dranchuk was found a short distance from the house, hiding in a field. There was blood on her clothing and she looked a little tired but beyond this, she appeared to be quite normal and surrendered quietly. The evidence against her was clear-cut and the inquest and preliminary hearing followed. She was committed to stand trial at the Fall Assizes.

The case attracted little attention, even in Edmonton, where the trial was held. The only newsworthy feature was that it was one of the last murder cases presented by veteran prosecutor Edward

Cogswell, who had gained considerable acclaim in the famous Vernon Booher case of 1929 and the successful prosecution of Fred and William McLean, the outlaw killers. Renowned for his attention to detail and his concise statements, Cogswell presented the Dranchuk case before Mr. Justice Ewing and jury on Monday, September 24, 1934.

In the two-day trial, Cogswell relied heavily on William Dranchuk's evidence, given through tears. The lad established that circumstances bound his mother and her alone to the crime. To deal with the only possible defence, Cogswell placed Dr. Charles Barager on the stand to testify that while she often acted strangely, Dina Dranchuk was not psychotic in the legal sense of the word; she could understand the consequences of her actions.

Although defence counsel Clare C. Darling had little to work with, he nevertheless managed to draw from Dranchuk neighbours several examples of Dina's strange behaviour. It was clear, however, that the Flat Lake witnesses were trying to minimize their involvement, and they were notable for their extreme reluctance to testify and the grudging manner in which they gave their evidence.

Darling's chief witness was Dr. C.D. Taylor, who had examined Dina through an interpreter since she spoke only Polish. While conceding that his testimony was clouded by this fact, Dr. Taylor felt that it was quite possible that she did not know what she was doing when she killed her husband.

Edward Cogswell took only seven minutes to point out that Dina had murdered her husband, that she knew what she was doing, and that it was wrong. She had demonstrated this by her flight from the farm and her attempt to hide in the field. He was followed by Mr. Darling for the defence, who devoted a scant five minutes to reminding the jurors that all the testimony from her children and neighbours went to prove that she had acted strangely for a number of years. This was partly supported by the Crown's own medical expert.

The only real issue before the jurors was whether Dina knew what she was doing and that it was wrong. After forty-five minutes of debate, they agreed that in the strict legal sense of the word insanity, she was guilty, but that in the broader sense of daily conduct she was strange indeed, and tempered their verdict with a strong recommendation to mercy on the latter grounds.

Dina, who had followed the testimony carefully through an interpreter, knew that if found guilty she would be sentenced to be hanged, and when the request came for her to speak to sentence she replied that it was of no concern to her. What mattered was what would happen to her children if they hanged her? In the kindest tones he could muster under the circumstances, His Lordship assured her that the boys would be cared for. This seemed to ease her mind and she lapsed back into the characteristic silence that had been her lot throughout the trial.

It was then ordered that she would be taken to the provincial prison at Fort Saskatchewan, where, on December 12, 1934, she would be hanged.

Though tension mounted in the prison and among the prison staff as the hours ticked away, Dina Dranchuk bore up remarkably well. When examined by psychiatrists appointed by the Department of Justice, she co-operated and displayed no deterioration of behaviour. In short, she was strange but not mentally ill. Nevertheless, despite the brutal savagery of her crime, Ottawa decided that the possibility of insanity existed, and that the degree to which this had motivated her was difficult to determine because of the language barrier. Rather than err, they decided to commute her sentence on December 9, just three days before her scheduled date with the hangman. She was removed from her death cell and held in the general cells to await transportation to the penitentiary.

Before that time there were no special facilities for women in local penitentiaries and all were incarcerated in the male penitentiary at Kingston. However, a women's penitentiary had been under construction for some time and it was officially opened on January 24, 1935, a few blocks from the male unit. Mrs. Dranchuk became the first female prisoner admitted to the new institution.

Her mental condition, however, had begun to deteriorate almost from the moment she was told that she would not be hanged, and her sanity slipped gradually with every passing week. She became more violent and reached the point where she could not be protected from herself or others from her, and on March 16, 1935, she was admitted to the Kingston Psychiatric Hospital for treatment. Though her condition improved somewhat, she remained there for the next forty-three years. By 1978 she was deemed capable of release and was paroled to a rest home associated with the Hospital. She remained there until her death in February 1981.

· · ·

Marie Desmeules

For Reasons Unknown

*C*ONSTABLE R. BENNETT was on duty at the Fort William, now Thunder Bay, Ontario, police station on the night of June 29, 1946, when the call came. Identifying herself as Mrs. Desmeules, the caller reported that there was a very sick woman at 121 Myle Street. In response to this, Bennett contacted a patrol car and dispatched it.

Within a few minutes of receiving their instructions at 11:45 PM, Constables Steene and Turner drew up at the two-storey house on Myle Street, which was dark except for a single lighted room on the ground floor. Leaving Turner in the cruiser, Constable Joseph Steene went to the front door and was admitted by a small, tousle-haired woman who identified herself as Mrs. Marie Desmeules. She was dressed in a kimono and slippers and there was the strong odour of liquor on her breath. Advising him that she thought there had been a murder, she led him to a downstairs room that served as a bedroom.

Entering the room, Constable Steene saw the body of a large, white-haired woman, about sixty-five, lying on the bed. Her head was bloody and one foot dangled over the edge, and there appeared to be splashes of blood on the wall beside her. The presence of reading glasses on her pillow and an open book near one hand suggested that she had been attacked while reading or had fallen asleep and then been assaulted. Returning to the patrol car, he reported the incident to headquarters and then brought Constable Turner to the scene.

Marie Desmeules told them that the victim was the owner of the house, Miss Susan Thoms. She had not notified the eight other boarders, all of whom lived upstairs. She occupied two rooms downstairs with her nineteen-month-old baby and had discovered the body when she opened the bedroom door to scrub the floor, a chore she often performed for her landlady. The presence of a mop and pail of dirty water in the bedroom seemed to confirm her story.

Marie said she had heard no noises and had no idea of who could have committed the gruesome murder.

Reinforcements arrived in the persons of Chief Charles E. Watkins, several detectives, and coroner Dr. Gillespie, and an investigation began. The upstairs boarders were awakened, but none had heard any noise during the evening. The doors, windows, and ground outside the home were checked for signs of forced entry, but none were found. The police then concentrated on the interior. A rubber glove was found on the kitchen floor behind the wood stove and revealed what seemed to be specks of blood. Its mate was located on a table in Mrs. Desmeules' sitting room. These were the only untoward items to show up.

Suspicion first focussed on Marie Desmeules following a curious incident in the kitchen. Constable Turner had taken the lid off the stove and removed a piece of birch kindling that had just started to burn. Marie, who had been hovering in the background, ran forward, grabbed the stick, and thrust it back into the fire. Startled by her action, Constable Turner shoved her aside roughly and rescued the log. When he reported the incident to the chief, he decided it might be wise to detain her and arrested her for obstructing the police. Curiously, one police officer later described her behaviour as that of a frightened woman, while another testified that she was calm and controlled. All agreed that she was coming down off a liquor binge.

The following day, June 30, Dr. Gillespie examined the dead woman and reported that the left side of her head had been broken by two blows, apparently struck by a round instrument. Bark removed from the cuts proved on analysis to be birch, suggesting that the log found in the woodstove might have been the weapon. Further checking of the ashes from the stove turned up buttons and a metal clasp, revealing that clothing had probably been burned. With this evidence in hand, the rubber gloves, Marie's kimono and other wearing apparel were sent with the log for analysis to Toronto and Marie was formally charged with the murder of Susan Thoms.

Very little was known about Marie Desmeules. She said she was thirty-eight, that she had been born in Quebec but had moved to Saskatchewan at the age of two. In 1943 she had married at Red Lake, Ontario, and lived there with her husband until March 13, 1946, at which time they had sold their house and she had moved to Fort William with her baby while her husband had gone to a mining camp north of Flin Flon, Manitoba, to look for work. She was to join him when he sent for her. The existence of this husband was never confirmed and he was never a factor in the case.

On August 1, a month after her arrest, Marie approached Mrs. Elma Filmer, matron of the jail, and asked to talk to Inspector George Marr of the local police, saying she wished to make a statement. After a formal warning, he proceeded to take a statement from her the following day in the presence of the matrons.

Marie stated that her bedroom adjoined Susan Thoms's and that she had been awakened on the night in question by the sound of voices in the landlady's room. She then heard someone come into the kitchen, which was lit only by a small, red light. "A small man came in. He was putting something in the stove and I got up and said: 'What are you doing?'" Upon which, he pulled her into the kitchen and threatened to kill her and her child if she did not do as he ordered. He would not let her look around, but made her take some papers and other articles from Miss Thoms's bedroom and put them in the stove. "I called Susie but she did not answer." He then made her begin to scrub the floor to clean up the mess. "I was bending down and when I raised my head to look at Susie, he kicked me from behind." After the floor had been scrubbed, he again threatened to return and kill her child if she told the police. He left then by the rear door.

Q: "What did this man look like?"

A: "I did not see his face. I just saw him when he was standing beside the stove. I cannot describe what the man was wearing. He seemed to be wearing a short jacket."

Asked why she had not told this to the investigating officers, she replied that she had been so frightened by the alleged murderer that she had kept quiet.

· · ·

Marie's trial opened on Monday, September 16, 1946, before Mr. Justice Daniel P. Kelly at Port Arthur. She was defended by S.E. Davis, a court-appointed counsel who had very little experience in criminal matters. Prosecutor P.V. Ibbetson had hoped that forensic evidence gathered from Marie's clothing and person might link her to the murder but Professor Joselyn's testimony on that score was inconclusive. The professor had examined twenty-eight exhibits for traces of human blood, but while blood had indeed been found on several of them, the amounts were such that they could not be identified as human. There was human blood on the kimono but not in sufficient quantity to type and compare with the blood of the victim. The piece of birch kindling, thought to be the murder weapon, had been subjected to so much heat that blood testing was rendered impossible.

The other weak link in the Crown's case was the lack of motive, and though prosecutor P.V. Ibbetson closely questioned the other boarders from the Thoms residence, all he learned was that while Marie and the victim had argued from time to time, their disagreements had been no more severe than several other roomers had experienced.

At the close of the prosecution's case, defence counsel S.E. Davis placed Marie on the stand to repeat her pathetic story of "the small man" who had invaded the rooming-house and threatened her and her child with harm if she did not obey his wishes. Clearly, nobody believed this account. What Mr. Davis failed to bring out in his direct examination, unfortunately, was any reference to the fact that she had been drinking heavily on the night of the murder. Also unexplored was a report that on admittance to the Fort William jail she had been found to be suffering from an advanced case of social disease, which could have affected her mind when combined with excessive alcoholic intake.

With none of this before them, the jury retired at 3:40 on the afternoon of September 20 and returned at 5:15 with a verdict of guilty. There was no recommendation to mercy by either the judge or the jurors and His Lordship sentenced her to be hanged on November 26.

When appeals to the Ontario Court of Appeals and to the Supreme Court of Canada were both denied, the matter was then clearly up to the Royal Prerogative of Mercy.

The Remission Service of the Department of Justice at Ottawa reviewed the case and had at its disposal not only the trial transcript but also confidential reports from the judge, the police, and doctors.

Among the doctors' comments was that it was just beginning to be known that the mental health of certain individuals was highly vulnerable to alcohol abuse, and that when the percentage of alcohol in the blood reached a specific level the person became mentally ill. When the alcoholic content dropped below that level, the person returned to sanity, sometimes with a vague recollection of what had happened; sometimes with complete lack of recall.

By the 1960s, knowledge of this phenomenon had increased to the point where psychiatrists, working in controlled settings, could bring on this spell of insanity in selected persons. When Marie Desmeules's case was being considered in 1946, this knowledge and these experiments were still in the future.

Acting on the assumption that she may have been mentally unbalanced by this combination of alcohol and social disease, the Remission Service recommended to the Minister of Justice that her sentence be commuted to life. Strengthening this "intuition" was the complete lack of motive as brought out by the evidence of the trial. Consequently, on November 22, 1946, she was whisked away to the Prison for Women at Kingston.

. . .

Love Triangles

Perhaps the motive most often associated with the female killer revolves around the love triangle, in which it is necessary for the murderers to dispose of one or two unwanted partners. It is possibly the easiest to understand and one of the simplest to demonstrate to a jury. Of the forty-nine women whose names appear here, nineteen were associated with this type of homicide. Of these, eight were hanged and eleven were spared. In ten of the cases, the woman was the actual perpetrator or played an active role in the slaying, while in the other nine instances she had foreknowledge of the crime and aided and abetted it in some manner. Only eight of the nineteen are dealt with in this section, since the remaining eleven are covered under other more significant categories.

The first for which any adequate records exist took place near Sydney, Cape Breton Island, in 1833, and though the court records have long been destroyed, a fairly detailed story was included in J.S. MacKinnon's Old Sydney, *published in 1918. The scanty archival material still remaining corroborates Mr. MacKinnon's narrative.*

Charlotte Flahaven
We Buried Him

J OHN FLAHAVEN owned a small roadhouse near North Sydney, where he dispensed liquor and provided shelter and food for the odd traveller on the road to Bras d'Or. Living with him were his wife, Charlotte, and two teenage daughters.

During the summer of 1833, a sailor named William Johnston was a frequent visitor at the tavern, and a friendship developed between him and Mrs. Flahaven. This was the subject of quarrels between the two men and the Flahaven girls were drawn into the friction as well, the younger siding with the father and the older with the mother.

A second man entered the picture that summer. Reuben Easman was a sailor from a ship that had been wrecked off North Sydney, and while waiting for a berth on a vessel back to his home in England, he had been doing odd jobs around town and in this way met William Johnston. He was described as "a quiet, inoffensive man" of apparently good upbringing, but for some reason, Johnston was able to weave a spell of dominance over him and lure him into a murder plot.

By the time Reuben Easman appeared on the scene, the friendship between Johnston and Charlotte Flahaven had progressed to sexual intimacy and somewhere along the route to this achievement it was decided to get rid of her husband. From the later behaviour of Mrs. Flahaven, it is entirely possible that she was the instigator of the plot and that she manipulated both Johnston and Easman.

On the day of the murder, Johnston and Easman came to the tavern early in the morning, planning to lure their victim away from the house and dispose of him in the nearby swamp. To this end, they loosened a prize cow that Flahaven had bought at Bras d'Or a short time before. Remembering its home, the animal started off at a stiff trot across country. The miscreants then went to advise John Flahaven that his cow had run into the woods, and as expected, he started in hot pursuit.

The fifteen-year-old daughter, who slept above the kitchen, was awakened by sounds of activity with the cow and saw the two men driving the animal away. She later observed her father go after the critter and no more than a minute passed before she saw Johnston and Easman enter the woods by a different route, one carrying an axe and the other a wooden club. Despite the suspicious nature of these activities, she dismissed them from her mind, thinking there must be a simple explanation for what she had seen. She went back to bed.

About half an hour later she was attracted by the sound of men's voices and noted Johnston and Easman returning. Her father was not with them. One of the men had what appeared to be blood on his hands. They entered the kitchen below her bedroom and she heard them talking with her mother. Gluing her eye to a crack in the rough floor planking, she saw one man go over to a wash-basin and wash blood off his hands.

She later testified to having overheard the following conversation. When her mother asked: "Have you seen my husband?" one of the men responded: "Yes, he will trouble us no more." Mrs. Flahaven questioned further: "What did you do with him?" and got the cryptic answer: "We buried him."

As Charlotte Flahaven began to serve breakfast for the two killers, one gestured upstairs with his hand towards the younger girl's bedroom. "What about her?"

Afraid for her life and terrified that her father had been murdered, the youngster crept back into bed and feigned sleep. Presently, the two men entered her room and stood looking down at her. Apparently reassured that she had seen or heard nothing, they left.

Moving with great stealth, the young girl slipped from her bed and gained the rear window. It was only six feet from the ground and she managed to lower herself without harm. She ran for the woods, directing her steps to the home of her paternal uncle some five kilometres (three miles) away at Sydney Mines. Avoiding the main trail, she remained in the woods for the entire distance. Her precaution was well taken, for as she emerged at her uncle's house, she saw the two men following along the road about 280 metres (300 yards) back.

Though stunned by her news, her uncle escorted her to the residence of Captain MacKinnon, a justice of the peace, and had her repeat the incredible story. Though sceptical, MacKinnon swore out a search warrant and dispatched three constables to the Flahaven Tavern to investigate. When they arrived, however, they found the building so heavily barricaded that they were unable to enter.

Convinced by this rebuff that there might be something to the girl's story, Magistrate MacKinnon swore in a larger posse and led them himself to the site. Faced with this show of force, Charlotte Flahaven, William Johnston, and Reuben Easman surrendered and were taken to the county jail, along with the older daughter. It quickly became obvious that the girl was not connected to her father's disappearance and she was permitted to return to the inn with her younger sister.

A search was begun for John Flahaven, but the terrain into which he had followed his cow was marshy and thick with underbrush and it was difficult to pick up tracks. After some hours, the searchers did discover an axe with blood on it. At this juncture they brought up Flahaven's dog and in short order the beast led them to a fallen log. From beneath a thick covering of leaves and moss, a single hand protruded. Following the hand, they uncovered a body ravaged by massive cuts and bruises caused by an axe and some other, duller instrument.

The three prisoners were arraigned before Judges Uniack and Hill on August 27, 1833, with twelve jurors in the box. Only nine witnesses were called and two of these were medical men; the rest were members of the family and the posses. Charlotte Flahaven's fifteen-year-old daughter, who had spread the alarm, was the key witness, and during her testimony her mother glared at her with a look of hatred on her face.

The elder daughter was called, but since she claimed to have slept through the entire sequence of events, she could add little to the picture. The last witness was the uncle, the first outsider to learn of the bloody crime.

The trial concluded the following day, August 28, and the jury had no problem returning guilty verdicts. Sentence was delayed to Friday, August 30, at which time all three were sentenced "to be taken hence and hanged by the neck until they are dead." The date was set for Thursday, September 19.

The Sydney prison, composed of logs, was not at that time the stoutest of structures. Fearing that ruffians from the ships in harbour might attempt to free the condemned trio, soldiers from the local barracks were brought in as sentries, but the days passed without incident. A special gallows capable of handling all three culprits simultaneously was constructed in the common marketplace, and on the morning of the execution, citizens and farmers thronged the area. Soldiers from the barracks militia formed an escort for the three as they were brought from the prison.

When the procession stopped at the foot of the gallows, the three were asked if they wished to make a statement or if they had any last wishes. Although the two men declined to speak, Charlotte Flahaven had one last request. She asked to say goodbye to her younger daughter. Suspicious of this apparent change of feelings, the sheriff refused to have the girl brought near. Mrs. Flahaven merely laughed, saying that if she had gotten her hands on the girl she would have killed her before any might intervene.

With that, the three were tied and lifted to the massive trap of the gallows. Fearful of reprisals if they assisted in the death of the sailor, no local man would volunteer to perform the doleful task, but the sheriff had found a sailor from a ship that had entered the harbour the evening before. He had been lodged for his own safety in the jail overnight and would be paid five dollars for his services.

Under the wide-eyed stares of the huge throng, the unknown hangman went efficiently about his task of affixing the ropes and at a signal from the sheriff pulled the lever that loosened the trap. While all eyes were riveted upon the swinging bodies, he quickly made his way through the crowd and disappeared in the direction of the harbour.

Charlotte Flahaven was the first and only woman hanged on Cape Breton Island for murder.

· · ·

Catherine Snow

The Ghost of Catherine Snow

*E*VEN AS THE JURORS in the Flahaven trial were delivering their fateful verdict, events were taking place eight hundred kilometres (five hundred miles) away that were to produce an almost identical pattern of murder. The coincidences were startling.

John Snow, a fisherman, had settled on a small cove of Conception Bay near Harbour Grace, Newfoundland, around 1813. He had married a young Catholic girl whose first name was Catherine, and over the next twenty years, they had seven children. An astute and industrious man, he had prospered moderately and by 1833 owned his own fishing boat and employed a young man, Arthur Spring, twenty-eight, to assist him. His wife, Catherine, took care of a large house with the help of a young woman named Kit White.

A frequent visitor at the Snow home was Tobias Mandeville, twenty-five, reputed to be Catherine's cousin, who lived at a community known as Bareneed. From time to time, he helped John Snow with clerical work. Mrs. Snow, though in her early forties, was still a handsome woman and in the spring of 1833, she became Tobias Mandeville's mistress. So strong was his passion for her that he plotted to rid her of her husband.

The young hired hand, Arthur Spring, was not a happy employee. He felt that he was being underpaid and complained to any who would listen that John Snow owed him a large sum in back wages, and he was merely waiting to collect it before being off in search of a better employer. Aware of the illicit relationship between Catherine and Tobias, his sympathies were naturally on their side. Somehow, he learned of their plan to murder the fisherman and fell in readily with the scheme when they promised to pay him his full back wages and increase his salary.

On the morning of August 31, 1833, John Snow left in his boat to bring Tobias Mandeville from Bareneed; they would not return until evening. Mrs. Snow sent her two oldest daughters, then in their teens, to an overnight wake in Harbour Grace; they were accompanied by the maid, Kit White. There remained at home only herself, Arthur Spring, and the five younger children, who were shunted off to bed before their father arrived back.

When Kit White and the two girls returned the following morning, they found that John Snow was still absent. They were told that he had gone fishing and would not be back for some time. This was not unusual, for he was often away for extended periods. As Kit White went about her duties, however, she was surprised to find a pair of men's pants in Catherine's bedroom. Readily identifying them as belonging to Tobias Mandeville, she said nothing of her discovery and the next morning they were gone.

Though John Snow was not a popular member of the fishing fraternity around Harbour Grace, he was a familiar figure, and by September 5 his absence was noticed. Police authorities began a search along the rocky coves and offshore waters. Their questioning turned up the fact that he had last been seen in the company of Tobias Mandeville on August 31. They also learned of Arthur Spring's discontent with his employer.

When they went to question Catherine Snow, they discovered that she had suddenly departed. Their suspicions aroused, they talked with Kit White and found out about the mysterious pair of pants. Suspecting foul play, they decided to arrest the hired man, Arthur Spring, and to question him at police headquarters in Harbour Grace.

No match for his interrogators, the young man soon told a tale of horror. It had been planned that when John Snow and Mandeville returned in the boat, Mandeville would contrive to step onto the dock first and be in the lead as the two walked up the pier towards the house. He, Spring, was to be waiting with a shotgun. At the crucial moment, Mandeville was to step aside and he was to shoot John Snow.

According to Spring, the plan worked—to a point. As the boat entered the cove, Catherine Snow handed him the shotgun and he went down the path. Mandeville stepped off first and came towards him with Snow following behind. As they approached to within a few feet, Mandeville moved aside, but, Spring claimed, he could not bring himself to pull the trigger and he threw the gun down. Mandeville snatched it up with a curse and fired, killing Snow instantly with a charge in the chest.

Wrapping the body with rope, the two men towed the corpse out into Conception Bay and there, weighing it with a small anchor, cut the rope and allowed it to sink. As the Bay was teeming with dogfish, they believed that the body would soon be stripped of its flesh.

Following this disclosure, a police posse went by boat to Bareneed and arrested Tobias Mandeville without opposition. Though he was of stouter fibre than his accomplice, on learning that Spring had confessed and named him as the actual killer, he made his own statement. His account tallied with Spring's up to the moment of murder, but he alleged that when he stepped aside at the last second, Spring had indeed fired the fatal shot.

An island-wide search for Mrs. Catherine Snow concluded a week later when she was apprehended at the home of some friends. She denied all knowledge of any murder plot.

The Session of the Supreme Court of Newfoundland that opened in early January 1834 was unusual in that no less than thirteen persons stood charged with murder. Among them were Catherine Snow, Tobias Mandeville, and Arthur Spring. In testimony given before the Grand Jury, neither man gave evidence that implicated her and she herself denied any knowledge of the crime. In his charge to the Grand Jury, however, Chief Justice Boulton paid particular attention to the charge against the woman:

In regard, however, to Catherine Snow, the widow of the deceased John Snow, it will be proper for you to inquire whether or not she instigated them to commit so unnatural and horrible a crime. In her case, you will observe that nothing said by either of the prisoners, Spring or Mandeville, upon their examinations can be admitted to implicate her in the act. If however, upon other evidence, you will find that she instigated one or both of them to murder her husband, you will indict her as an accessory before the fact.

In response, the Grand Jury returned indictments for murder against Spring and Mandeville and a charge of being an accessory against Mrs. Snow. The trio stood trial on the morning of Friday, January 10, 1834.

Trials in early frontier days were marked with the same swiftness that attended punishment. Seldom did a murder trial extend beyond one day and thus it was in the instance of these three people. An all-day session heard testimony from Kit White and the two eldest Snow girls, along with the statements given by Arthur Spring and Tobias Mandeville. Mrs. Snow continued to maintain her innocence. The jury retired at 10:30 that evening and when they returned at 11:00 their verdict was guilty in all three indictments. Chief Justice Boulton ordered all three to be hanged the following Monday, January 13.

At this point, Mrs. Snow's lawyer rose and announced that she was pregnant. Court was adjourned to allow a panel of married women to confirm the fact, and when it met again on Saturday morning, Catherine Snow's sentence was respited to the fall sitting of the court.

The prisoners were held in large basement rooms of the old courthouse at St. John's, which one visitor reported were no better than small cellars. Some contained as many as ten prisoners awaiting trial. A small measure of propriety was maintained by having female prisoners isolated in one end of the basement. On the morning of Monday, January 13, Catherine Snow watched from her cubicle as her two companions were led to their deaths.

In its issue of January 14, *The Public Ledger* noted:

Mandeville made his exit from this world with but very little suffering and passed into eternity with scarcely more than a struggle; his miserable companion endured a strife with human nature for nearly three minutes before animal life became extinct; and after hanging for the space of about half-an-hour both bodies were taken down and committed to their coffins. It is intended that they shall be gibbeted at Spectacle Hill, in the neighbourhood of the place where the murder was committed, as a salutary warning of the awful consequences of crime.

Following the birth of her child, which was assumed to have been fathered by Tobias Mandeville, Catherine Snow was in poor health. Normally, she would have been returned almost immediately to court for a new sentence date, but her illness postponed that fateful moment. It was not until Thursday, July 10, 1834, that she was brought before a panel of judges composed of Chief Justice Boulton, Judge Brenton, and Judge Archibald. With no sign of contrition, she again stoutly denied her involvement in the murder. Nonetheless, she was sentenced to be hanged on Monday, July 21.

The unusually long period between sentence and execution gave hope to the priests who attended the condemned woman that some further respite might be granted. Accordingly, they drew up a petition and circulated it throughout St. John's, alleging that the jury had erred in condemning her. Few signed it. The general feeling was that even though no whit of evidence connected her to the murder of her husband, the very fact of her sexual relationship with Mandeville was sufficient to denounce her. After her death, the editor of *The Public Ledger* wrote:

> Had the promoters of it pursued a difference course and grounded their appeal upon the simple attribute of mercy towards the weaker sex . . . they would have more than probably have had a very numerous accession to their list of signatures . . .

Even so, the editor doubted that such a course would have swayed the dispensers of mercy. In any event, the petition was refused and the unfortunate woman was led to the scaffold that extended from the second-storey window of the building. Attended by priests, she mounted the gallows with a firm step and went to her death still protesting her innocence.

In other circumstances, the body of Catherine Snow would have been transported to Harbour Grace and, after being tarred to preserve the flesh, would have been hung on Spectacle Hill as a deterrent to others. The Catholic priests, however, would have none of this. Convinced of her innocence, they removed her body from the prison and buried it that night in the Catholic burial ground. She was the last woman to be hanged in Newfoundland.

. . .

There was a fascinating sequel to the story. The original stone courthouse, built in the days of Governor Osborne in the 1730s, was destroyed in the great fire of June 9, 1846. A new, crude structure, known as the Market House, was built to the west and included a jail and courthouse.

In his work *A Seaport Legacy,** historian Paul O'Neill writes that on February 15, 1890, a ghost was seen walking in the courthouse. Many felt that it was the spirit of Catherine Snow, still protesting her innocence from the other side of the grave. Others thought that the court officials who reported the sighting had hoisted one too many drinks that night.

The guilt of Catherine Snow remains a moot question. While in their original confessions to the police at Harbour Grace, both men had involved her in the plot, their later statements exonerated her completely. Her only connection was to confess that she had handed a shotgun to Arthur Spring that terrible evening of August 31, 1833, thinking he intended to shoot some game. Be that as it may . . .

. . .

Marie Ann Crispin
I'll Not Go Quietly

*I*N THE DAYS when men and women were hanged publicly in Canada, it was almost an unwritten rule that the victim should do nothing to disturb the pleasure of the crowds that clustered around the foot of the scaffold. The audience

---

* Paul O'Neill, *A Seaport Legacy,* vol. 2, Don Mills, Ontario, page 571.

anticipated that at the appointed time the victim would be brought from the prison and would walk quietly to the scaffold in the company of the hooded hangman. Sometimes the prisoner would need help mounting the steps to the gallows, sometimes he or she would climb steadily. The brief pause at the top was normally a time for confession—quite often a letter read by a priest or minister—and then, with the recitation of the Lord's Prayer, the County Kerchief would be lowered and the body would plunge through the trap. The whole ritualized affair was so impersonal that the viewer could walk away with a sense of detachment and the satisfaction of having been entertained. It was almost like watching the smooth performance of a play in which all the actors performed their roles without faltering.

The death of Marie Ann Crispin at Montreal on Friday, June 15, 1858, did not conform to this pattern.

Marie Ann had been born on a farm near the tiny village of St. Jerome about forty kilometres (twenty-five miles) north of Montreal. A girl of generous proportions—she stood six feet—she was an attractive woman and was the object of a good deal of male attention as she grew up. She was known as a woman of sharp tongue and was a fierce battler. Few dared to cross her. The man who finally won her hand in marriage was a farmer named Jean Belisle, who owned property in the vicinity of St. Jerome.

Before marriage, Marie Ann had been carrying on an adulterous relationship with a man named Antoine Desforges, who lived with his wife, Catherine, in the village. Catherine was of sickly disposition and quite unable to meet her husband's sexual needs. Marie Ann bore a male child by Antoine and it was sent to live with his relatives a day's journey away. After her marriage to Belisle, Marie Ann maintained contact with her lover.

Jean Belisle was much older than Marie Ann but took delight in displaying her at public functions. If he knew she was still involved with Antoine Desforges, he gave no outward indication. The affair, however, was an open secret in St. Jerome and the surrounding districts, and Marie Ann and Antoine met as frequently as possible at the home of his brother, Jean Baptiste Desforges, in the village.

The situation continued for several months, until in the spring of 1856, Jean Belisle died suddenly. Tongues wagged and there were hints that his death had been murder. Suspicion fell naturally upon Marie Ann and her paramour, but an autopsy appeared to show that the death was natural and a certificate of death was issued to this effect. When Marie inherited a large estate composed of two farms and other properties, the police made a note to keep their eyes on her activities. Since she was not yet thirty, there was a steady stream of suitors calling at her farm.

The situation continued through the balance of 1856 and well into 1857. While several swains boasted of an evening spent with Marie Ann, none lasted the distance and she always returned to her illicit affair with Antoine Desforges. It was not known whether his wife, Catherine, was aware of her husband's escapades, but it was common knowledge in the village that she disliked Marie Ann intensely.

The police later alleged, but were never able to prove, that one day in late December 1857, Marie Ann and Antoine went to Jean Baptiste's home in St. Jerome. The three were believed to have been planning for some time to murder Catherine Desforges to clear the way for marriage between the adulterous pair and this meeting was to finalize preparations.

It is known that on leaving his brother's house, Antoine told several villagers that he was going to visit his relatives in a village some forty-five kilometres (twenty-eight miles) distant. It was a trip that normally took three days to complete, there and back. He then drove off in his horse and cutter.

Marie Ann went directly from her meeting with Jean Baptiste to Antoine's house, allegedly to care for Catherine during her husband's absence. She was seen about the premises several times that afternoon.

That night, Jean Baptiste Desforges made his way undetected to the home of his brother. While Marie Ann held Catherine's legs, he smothered her with a straw pillow. Then they sat on her to make sure she was dead. He then returned to his own home while Marie Ann remained with the corpse.

After driving some distance out into the country, Antoine Desforges turned around and made his way to a country inn about ten kilometres (six miles) from St. Jerome. There he took a room for the night, though he could easily have driven home. He made every effort to be remembered at the inn, even creating noises in his room well into the morning hours. In the morning, while breakfasting with the innkeeper and his wife, he apologized for the noise, saying that he had been awake all night thinking of his poor wife, who was so ill that she would not last long. He added that when she did die, he planned to marry a much younger and healthier woman.

Antoine Desforges then returned home to find the body of his wife. Shortly after noon, he went to the home of Madame Urbaine, who lived a short distance away in the village. There being no undertaker in the area, she was the only person skilled in laying out bodies for burial. Advising her that his wife had died in her sleep the night before, he asked her to prepare the body.

Knowing that Catherine's death had been only a matter of time, Madame Urbaine was not suspicious as she went with him. She was met at the door by Marie Ann Crispin, who informed her that Catherine had asked her to stay the night as she was not feeling well, and she had remained, sleeping in the same bed. On awakening, she had discovered that Catherine had passed away in her sleep. Madame Urbaine, who knew of Catherine's animosity towards Marie Ann, thought this was odd.

Her suspicions deepened when she entered the bedroom. The bed gave no indication that it had been slept in by two people. The dead woman was lying on her back, one arm crossed peacefully over her chest and the other stretched by her side. As she later testified, the whole scene looked "too artificial." The room and bed were too neat. Keeping her thoughts to herself, she prepared the dead woman for burial in her best clothing and then took her leave.

Going directly to the home of the parish priest, Madame Urbaine confided her concerns to him. Well aware of the ugly gossip that linked the names of Antoine and Marie, he went to Montreal and contacted the police. They still had a file open on the mysterious death of Jean Belisle in 1856 and with news of this second death involving Marie Ann, they hastened to St. Jerome. A doctor was called to look at the dead woman and his preliminary report stated that she had not died naturally.

The murder had been stupidly constructed and the plot began to fall apart almost with the first questions asked by the police. Learning that Antoine Desforges had left the previous afternoon to visit his natural son, they asked him why he was back in St. Jerome within twenty-four hours. Antoine could give no immediate explanation for his presence in the village.

When a more complete medical examination revealed that Catherine Desforges had died of asphyxiation, the police moved quickly to arrest Marie Ann Crispin, who had, by her own admission, been in the house continuously and must have been there when the murder was committed. While they strongly suspected that Antoine was also involved, his alibi was so air-tight that nothing could be proven. In order to hold him for questioning, however, they arrested him on suspicion of complicity in the murder of Jean Belisle, Marie Ann's husband. Both prisoners were taken to jail in Montreal. At that point, no one had connected Jean Baptiste with the death.

Under stern questioning, Antoine Desforges stoutly denied any part in his wife's death. He finally remembered that he had decided not to visit his son and had turned back towards St. Jerome. When his horse became tired, he had stopped at the inn to rest the animal. While there were gaps in his story, a check at the inn proved his alibi to be ironclad.

Marie Ann, however, cracked under the pressure of questioning and eventually admitted that she and Jean Baptiste had carried out the brutal murder to clear the way for her marriage to Antoine. She did not implicate her lover. On the strength of this, Jean Baptiste was arrested and he admitted his part but refused to incriminate his brother.

Marie Ann and Jean Baptiste were tried for murder at Montreal on January 18, 1858, and although the case against them was circumstantial—neither took the stand—their confessions were admitted and the jury returned a guilty verdict against them. They were sentenced to be hanged within the week.

The police, who were still trying to build a case against Antoine for the murder of either his wife or Jean Belisle, secured a respite, hoping that Marie Ann would finally tell the true story of her husband's death. Although this did not happen, they did not release Antoine.

Several more respites were granted the couple based upon this and the fact that there was a repugnance to hanging a woman in public. However, the nature of the callous crime was such that executive clemency was denied and a final date was set for June 25. Preparations proceeded and a scaffold was erected on the street just outside the old Montreal Prison. Announcements were posted in the public markets.

. . .

Marie Ann Crispin was not the first woman to face the gallows in Montreal. In 1826, Marie Belanger had been sentenced to death for horse stealing but her sentence had been respited and she had been banished to Bermuda. Judith Couture had been convicted in January 1829 of the murder of her five children, but the penalty had been commuted to a short term in prison. Two women, Mary Manning and Mary McNaughton, had been condemned in 1830 for robbery but had escaped the gallows and received light prison sentences. The last woman, Betsy Williams, had been convicted of murder and was to hang on April 16, 1840, but this likewise had been converted to a term of imprisonment.

On the morning of the executions, a huge crowd estimated at fifteen thousand people gathered on the street to watch the first woman hang. Many from the countryside had brought their picnic lunches and had secured good seats. Reverend Mr. Villeneuve and the Sisters of Mercy, who had spent the night with the condemned couple, remained with them to the end.

Brought first from the prison, Jean Baptiste mounted the gallows with a steady step. He confessed his awful crime, and went to his death bravely. After allowing him to hang for twenty minutes, officials cut him down and the hangman went for Marie Ann.

Marie Ann's departure was filled with a horror that struck a chill into the hearts of everyone present. When the hangman arrived at her cell to pinion her arms and lead her out, he was met with a burst of curses and swinging fists. The Sisters of Mercy scattered and guards came running to overpower the crazed prisoner. The hangman was knocked down several times before he finally secured ropes around her arms. Kicking and cursing, Marie Ann was then dragged from her cell through the door leading to the yard.

As she was half carried, half dragged across the yard to the prison gate, the convicts whose cell windows looked down on the scene roared their encouragement of her desperate struggle. As the death party emerged from the yard into the street, the vast crowd that had been buzzing with anticipation of their second execution, suddenly fell silent, almost as if they were realizing for the first time the gravity of the event.

Marie Ann's struggles intensified as she was forced up the steps and she managed to shove several guards off the platform before she was finally overpowered and her legs securely bound. Only then did she resign herself. By this time, a murmur of "No, No" had begun to course through the crowd, and people began to press against the cordon of police and soldiers that had been drawn up around the stage. Realizing that the spectators were turning ugly, the Sheriff of Montreal urged the hangman to finish his work quickly. The man bungled the job, however, and when Marie Ann dropped through the trap she was not executed cleanly but ended her life by strangulation.

Prevented from reaching the gallows, the crowd vented its anger by racing through the streets leading from the prison, smashing windows, tearing down signs, and setting fires. Several stores were burned and looted. It was hours before the police were able to quell the disturbance caused by the first execution of a woman in Montreal.

After a few days, when the furore had died down, the forgotten man in the drama, Antoine Desforges, was quietly released from prison, all charges against him dropped.

. . .

Johanna Hamilton
The Body in the Pit

*T*HE TRIAL OF PATRICK GEEHAN and Johanna Hamilton for the murder of Garrett Sears was beyond doubt one of the most sensational ever held in St. John's, Newfoundland. The savage nature of the crime riveted public attention on the scene, and the unusual direction taken by the defence gave it an aura seldom found in capital cases. It began in late 1871 but the final act in the drama was not played out until 1880.

The stage was Patrick Geehan's two-storey house located at the south end of Harbour Grace. The building was surrounded by a stone fence that enclosed a barn, some small corrals, and a shed, all of which were partially shielded from the gaze of neighbours by clumps of trees, which gave the farmyard the look of seclusion.

The house was occupied by Patrick Geehan, farmer-fisherman, about thirty-five years of age, and his wife Jane, who was considerably older. Three children had been born to them but all had died some years before. Living with them was elderly Garrett Sears, brother to Jane. The fourth member of the household was Johanna Hamilton, twenty-five, a young woman from Harbour Grace who served as their maid. Newspaper accounts described her as five feet, two inches tall, black haired, and of fair complexion.

Outwardly, there was harmony in the household, and all members bore good reputations in the community. The husband, Patrick Geehan, had been a heavy drinker in the past but over the last three years had modified his drinking and had joined a temperance group. During the summers, the Geehans and Garrett Sears had made an annual pilgrimage to Labrador for fishing. When failing health forced Mrs. Geehan to abandon this practice, her place had been taken by Johanna Hamilton. At the end of the 1871 session, Geehan, Sears, and Hamilton had returned to the farm around the second week in November.

On the morning of Sunday, November 19, Daniel Shougharoo, a neighbour who lived about 400 metres (440 yards) from them, paid a short social visit and chatted with the Geehans. That afternoon, Patrick Geehan called at the Shougharoo home and mentioned that Garrett Sears, the old man, was going up to St. John's to have his toes fixed, and that Mrs. Geehan would be accompanying him as far as Turks Gut, where he would catch a boat to the capital. Mrs. Geehan, he went on, planned to go on and visit friends and relatives. Daniel Shougharoo thought it strange that nothing had been said about these arrangements during his visit that morning. Also, Geehan's sole motive in visiting seemed to be to convey this information.

That evening, Johanna's sister, Catherine, arrived from Harbour Grace and remained for several hours. Again, neither Jane Geehan nor Garrett Sears said anything about planning a trip. As Catherine was leaving, Johanna followed her into the yard and casually mentioned the proposed trip.

The next day, Monday, about one o'clock in the afternoon, several neighbours heard a shot from the direction of Patrick Geehan's establishment. Two of these, John Fitzgerald and his wife, also thought they heard Garrett cry out: "Oh, my God, Pat!" or words to that effect. Since gunfire was not unusual on the cape, no one went to investigate and the incident passed off without alarm.

On Tuesday morning, Daniel Shougharoo saw Patrick Geehan working at a fish pit near the back of his property. He walked over to ask his assistance in butchering a pig, noting at the same time that Geehan had scratches on his face that had not been there the night before. Geehan said he had scratched himself on a bush. While they were slaughtering the pig, Geehan mentioned that Garrett Sears and Mrs. Geehan had gone up to Harbour Grace on their way to St. John's. He also explained the gunfire by saying that he had fired at a hawk, but missed.

The next development in the case came the following day. A man walking down Spaniard's Bay road towards Harbour Grace noticed a woman lying in a gravel pit a short distance off the road. He reported the matter immediately to Sergeant George Winslow of the Harbour Grace police. The body was identified as that of Jane Geehan, wife of Patrick Geehan, and since there were no marks of violence it was placed on a cart and taken to her home. The doctor who was called to examine her concluded after a careful examination that Mrs. Geehan had died of a heart attack. The only wound on her body was a small cut on her forehead that could have been made when she fell.

When news of the discovery reached St. John's later in the day, Inspector Thomas Foley, head of the Newfoundland Constabulary, decided to investigate for himself. He was acting purely on a hunch. A former chief of the Royal Irish Constabulary, he had been appointed only a few months before to organize the Newfoundland force and brought with him the wisdom of more than thirty years of police work.

Arriving at the Geehan home on Friday, November 24, he learned that Garrett Sears and Jane Geehan had left for St. John's on Tuesday, the 21. Johanna Hamilton, the maid, confirmed this. In company with Magistrate R.R.W. Lilly, Inspector Foley examined the body and was immediately struck with a suspicious circumstance: The body gave no indication that it had lain in the open for nearly forty-eight hours before discovery. Also, it was highly improbable that no one would have seen it during that time since it was completely exposed to public view. As a result of this observation, he ordered a complete post-mortem, and at the same time, he instructed the local constable to keep a close watch on Patrick Geehan's movements.

The autopsy performed the following day by Dr. William Allan confirmed death from heart seizure and the coroner's jury returned a verdict of "death from natural causes and not otherwise."

Still not satisfied, Inspector Foley continued his investigation. His agents reported that after burying his wife, Patrick Geehan had visited Harbour Grace and Turks Gut, asking if anyone had seen his brother-in-law, Garrett Sears. They also informed him that no one remembered seeing either Mrs. Geehan or her brother after Sunday, November 19. On learning of the mysterious gunshot from the Geehan place, Foley questioned neighbours and was told that no one had seen a hawk in the vicinity for some time.

Convinced that Patrick Geehan and Johanna Hamilton were concealing information, and that the missing Garrett Sears had been killed, Inspector Foley arrested the pair on December 4 and lodged them in the jail at Harbour Grace. With the way clear, he began a minute examination of the Geehan house and yard and found a shotgun, recently cleaned, in the house. The tailgate of a wooden cart in the yard yielded up pellets of lead that corresponded with shotgun shells on the premises. Some straw in the stable was stained with what appeared to be blood, and a pitchfork also had brown stains on it.

The search was widened and on December 6 the police came upon a fish pit that had been dug in a back section of the farm. It was filled with fish offal and clay. Using a ramrod to probe into the soft dirt, Inspector Foley struck an object about two feet from the surface. Ordering two policemen to carefully excavate the pit, he watched as they cleared away the slime to reveal an object they at first thought was a squid. On closer examination, it proved to be a head. Foley ordered the digging stopped and sent for the coroner.

The body of Garrett Sears was removed from the pit and taken to the kitchen, where it was stretched out on the same table that had borne the body of his sister a few days before. The head and upper portion of the body were horribly mutilated, bearing no less than thirteen wounds. Two, in one arm, had been made by shotgun pellets, while the others had been inflicted by two instruments, one long and sharp and the other blunt. Death had been caused—not by the shotgun pellets—but by the other weapons. A coroner's jury had no difficulty ascribing his death to murder and naming Johanna Hamilton and Patrick Geehan as probable suspects.

Both Patrick and Johanna made voluntary statements before Coroner Peters. Geehan's was a simple repetition of what he had said previously: His wife and her brother had left for St. John's on Tuesday, November 21; the next day he had worked in the fish pit and helped a neighbour slaughter a pig; after the burial of his wife, when his brother-in-law did not show up, he made inquiries, but to no avail. That was all he knew of the affair.

Johanna's statement was more damaging and a little closer to the known facts. She told them that Patrick and Garrett quarrelled frequently and that on the morning of November 20 they had another family quarrel. Having prepared dinner for the four of them, she had called Garrett to come and eat and had gone back inside. Mrs. Geehan, who had been drinking heavily, was sitting in the kitchen.

Hearing a shot, she said, she had run into the yard and found Sears dead. Later, she had helped carry the body into the stable and afterwards, from fear, had helped Patrick bury it in the offal heap. She offered the explanation that when Mrs. Geehan heard that her brother was dead, she had screamed and fainted. In falling, she had struck her head on the corner of the woodbox and when they examined her, they found that she was dead. Two nights later, they had placed her body in the gravel pit, where it had been found the next morning.

The two prisoners were removed to the penitentiary at St. John's, where they were held for trial. While there, Patrick evidently had second thoughts about the statement given by his accomplice, and on January 27 he sent for Magistrate R.R.W. Lilly and dictated a new confession. In this he maintained that he had been stalking a hawk that morning and that the bird had landed on the wooden cart. Just as he fired, Garrett had come around the corner and the shot had struck him. Johanna then came running from the house, and believing that Sears was dying but not yet dead, had cried out that they would both be hanged and handed him the pitchfork. Thinking that killing a man by accident was as bad as murder, he had taken the pitchfork and driven it into his brother-in-law's head. That had killed him. Later, they had buried him. His account of Jane Geehan's death corroborated that given by the maid.

Two days later, Patrick again sent for the magistrate and told him that part of his last statement was untrue and that he wanted to correct it. His new version was that Johanna had not given him the fork. Rather, seeing that Sears was dead from the gunshot wound, they had taken his body to the stable. Later that night, he had gone out and discovered that the pigs were tearing at Sear's head and had bitten off one ear and caused other wounds. Snatching up a pitch-fork to drive off the pigs, he had accidentally struck the dead man in the head. Johanna was innocent of any wrongdoing.

In mid-May 1872, the pair were jointly indicted by a Grand Jury at St. John's, with their trial fixed for May 29. Since Johanna had no money for a lawyer, Prescott Emerson was appointed by the court. Patrick Geehan opted to be represented by Richard Raftus, who had just been admitted to the bar and had never undertaken a case, let alone one for murder.

The trial opened before Mr. Justice Robinson, sitting with two associates and a jury of twelve. Some evidence was taken that afternoon before it was found that one of the panel had been wrongly sworn in. A new trial was ordered and it began the following day. The Crown's case as presented by Mr. Carter was based on an alleged sexual intimacy between the two, from which had arisen a plan to dispose of Mrs. Geehan and her brother. Medical testimony showed that the "accidental" gunshot wounds—only two in number—were harmless by themselves. Death had been caused by a savage beating about the head with a blunt instrument, and from the penetration of a wound probably inflicted with a pitchfork. Either of the latter two would have been fatal.

The prosecution emphasized the story they told before the deaths that the brother and sister were going to St. John's and pointed out that no neighbours had heard of this proposed journey from either of the victims. The statements made by the prisoners at Harbour Grace and Patrick's two revisions were admitted as evidence and these were powerful pieces of information.

The Crown's case was completed on June 1 and the defence decided not to call witnesses. Mr. Emerson, addressing the jury on behalf of his client, Johanna Hamilton, ridiculed the idea that there had been any intimacy between Patrick and Johanna, and declared that Hamilton had only assisted in the disposal of the bodies from fear of her employer, and then only after she believed that the older man's death had been an accident. The death of Mrs. Geehan, he pointed out, though not a matter of trial, had been caused by heart failure brought on by the realization of her brother's death.

There was little that young Mr. Raftus could say on behalf of Patrick Geehan. The confession sank him.

The argument of Mr. Carter for the Crown and His Lordship's charge to the jurors occupied most of the session on Monday, June 3, with His Lordship summing up mercifully in the woman's case. The jurors retired at 6:30, taking with them an overwhelming body of evidence against the man, but little concerning his alleged accomplice. It was therefore assumed by many in the courtroom that if she was found guilty it would be of a lesser offence. Nevertheless, when the twelve returned at 8:30, they rendered guilty verdicts in both instances, although they did advance a strong recommendation to mercy for the woman.

In replying to sentence, Patrick Geehan gave such an incoherent and rambling response that many realized for the first time that though the Crown had described him as a cunning and intelligent man, he was in truth a simple, ignorant soul; his plea that he thought accident and murder were the same might well be true. Johanna's response was pitiful: "Keep me in prison all my days but don't put a rope around my neck. Oh God, must I be hung? Let me crawl upon my knees to the Judge."

At this solemn moment Prescott Emerson informed the court that the young lady was pregnant. Court was adjourned so the truth of the matter might be ascertained.

When it was confirmed that Johanna was indeed six and a half months pregnant, her sentence was held over until November 20. Patrick Geehan, however, was ordered to be hanged on July 1. A quick calculation by the women in the audience estimated that the pregnancy must have taken place in November of the previous year, coinciding closely with the deaths of Sears and Mrs. Geehan.

Before going to the gallows built within the penitentiary walls, Patrick Geehan made another full confession. In it he stated that his wife and her brother had made his life a perpetual hell and that he had decided to kill Sears and rid himself of the turmoil. Jane Geehan had been drunk that morning and had fallen and struck her head; the fall had killed her. He had met Garrett Sears in the yard a few moments later and shot him. Seeing that he was not dead, he had struck him with the butt of the gun. The other wounds had been inflicted, as he claimed earlier, by the pigs in the stable. Johanna Hamilton had no foreknowledge of his designs and had become involved only through her fear and loyalty to him.

Despite Geehan's last-ditch efforts to exculpate her, there was little doubt that she had been a party to the murder plot and possibly even a participant. Some time before the murders, she had bragged while drunk that Jane Geehan would not live through Christmas and that she would be the new Mrs. Geehan. It was entirely possible that she even knew the date of the murders, for the previous evening she had told her own sister of Jane and Garrett's impending but entirely fictitious journey to St. John's.

Patrick Geehan was the first man to be hanged at the penitentiary. The execution went off flawlessly and he was buried within the prison compound, where he remains to this day.

As for Johanna Hamilton, scheduled to be executed on November 20, her sentence was commuted to life imprisonment on October 21. By this time the question of guilt or innocence was almost a forgotten issue and the emphasis was upon rendering pity rather than justice. After serving just under eight years, she was paroled on May 24, 1880. It is said that both the commutation and eventual early release found favour with those people who had long believed that, at worst, she had merely been the pawn of a desperate but befuddled killer.

· · ·

Angele Poulin
The Most Guilty

A NGELE POULIN, forty-eight, of Caraquet Island, New Brunswick, was typical of the majority of Canada's female killers. Born near Bathurst in 1826, she grew up without benefit of schooling. Poverty and hunger were everyday companions, and even the usual social graces were not a part of her world. She was not even blessed with good looks. At the time of her trial, newspaper reporters constantly referred to her as "unprepossessing" and even "repulsive." It is little wonder, then, that she did not marry until she was twenty-three, and then to a backwoods man twelve years her senior.

Angele married Xavier Poulin around 1850 and over the ensuing fourteen years bore him eight children. In 1864, however, Xavier came down with a malignant disease, thought to be leprosy, which was common in the Maritimes at that time. He was consequently forbidden by his parish priest to have intercourse with his wife. As his condition worsened, he was also unable to work at his craft of woodcutting and he and his family became wards of the parish.

In this destitute state, they were befriended by a young man named Oliver Gallien, about twenty-five years of age, who lived in a one-roomed cabin on Caraquet Island. He was a husky, dark-faced chap with features bespeaking Indian ancestry. Despite his own poverty, he invited them to live with him, and for the next ten years they shared his meagre fortunes. It was not unexpected, therefore, that Angele's next two children were fathered by Oliver.

The span between 1864 and 1874 were years of misery for Xavier Poulin. He was frequently confined to bed, his body covered with gross sores and his bones racked with agony. In the spring of 1874, however, his condition began to improve, and he moved from his bed to a chair and finally managed to walk with the aid of a stout stick. When weather permitted, he went for short walks in the surrounding woods and even tried to do some light wood-chopping. By this time, Angele was about three months pregnant with her third child by Oliver Gallien.

According to later statements by Gallien, Angele had been hinting for nearly two years that he should murder her husband, but he ignored the insinuations. With Xavier's return to better health, however, Angele increased the pressure.

Gallien's story was supported by other people. A woman named Victoria Dugay, who visited the cabin in mid-April 1874, reported two separate incidents. In the first, she related while Xavier was off on his customary walk in the woods, Oliver Gallien and Angele Poulin had sharpened a knife. She said Gallien had put it in his pocket and followed Xavier. Dugay went on to elaborate that when Gallien returned a short time later, Angele asked him if he had "killed him" and he said "no, his heart did not permit him."

In the second episode, Dugay vouched she heard Angele say to Gallien: "Go and see if Xavier is sleeping and if not sleeping give him a good blow so that he will not get up for some time. No, just choke him. People will think he died of a weak fit."*

Then Miss Dugay heard Xavier whisper that he was awake and that he was just as cunning as they were.

On Monday, April 20, Delina Gallien, Oliver's sister, was at the cabin. She later testified that about ten o'clock in the morning, Xavier Poulin left with an axe to try to do some cutting in the woods. About an hour later, Oliver left, and when he returned, he spoke with Angele, but Miss Gallien could not hear their conversation since they were in the yard. Oliver then went back into the woods

---

* All quotes in this work are from the Capital Case Files of the accused persons, unless otherwise recorded.

and was absent about half an hour. His sister reported that upon his return, "He seemed sorry." Then Angele disappeared into the forest and was gone about half an hour as well. When she returned, Oliver washed himself and changed his clothes; Angele took the discarded clothes and threw them into the loft of the cabin.

About four in the afternoon, concerned about the old man's continued absence, Delina Gallien asked Angele where he was. Angele gave her directions and she went into the woods and found Xavier lying dead in an open clearing. His battered head suggested that he might have been killed with an axe. She looked but could not find one. When she sounded the alarm back at the cabin, her brother seemed distressed, but Angele Poulin was her usual, taciturn self. With the assistance of a neighbour, Augustine Murray, Oliver Gallien brought the body to the cabin on a cart. Angele washed off the blood and tied a white bandana around his head to hide the wounds.

Several times that evening, Oliver made a point of saying that he was not the killer, but he was obviously troubled.

The inquest held on April 23 was inconclusive and attached no blame. However, the next day Oliver Gallien sought out Magistrate J.C. Blackhole and in the presence of several witnesses announced: "I did the deed." The magistrate cautioned him to say nothing more, but Gallien continued: "I would not have done it if I had not been incited by Angele Poulin. I killed him with a stick and my fists and not with an axe."

This was apparently in contradiction to medical evidence, which indicated that some of the fatal wounds might have been made with the blunt edge of an axe head.

Gallien was placed under arrest and lodged in the jail at Bathurst, where he continued to make short, succinct statements. To Constable Alphonse Landry, he related that Angele had been after him for two years, warning that if he did not kill her husband, she would. He confessed that he had followed Xavier into the woods and attacked him with a stick. He said Xavier begged him to stop, but he had to do it. He had hit him several times and then walked away. When he left, the sixty-year-old man was on his hands and knees trying to crawl.

On the strength of these statements, Angele Poulin was arrested and charged with the murder of her husband. The police believed that when Oliver returned from beating Xavier, Angele went into the woods and attacked him with the axe, but they could not prove this.

Gallien's one-day trial was held at Bathurst on September 3, 1874, with Mr. Justice J.W. Weldon on the bench. Crown Prosecutor F.W. Morrison presented a series of witnesses, among them Gallien's sister Delina, to prove the circumstances of the murder. The most telling evidence was the series of confessions the accused had made to various police authorities. J.S. Barbrie, for the prisoner, was unable to offer any witnesses or evidence to lessen his guilt. Taking only twenty minutes to reach their verdict, the jury softened it by a recommendation to mercy based on the fact that "he had confessed and said he was sorry."

Angele Poulin's trial followed immediately with the same judge, prosecutor and defence counsel. With no conclusive evidence of her actual participation in the murder, she was charged with being an accessory before the fact. The evidence followed the pattern of her lover's trial, with the exception that Gallien was placed on the stand to testify against her. His evidence, however, consisted of responding "I don't know" or "I can't remember." After a futile effort to extract testimony from him, he was dismissed. His Lordship later commented that the prisoner's influence over the man was apparently still as strong as ever.

The jury took an hour to find her guilty and there was no recommendation to mercy.

Brought back into the courtroom on September 5, both prisoners were sentenced to death. Oliver Gallien was to be executed at Bathurst on October 29 while Angele, because she was pregnant, had her term delayed until January 5. Reporters in the courtroom were amazed that neither prisoner expressed the slightest concern as the dreaded words rang through the courtroom. It was some time before an explanation was forthcoming. His Lordship had delivered the sentence in English and the interpreter had been so awed by the solemnity of the occasion that he forgot to translate the jurist's words into French! Thus, both were led from the room unaware of what fate lay in store for them. It was some hours before someone realized what had happened and hastened to translate the sentences.

In his report to the Minister of Justice, His Lordship recorded that in the instance of Gallien, despite the recommendation of the jury, he could "see nothing in the evidence or in the conduct of the prisoner which would justify me in saying anything to call for the interference of the merciful Prerogative of the Crown." As for Angele Poulin, he added: "I am of the opinion that she was the most guilty of the two."

There was no mercy for Oliver Gallien and he was hanged on October 29 by Sheriff Vail in a special enclosure built outside the front wall of the prison.

The day before, he was permitted a short interview with Angele. When she asked him if he forgave her for involving him in the crime, he replied stoically: "God will take care of that." Angele, who still protested her innocence, kept her face frozen in an unrevealing mask as he was led to his execution, but later, when his body was removed from the prison for burial, she broke down and cried. It was the only expression of emotion her jailers noted on their records.

As for Angele, following the birth of her child, she had her sentence commuted on December 22, 1834, to life in Dorchester Penitentiary, where she remained for the next ten and a half years. However, in 1885 the Penitentiary Service adopted a new policy under which all female federal prisoners were concentrated in Kingston. In the case of Angele at Dorchester, the warden suggested that it would be better to "clear her out by pardon." Before acting on the recommendation, the Minister contacted Judge Weldon, whose original remarks regarding Poulin had been most scathing. Weldon, who had either mellowed through the years or had forgotten his earlier condemnation, supported the plan. "The convict appears to be a poor, half-witted person," he observed, and indicated that had the law permitted it in 1874, he would have imposed a lesser penalty.

The Secretary of State concurred with the recommendation and on June 29, 1885, Angele Poulin was pardoned into the care of one of her married daughters.

· · ·

Elizabeth Ward

The New River Murder

S IX PEOPLE FORMED THE HOUSEHOLD of Thomas Edward Ward in September 1878, and they were a strange group. Titular head of the family was Thomas Ward, sixty-three, farmer and part-time fisherman. His wife, Elizabeth, was much younger and was known in the district as a "hard character." There were two children at home—Annie, seventeen, and Susan, four. Boarding with them was a man of forty named Thomas Dowd, who did odd jobs in the neighbourhood. The last member of the menage was David McCarthy, a man in his early twenties, who was merely boarding there until he found steady employment. Before the tragic affair was over, each member would be tainted with some scandal, except four-year-old Susan, and even she would have the unique experience of being locked up in a debtor's cell.

Thomas Ward had been born at Gagetown, New Brunswick, in 1815, the eldest son of Myer Ward, and grew up in the district. When the family moved to Saint John, he went with them. At Saint John he met a young woman and married her. They had three children. Then suddenly and without warning, he deserted her and the family in 1854. They did not hear of him again until 1878.

Thomas Ward next turned up at Digdeguash, a farming community in Charlotte County in the southwest section of the province. Here, without benefit of divorce from his first wife, he married Elizabeth Summers at St. Stephens in 1859. They moved to Boston for a period of four years, but then returned to farm at Digdeguash, where they remained until November 1868. At that time they moved south to New River, a short distance from St. Andrews, and rented a five-room house from a Mrs. McGowan. Though they were reputed to have had nine children, only Annie and Susan were living with them at the time of the tragedy ten years later.

The weekend of September 7, 1878, was a hectic one at the Ward home. Thomas, known to his neighbours as a mild-mannered, nice guy, kicked over the traces. First, he accused young David McCarthy of seducing his daughter, Annie, and ordered him to leave immediately. The youth departed so promptly that he left some of his personal belongings behind. Ward next turned his wrath against Annie, telling her to get out and never return. She left and sought refuge with a family in New River.

Thomas Ward did not stop there. For several weeks he had suspected that something was going on between his wife and their star boarder, Thomas Dowd, and had mentioned to friends that he had seen them "hugging and kissing." He ended his weekend emotional rampage by telling Dowd that he would have to find another place to board, and the sooner the better.

On Monday morning, September 9, Thomas Dowd went berry-picking in some bushes lining a pasture south of the house. About twenty minutes later, Thomas Ward left to do some bridge repairs to a structure across a stream half a mile away. Since he intended after repairing the bridge to carry on to the pasture and pitch some hay, he carried with him an axe belonging to David McCarthy and also a pitchfork.

Towards eleven that morning, Mrs. Taylor, a neighbour, stopped by to visit Thomas Ward. There was no one at home, but as she was about to leave she saw Mrs. Ward, Thomas Dowd, and the child Susan coming towards the yard from the direction of the pasture and the bridge. Dowd was carrying a pail of berries. Mrs. Taylor said that she wanted to speak to Mr. Ward but was told by Mrs. Ward that her husband was away. She then took her leave. Afterwards, she could not remember whether Elizabeth had said Thomas was away from the district or just temporarily away from the house.

Over the next couple of days, Thomas Ward was not seen around the farm or in the village. When asked, Mrs. Ward let it be known that her husband had walked out on the family; it was not the first time he had taken off without telling anyone. Thomas Dowd confirmed the story and as to emphasize that the absence was permanent, the daughter Annie returned home from the village.

On September 20, a farmer named Thomas Mulbern was searching for some cows along a stretch of lane leading to the wooden bridge when he heard his dog barking. On investigating, he found the animal yelping around a small mound of sod covered with branches, and as he approached, he detected a sweet odour. His first thought was that an animal must have been buried there, and he turned aside to continue his search for the cattle without checking further. That evening, after thinking it over, he told some friends about the funny smell "near the Ward farm" and their curiosity was also aroused.

The next afternoon, Mulbern returned to the spot with three companions and carefully removed the brush covering the mound of dirt. As they brushed this aside, they came upon a human foot. Convinced that they had found Thomas Ward, they did not disturb the site further but spread the alarm. The coroner and police were called to complete the gruesome task of unearthing the cadaver. The body was that of Ward and the battered condition of his head left no doubt that he was a murder victim.

Suspicion immediately fell upon Thomas Dowd and Elizabeth Ward, and police went to the farm and arrested them. Dowd was conveyed to a hotel at Lepreaux to await the inquest, but Mrs. Ward was allowed to remain at home under house arrest to care for her children. A constable was stationed there to watch over her and her daughters.

The suspected killer, Thomas Dowd, was then a man of about forty, slender but athletic. Born in Saint John, he had moved to Charlotte County with his family at the age of three. After a varied career, which included a stint as an American soldier, he had returned to Charlotte County and eventually ended up boarding at the Ward home.

At the inquest, Elizabeth Ward told a simple, straightforward story. There had been quarrelling over the weekend and her husband had ordered David McCarthy and Annie to leave the house. He had also told Dowd to find another place. The next day, Dowd had left to pick berries and a few minutes later her husband had departed to do some haying and fix the bridge. About eleven, she had taken Susan and walked towards the south field where the men were supposed to be working. She could not locate her husband and suspected that he had gone to the village. She went on to meet Dowd and they returned to the farm to find Mrs. Taylor waiting.

She was not alarmed when her husband did not return for dinner; following past arguments he had often gone away without telling anyone his destination and stayed away for days until he cooled off. She told the inquiry that while they were a poor family, they got along well financially. When her husband did not return after two days, she supposed that he had deserted them, so she went to the village and persuaded her daughter, Annie, to come home with her.

The story related by Thomas Dowd, however, immediately focussed attention on him. After picking his berries, he had started for the house, and near the bridge he had come upon the older man. They started quarrelling again and Thomas Ward had become belligerent and lunged at him with a pitchfork. He managed to evade the first attack, but Ward had come at him again. In desperation, he had snatched up McCarthy's axe and struck Ward across the side of the head. At that point he had started to run away, but fear of retaliation swept over him and he returned and delivered a second blow with the axe to make sure the man was dead. Then he dug a shallow grave and covered the body with dirt and branches. He insisted that Mrs. Ward knew nothing of this and had no part in it.

Coroner's inquests have much more latitude than regular courts of law, and at this session some hearsay evidence was allowed. Several witnesses said that the dead man had frequently complained that something was going on between Elizabeth and Dowd. This, plus Mrs. Taylor's testimony that Elizabeth had told her within minutes of the murder that her husband had gone away, focussed attention on her. On September 29, the jury found that Thomas Ward had come to his death at the hands of Thomas Dowd and that Elizabeth Ward was an accomplice to the murder.

Both prisoners were then taken to the county jail at St. Andrews. Elizabeth was housed in the debtor's cell and it was arranged that four-year-old Susan might occupy this with her.

When trial opened before Mr. Justice Weldon at St. Andrews on November 15, 1878, the Crown was represented by the province's Attorney General but no defence counsel was present. Considering the case to be hopeless and having their reputations to think about, all the lawyers had taken pains to be absent from town. The two accused had to defend themselves.

The jurors did not believe Dowd's story that he had acted only in self-defence, and his statement about striking him once with the axe and returning for a second blow told heavily against him. In their minds, it removed the case from simple, justifiable homicide to the realm of murder. Likewise, they did not accept Mrs. Ward's assertion that she knew nothing of the affair. Crown testimony centred on Ward's suspicions that Dowd and his wife were lovers and on Mrs. Taylor's statement that she had been told that morning by Mrs. Ward that her husband had gone away. This did not agree with the statement that she had not missed her husband until supper that evening.

They found both prisoners guilty—Dowd of murder and Ward of being his accomplice. No recommendation was advanced in either case and Mr. Justice Weldon sentenced them to be executed on January 14, 1879.

With the key issue out of the way, the lawyers who had vacated town to escape being called to act now came forward and mounted a clemency campaign for the woman. Several petitions were forwarded to the Secretary of State on her behalf, and in an unusual move, the woman's death sentence was commuted in early January 1879, but no indication was given as to what the new sentence would be.

Thomas Dowd, in a statement made the day before his execution, reaffirmed that Elizabeth had no part in the murder and denied that there had been any improper relationship between them. He still contended that he had acted only in self-defence and there were many in the community who believed him. Among these were the Roman Catholic priests, who declared that because of their views, they would accord him a regular funeral and burial afterwards in sacred ground.

· · ·

The method of execution in New Brunswick in the 1870s was quite different from that practised in other parts of Canada. Instead of mounting an elevated platform to drop through a trapdoor, the condemned were positioned on the ground with a rope around their neck. This rope ran through an overhead pulley and through a window into the prison. After passing over another pulley, the rope was attached to a heavy weight, which was in turn suspended by a second rope from the ceiling. The apparatus was put into motion by cutting this second rope and allowing the weight to fall. The result was that the victims were jerked upwards into the air, hopefully breaking their necks. The whole procedure was tricky, involving a good deal of precise measurement, and was seldom successful. After a few years of experimentation, and a number of unfortunate incidents, the idea was dropped in favour of the more traditional method of execution.

Thomas Dowd was executed by the rope-and-pulley method on the morning of January 14, 1879, at St. Andrews. The next day, after his funeral, word was received from the Governor-General's office that Elizabeth's sentence had been commuted to seven years imprisonment. The authorities had indeed taken a merciful view of her case.

She actually spent very little time in custody. On February 28, 1879—six weeks later—the Minister of Justice, John A. Macdonald, wrote to the Secretary of State that he considered the evidence against her most unsatisfactory and insufficient. As a consequence, he recommended her immediate discharge from prison. On March 3, the Secretary of State approved the move and Elizabeth Ward was released.

. . .

Cordelia Viau

Kill Him! Kill Him!

S UNDAY, NOVEMBER 21, 1897, should have been a happy, peaceful day in the little village of St. Canut, northeast of Montreal. The sun was shining and the snow lay crisp and unbroken in the fields. However, as Father Pinault finished his morning service and stood at the church door, shaking hands and chatting with his congregation as they left, he noted with sadness that the last two to depart were his organist, Cordelia Viau, and one of his choir members, Samuel Parslow.

Cordelia Viau was married to Isidore Porier, local carpenter and builder. Childless, they had adopted a young girl to brighten their lives. Sam Parslow was a farm-hand, single, and one of several sons of a large, old-time family in the district. Parslow and Viau had been carrying on an immoral relationship for over two years and their alliance was the talk of the parish. It had started when the woman's husband, Isidore Porier, had gone to California in 1895. George Parslow, Sam's brother, had asked Father Pinault to do something about it, and he had written to Isidore asking him to either return home or take his wife away from St. Canut. Porier's answer had been noncommittal and when he later returned to the village, the liaison had continued underground.

That morning, Father Pinault would have been stunned had he known the thoughts that were passing through the minds of his organist and choir member as they left the church.

Cordelia Viau later stated that she had returned home after church to find her husband depressed and drinking. He had often told his friends that one of these days he was going to kill himself. Sam Parslow and other friends had arrived around one o'clock and the drinking had continued into the afternoon. When the others left, she, Parslow, and her husband kept tilting the cup. Isidore finally passed out and she had put him to bed. Then she got ready to visit her father in another village. Sam had helped harness the horse and she had left, taking the adopted child with her.

She did not return until the following day, and her arrival was noted by Noel Courvrette, the village blacksmith, whose house stood opposite hers. Her child was not with her. She started to walk towards her front door, but hesitated, and then stopped. Instead, she turned and came to his door saying she sensed something was wrong in her house but that she had to hurry to the church to play the organ for a wedding. She promised to be right back.

After the wedding, Noel Courvrette accompanied her home, where they found Isidore lying across his bed with his throat cut in several places. A butcher knife, which she identified as one from her kitchen, was lying near his hand. There was a bloody footprint in a pool of blood on the floor beside the bed. At first glance, Isidore seemed to have carried out his promise to destroy himself.

The coroner, Dr. P.Z. Mignault, arrived at St. Canut that evening, and after examining the body reached the conclusion that Isidore could not have committed suicide. The cuts on his neck were too deep and extensive to have been self-administered with the weapon at hand. He posted a guard on the house, notified the police, and arranged for an inquest.

The inquest was thorough and brought to light details of Cordelia's supposed liaison with Samuel Parslow. Though she vigorously denied that anything improper had occurred, she insisted that her husband must have committed suicide. Beyond the love triangle, the only other potential motive was that he carried a $2,000 life insurance policy in her favour.

Detective Kenneth McCaskill arrived from Montreal to look into the matter, and after examining the body and the bloodstained bedroom, conferred with the coroner. The bloody footprint on the bedroom floor was proof that someone else had been in the room either during or shortly after the attack on Porier, yet no one had come forward. His interview with Cordelia convinced him that murder had been done, and after a second conference with Dr. Mignault, he decided there was sufficient cause to arrest both Cordelia and Sam.

The pair were taken into custody on November 25 and escorted to the district prison at St. Scholastique, sixteen kilometres (seven miles) south—Cordelia in the afternoon and Sam a few hours later.

When she learned that Parslow had been arrested, Cordelia sent word that she wished to speak with Detective McCaskill, who agreed to meet with her that evening. Her first question was whether Parslow had confessed. When he said no, she told him that Parslow had been after her for some time to kill her husband and had even gone to Montreal to purchase a revolver. On Sunday afternoon, after her husband had passed out, Parslow had told her to kiss him goodbye as she would not see him alive again. She did not believe him and went to visit her father. When she came back the next day, Parslow had met her at the outskirts of the village and told her what he had done, warning her to say that it was suicide. She had then gone to the church for the wedding and then went with Noel Courvrette to find the body.

Realizing that they were alone and that she could later deny any statement, Detective McCaskill asked her if she would go over it again later. When she agreed, he arranged for Dr. Mignault and a policeman to hide in an adjoining room and listen. When he took her through her story again, she told essentially the same tale.

Faced with her accusation, Samuel Parslow gave a different version, maintaining that Cordelia had been constantly after him to kill Porier. He had indeed purchased a revolver, but she had vetoed this method, saying it would make too much noise. On Sunday, when Porier passed out, Cordelia had gotten a kitchen knife and thrust it into his hand. "Kill him! Kill him!" she had urged, upon which he had rushed into the bedroom and struck the unconscious man. When Porier had risen from the bed, he had slashed him again, at which point Porier had fallen over on the bed and lay still. Parslow said that his mind was a blank after that.

At the December preliminary hearing, Judge Martigny placed a ban on the publication of any evidence by either the press or witnesses. Because of the parish's limited population, he did not wish to contaminate any potential veniremen. He also cleared the room of all spectators. Both Parslow and Viau pleaded not guilty, but after nearly ten days of testimony they were both committed to stand trial.

Courtroom seats were at a premium when Cordelia Viau went on trial before Judge Taschereau on January 17, 1898. Crown Prosecutor F. Xavier Mathieu introduced medical testimony to indicate that three of the numerous wounds on the victim's throat would have caused death. This suggested that suicide was out because Porier would not have had the strength to inflict these deep cuts on himself. Mathieu then followed with a series of witnesses to establish the illicit relationship between the accused and Parslow.

The highlight came on January 25, when the Crown tried to introduce the second statement Cordelia had made to Detective McCaskill, which had been overheard by hidden witnesses. After considerable argument and strong protests from defence counsel A.E. Porier, His Lordship decided to admit the statements, remarking that the Court of Appeal could rule on his judgement later. It was a telling blow for the Crown.

The defence suffered a second setback when Mr. Belanger, a reporter for Montreal's *La Patrie* newspaper, testified that he had visited Cordelia in prison the day after she spoke to Detective McCaskill and she had told him virtually the same version. This, basically, concluded the Crown's case. Though the defence lawyer had wrung admissions from witnesses that Isidore Porier had on many occasions threatened to take his own life, he had not shaken the main body of evidence against Mrs. Viau.

Presenting no evidence for the defence, Mr. Porier made an impassioned plea to the jurors that the confession had been tricked from his client and that her husband had indeed taken his own life. Just as emphatically, Crown Prosecutor F. Xavier Mathieu argued that Isidore could not have killed himself, and that Cordelia's confessions linked her to the crime. On February 2, after listening to a three-and-a-half-hour charge from the bench that went strongly against the accused, the jurors took only a short time to find her guilty of the charge.

Reserving sentence, Mr. Justice Taschereau advised the defence to immediately prepare an appeal based upon the admissibility of the confessions. While this was going forward, no action was taken to bring Samuel Parslow to trial.

When the Quebec Court of Appeal ruled that there was sufficient uncertainty about the confessions to warrant a new hearing,
the Crown immediately appealed this judgement to the Supreme
Court of Canada, which heard and rejected it on October 13, 1898.
It also ruled that a new trial should take place.

Cordelia Viau's second trial opened at St. Scholastique on
December 5 with Mr. Justice Taschereau again on the bench. Her
original lawyer, A.E. Porier, had withdrawn from the case, leaving
her interests in the hands of J.D. Leduc. Likewise, Crown Prosecutor
F. Xavier Matheiu was replaced by J.A.N. Mackay. The trial moved
forward smoothly with much of the previous evidence condensed,
and as before, both confessions were argued but admitted. An effort
was made on December 9 to have Sam Parslow testify, but he
thwarted this; though placed in the box, his standard response
during his ten-minute appearance was: "I will not answer."

Sheriff Lapointe, who had charge of the prison at St.
Scholastique, took the stand as a surprise witness on December 13.
He stated he had had a conversation with Cordelia about two
months after her first trial. Asking him "to accept this in secret," she
mentioned the footprint in the blood on the bedroom floor. It was
hers, she said; she had been present when Parslow killed her
husband. The defence was unable to exclude this testimony or to
negate its effect on the jurors.

After ten full days of trial, the Crown concluded its case on the
evening of December 14. When the defence indicated that it would
not be calling witnesses, another attempt was made to have Samuel
Parslow testify, but this only evoked another series of refusals and
the Crown closed its presentation. It is possible that the Crown saw
Cordelia as the instigator of the crime and that they were willing to
exchange mercy for his testimony. In the light of further developments, it is interesting to wonder what Parslow's fate might have
been had he co-operated.

Mr. Leduc's address to the jury the following morning was a
masterpiece of passion and argument. Depicting his client as the
dupe of her murderous and domineering paramour, he contended
that she was merely a pawn in the man's consuming lust to possess
her. As he concluded, Cordelia's sobs could be heard throughout
the courtroom. In contrast, the cold, dispassionate logic of prosecutor Mackay and His Lordship tied her to the brutal crime, if not as
the instigator, certainly as a more than willing accomplice. Un-

swayed by Mr. Leduc's emotional appeal, the jury found her guilty and expressed the general feeling of the community when they did not add a recommendation to mercy.

She was sentenced to be hanged at St. Scholastique on Friday, March 10, 1899.

Samuel Parslow, who had languished in prison for almost a year awaiting the appeals on behalf of his accomplice, came to trial December 19, 1898. Defence counsel's first move was to ask for a delay in order that medical men might examine the state of his client's mind, an obvious ploy to gain time so that the emotion-filled trial of Cordelia Viau might fade slightly in the public memory. His Lordship sternly refused it and cautioned him to get on with the business at hand.

The trial followed basically the same format as that of his accomplice, but with his own confession telling heavily against him. After a court recess for Christmas the session resumed on December 28 and the jury needed only fifteen minutes to decide on a verdict. Without leaving the box, they signed a petition asking for clemency.

The twin cases were reviewed by the Department of Justice and the Secretary of State, but on March 6, 1899, Mr. David Mills, Minister of Justice, announced that no clemency was forthcoming and that the death warrants had been issued.

The double execution of Cordelia Viau and Samuel Parslow at St. Scholastique on March 10, 1899, was one of the most disgraceful public spectacles in Canada's history. Attendance at the hanging was limited to two hundred and these were by invitation only. By the evening before the hanging, however, excursion trains, sleighs, and cutters had brought nearly two thousand people from Montreal and surrounding area. They were professional men, mostly medical students, lawyers, and businessmen. As the hour approached, the uninvited throng pressed around the outside gate that led to the prison yard. Though the stone fence was fourteen feet high, several tried to scale it.

Recently passed regulations dictated that prison, or church, bells were to begin ringing fifteen minutes before the ceremony and continue for fifteen minutes afterwards. As these began their soulful dirge, the crowd around the gate made a determined effort to break into the prison yard, launching a battering ram against the entrance. Only after the police had fired several warning shots into the air did the men, women, and children fall back.

The unhappy pair were brought from the prison to the gallows, which had been erected close to the doorway, and placed back to back on the trap with a grey blanket concealing each from the other. Cordelia Viau was calm and resolute, while Parslow needed the assistance of hangman Radclive to climb the two steep flights of stairs that led to the platform. A black curtain shrouded the area below the scaffold, concealing the space into which they would drop.

With practised ease, Radclive bound Mrs. Viau, hooded her and dropped the noose into position. Then he went around the blanket and repeated the performance with Parslow. At a sign from the sheriff, he pulled the bolt and both victims died instantly.

Scarcely had the twin ropes tightened when the crowd inside the prison yard surged forward and tore away the black shroud below the platform. As the bells resumed their death knell, these watched in fascination as the two bodies twisted slowly and hypnotically below the gaping trap. A black flag was run to the top of the prison flag-pole and a notice was posted on the front door announcing to the world that the pair had expiated their crime.

After hanging for twenty minutes, the bodies were taken into the prison and an inquest was held. Later in the afternoon, relatives conveyed them to the cemetery at St. Canut for burial. By that time, the streets of St. Scholastique were quiet again.

. . .

Mary Cowan

The Temptress

THE TINY COMMUNITY of Barry's Bay lay at the head of Kamaniskeg Lake and was situated some fifty kilometres (thirty miles) west of Renfrew, Ontario. Comprised of about five hundred people in 1935, it was a beautiful, secluded setting surrounded by rivers, lakes, and forests. It was an unlikely place for a murder, but then homicide is never particular about its surroundings. A detachment of Ontario Provincial Police had been established there in 1928, but its main duties had consisted of enforcing game laws and investigating the occasional break-in of an isolated cabin. By 1935, the detachment was closed and police duties were carried out from Renfrew or Pembroke.

On Sunday morning, July 21, 1935, a phone call was received at the Renfrew office of the OPP stating that a man named Albert Cowan had died around five-thirty that morning from a gunshot wound to the head. Constable William Johnston responded to the call and arrived at Barry's Bay about eleven o'clock.

He was already familiar with the Cowan family. About nine months earlier, following an anonymous call, he had gone to their home and found Allan Cowan, the dead man's brother, and Mary Cowan, the victim's wife, drinking liquor. From his observations at the time, Constable Johnston suspected that an illicit sexual relationship existed between the two. He had charged Allan with possession of illegal liquor and the young man had been convicted on October 5, 1934.

On this Sunday morning, he found about one hundred people milling around when he pulled up in front of the storey-and-a-half shanty on the lakeshore on the outskirts of town. Inside, he found the body of Albert Cowan, twenty-six, lying on a bed in a downstairs bedroom. The bed was about two feet from an open window, outside of which were the clear imprints of large shoes in the soft ground. Johnston assumed that the killer had stood here and fired through the opening. The entrance wound of a small calibre bullet was half-hidden in the hair at the back of the man's head.

Mary Cowan, twenty-six, wife of the deceased, told him that her husband had come home around six-thirty Saturday evening and they had drunk some wine together. After he had left to visit a neighbour, Antoine Arcand, she had gone out around nine to see her parents, the Kubeshacks. Returning home around three o'clock in the morning, while getting into bed, she had discovered that her husband was unconscious with blood on his head. She had run to the home of his parents, Fred and Bridget Cowan, and told them that Albert had been murdered.

Going with her, his parents found that Albert was still alive. Dr. P.P. Smythe was called, but under the impression that Albert was suffering from a severe hangover and had been in a fight, he gave them instructions for his care and departed. An hour later, while bathing her son's head, Bridget Cowan discovered the bullet hole in the back of his skull. An emergency call had been sent out for Dr.

Smythe, but by the time he arrived, Albert Cowan had died.

Mary Cowan's complete lack of distress over her husband's death triggered suspicion in Constable Johnston's mind, and after a preliminary examination of the house and corpse he decided to check her story. Calling at the home of her parents, he learned that she had not been there at all the previous night. Confronted with this lie, Mary said that she had merely walked to her parents' home but had not gone in. When Johnston asked her why it had taken her six hours to walk the ten kilometres (six miles) there and back. Mary blithely replied: "I sat on a fence for a while."

Reinforced by officers from other detachments, Constable Johnston continued his investigation and found a pair of overshoes discarded under a bush a short distance from the house; they matched the prints under the bedroom window. He also found a white hat with a blue band crammed down behind the kitchen stove with spots on it that looked suspiciously like blood. In another part of the house, he unearthed a blue dress, partly hidden, with similar spots on it. Mary identified the clothes as those she had worn the previous evening. There were no guns on the premises.

Towards nine o'clock Sunday evening, after completing his inquiries, Johnston took Mary Cowan into custody as a material witness and drove her to Renfrew. Mary was a very talkative passenger, and by the time they drew up in front of the detachment house, Constable Johnston had a solid picture of the events of Saturday night.

According to Mary, she had been carrying on an adulterous affair with Allan Cowan, seventeen-year-old brother of the murdered man. She had met Allan that Saturday night beside the church and they had watched as her husband went to visit Antoine Arcand, who lived on a deserted scow on the beach between her home and that of Fred and Bridget Cowan. Seeing that Albert was occupied drinking wine with the old fisherman, she had sent Allan to her house to open the downstairs bedroom window. When her husband left Arcand's boat, Allan had slipped into the wheelhouse and stolen a rifle that had originally belonged to Albert. He had recently traded it to Arcand in exchange for some animal traps.

Mary had searched her home for bullets for the gun, but had only been able to find one, which she gave to Allan. When her husband was asleep, Allan had slipped up to the window, wearing the pair of oversized shoes to conceal the size of his own feet, and had shot Albert. He had thrown the rifle in the lake before rejoining her beside the church. Around three o'clock, Allan had returned to his room at the home of his parents and she had gone back to her own house. At that point, she had gone to the Cowans to tell them that someone had murdered her husband.

Mary interspersed her narrative with giggles and accounts of sexual exploits, explaining that she had no compunction about sex outside marriage since her husband was also active in that respect. He had an illegitimate baby by her own sister, Irene, and was wild-catting with several other women in town.

After locking Mary in the detachment cells, Johnston turned around and drove back to Barry's Bay, where he found Allan Cowan at home. With the information supplied by Mary, he had little difficulty obtaining a verbal confession, which corroborated most of what his sister-in-law had said.

Bridget Cowan turned over a series of letters written by Mary to her son, which contained several references to a murder. While mending Allan's pants about two weeks previously, she had found them in a back pocket. Unable to read, she had one of her daughters read them to her. She had kept them.

After arresting Allan Cowan for the murder of his brother, Constable Johnston drove him to Renfrew, arriving in the small hours of Monday morning, July 22. There, Allan gladly gave a statement, which was written down and from which the police officer got one piece of information he did not already have. Allan said that when he met Mary Cowan at the church, he questioned going through with the plan. Mary had laughed and said that if he didn't, she had someone else who would kill her husband. That had convinced him to go through with the crime.

Once finished with Allan's written statement, Constable Johnston brought Mary Cowan to the office. Faced with her boyfriend's confession, she made the following admission:

> Allan has told me more than once he wished I was his. He loved me so much, that's why we both made the arrangements to kill him, shoot him, or do something else. I have told Allan to get rid of Albert because Allan was better to me than Albert was. Allan said he might get a .22 gun and asked me to get a bullet. I got one—all that was in my house, my own home. I gave it to him Saturday night and said: Here is the bullet if you want it, and I told him to make a good job of killing Albert.

Q. Did you ever say to Allan that if he didn't do it, you'd get someone else to do it?

A. Yes.

Q. After Albert's death, did you want to marry Allan?

A. No, I just wanted him for company. He was good to me. He bought me everything.

Then, after almost thirty-six hours of continuous investigation, Constable Johnston went home and got some sleep.

· · ·

There was one more macabre element to be added to the grim tale of Albert Cowan's murder. On August 11, Antoine Arcand was travelling in a rowboat near the beached scow that served as his home when he caught a glimpse of a rifle lying in shallow water a few metres offshore. Responding to his call, police brought up a .22 rifle, which he quickly identified as his. There was still a shell casing lodged in the chamber.

On examining the casing, Constable Johnston noted that there were three separate firing-pin impressions on the impact surface. Forming his own conclusions, he questioned Allan about them. The young man told him that the first time he pulled the trigger, the shell did not explode, so he took the bullet out and turned it around. Again it failed to go off and he extracted it once more, turned it a little more and reinserted it in the breech. The third time, the gun had gone off. Even Johnston, hardened by previous revelations in the case, was disturbed by the calm recital of Allan's explanation.

After the preliminary hearing at Pembroke on August 6, both suspects were bound over for trial. Allan's, which was held first, concluded on December 11, 1935, with the anticipated verdict of guilty. His own confession swung the scales against him. Curiously, the jury made no recommendation to mercy despite his tender age.

Mary Cowan's trial opened immediately afterwards before Mr. Justice J.K. MacKay, with James A. Malony of Renfrew mounting a valiant defence. Mr. C. Snyder, for the Crown, had hoped to link her directly to the crime through bloodstains on the hat and dress she had worn that night, but while both articles revealed bloodstains, it was impossible to determine that they were human. Though Mary had been quite voluble in her conversations with Constable Johnston, His Lordship refused to admit these. However, she had made a voluntary, written confession before a magistrate at Pembroke on July 22, and this was admitted.

Mr. Snyder's star witness proved to be Allan Cowan, who took the stand on the second day of the trial and gave his answers clearly and distinctly. He had no hesitation in implicating his lover, and his evidence, together with her confession, sealed her fate. Again, in returning its verdict, the jury made no recommendation to mercy.

Both prisoners were sentenced to be executed at Pembroke on Thursday, February 27, 1936.

There was no appeal to a higher court on behalf of either and the struggle to save them from the noose was conducted with a view to executive clemency. Dr. C.D. Tennant examined both and concluded that Mary Cowan was faking most of her responses to his questions. Though finding her quite sane, he felt that she was "a moron and a sexual delinquent." Allan, though of slightly higher intelligence, he found to be a submissive and easily led youth. "It is not surprising that a woman ten years his senior who has been gratifying his sexual appetite, can control him quite readily." Dr. E.R. Frankish, another psychiatrist, concurred with Dr. Tennant's opinion.

In mid-February, as the execution date drew near and a decision had to be made, Dr. Harry Clare examined Mary Cowan, and concluding that she was too dangerous to be at large in any community, recommended that she be confined in an institution for mental defectives.

Officials had little difficulty making the decision to commute the sentence of Allan Cowan, now eighteen. Though the jury had not recommended mercy and the trial judge had made no comment in this respect, his youth and degree of mental impairment convinced them that he should not be hanged. His sentence was altered to life on February 24, 1936, and after spending just over fifteen years in Kingston Penitentiary, he was paroled on November 2, 1951.

The question of Mary Cowan was a different matter. In the mid-February 1936 report submitted by the Remission Service to Mr. Ernest Lapointe, Minister of Justice, the tenor was definitely to allow the execution to go forward. Mr. Lapointe carried the case to the Privy Council, and after much debate it was decided to recommend commutation to the Governor-General, but only on one condition. Writing on March 13, Mr. Lapointe noted: "When Council advised commutation of the death sentence, it proceeded upon the assumption that Mary Cowan would never again be a menace to society."

This admonition remained on Mary Cowan's file and over the next forty-five years thwarted every effort to secure her release. Finally, on January 3, 1961, the newly formed National Parole Board reviewed her case and recommended to Parliament that she be liberated. She was released to the city of Kingston at the age of seventy-two and died there shortly afterwards.

. . .

Christine Pogmore
I've Changed My Mind

*A*LTHOUGH ORIGINALLY FROM SCOTLAND, the Pogmores some time in the distant past moved to London, England, and in 1905, seduced by the high-class propaganda campaign sponsored by the Canadian government and the Canadian Pacific Railroad, they were lured to the New World. They settled in the Byemoor district in the centre of Alberta, north of present-day Hanna. The eldest son, James, took up a homestead eleven kilometres (seven miles) south of the village, and when the next in line, George, filed for land adjacent to his brother's, the Pogmore clan were well-established Albertans. The land around them was hilly and dry, with thick clumps of trees surrounded by short-grass prairie, and the soil, while not the most fertile in the West, was well suited for grain.

In 1917, George Pogmore met a dark-haired, slender, and attractive nineteen-year-old girl, Christine Maud, who was visiting from Kingston, Ontario. He married her and took her to the homestead, and together they brought six children into the world, five girls and a boy. They were both dedicated and hard workers and built their holding into a modest-sized farm.

By the early 1930s, the trucking industry was just getting a toehold in rural Alberta and George became one of its pioneers. Byemoor was a distribution point for several smaller communities and thus ideal for headquarters. He worked from there. Since it kept him on the road a good deal, he employed one, and sometimes two, hired men to keep the farm operating.

One of the first was Emanuel Ernst, a tall, clean-shaven, blue-eyed Russian, who came to work on the Pogmore farm in 1934. As a youth, he had accidentally drunk formaldehyde, thinking it was water. The resulting scars and burns left him in poor health, affecting his speech and causing lapses of memory and other inappropriate behaviour. He was an experienced farmhand, however, having worked in the Craigmyle-Hanna district for some time. Though he was known as "Happy" to his friends, he was a distressed man.

Tiny, bespectacled Christine Pogmore was attracted to the hired man, and because of her husband's frequent absences on trucking business, they were thrown together a lot. It was the old story of familiarity breeds attempt, and she allowed her liking to ripen into sexual intimacy, and then began to think in terms of getting rid of her husband so she could continue the relationship.

· · ·

The final tragedy may have had its beginning in September 1936. Just before leaving on one of his extended trips, George Pogmore gave Happy Ernst specific instructions to move a granary from one part of the farm to another. Ernst forgot. When George returned on September 15, he became angry, and in the ensuing argument he fired the hired man. Emanuel Ernst took his back pay and rode his bicycle to Craigmyle, thirty-two kilometres (twenty miles) to the south, where he checked into the local hotel.

With the heavy harvest work over, there was not much spare work in the district and Ernst hung around the hotel. He was not much on letter-writing, but Christine Pogmore was; in all she wrote nineteen letters to her lover, none of them dated. Most contained some reference to the fact that she wanted him to kill her husband. Emanuel kept the letters in a trunk in his hotel room.

He found this method of communication unsatisfactory, however, and on Thursday, October 15, Ernst rode his bicycle to the Pogmore farm south of Byemoor. He was seen by several people along the way. For two days he hid in a wooded bluff, where Christine brought him a blanket and food, and there they finalized details of the murder.

Christine, however, began to have second thoughts about the

relationship and the morass into which it was drawing them, and she met with him Saturday night. In the company of her daughter, Margaret, eighteen, she told him that she had changed her mind; she did not want her husband killed and thought it would be best if he stayed away from her.

Ernst went back to his hotel room in Craigmyle that night with quite a different understanding of this meeting with her. He believed that the plot was still alive. The next day, Sunday, October 18, he rode back to the Pogmore farm and hid in the bluff near the farmyard. This time he carried a .32 rifle in a canvas sheath.

Paul Portula, the hired man who had replaced Ernst, was the chief source of information for what happened that evening. He said that after completing his chores Sunday evening he sat down at the kitchen table with George Pogmore, Arthur Jones (the second hired man), and Frank Willis, a schoolteacher, to play whist. George was sitting with his back to the kitchen window.

Paul Portula recalled that about ten-thirty Mrs. Pogmore came downstairs from her bedroom and went outside. She was absent for ten or fifteen minutes before returning and going back upstairs to her room. The children were already in bed on the second floor.

About fifteen minutes later, a bullet came crashing through the kitchen window, striking George Pogmore in the head. Mrs. Pogmore came running downstairs in a panic, and when she saw her fallen husband, she sat beside him and held his head in her lap until he died. She looked and acted as if she were in shock. The children, awakened by the shot, came downstairs and sat huddled around her. The men, frightened that the killer might be lurking, waited but finally ventured outside. They could see nothing in the darkness. Later, footprints were found in the soft ground outside the kitchen window.

Christine Pogmore was to testify that she had gone outside to meet with Emanuel Ernst at ten-thirty. She maintained that she had told Ernst to go away, repeating that she had changed her mind and did not want her husband killed. Ernst was to swear with equal sincerity that she was still in favour of the murder.

· · ·

Constable (later Staff Sergeant) David Beeching, RCMP, was placed in charge of the investigation and was quickly convinced that the evidence pointed to the tall, former hired man, Emanuel Ernst. He learned that the man had been dismissed by Pogmore a month earlier, but that he had been seen riding a bicycle near the farm on two recent occasions. It was known that he was staying at the two-storey hotel in Craigmyle.

Taking several officers with him, Beeching drove to Craigmyle. They overtook the suspect walking along the road towards the town. His bike had broken down and he had proceeded on foot.

They took him to the Craigmyle Hotel, where, in the presence of three officers, he made a statement admitting the murder and implicating Mrs. Pogmore. He was then placed under arrest. In support of his story, he turned over the incriminating letters she had written.

As they were leaving the hotel to drive to Byemoor, they met a Mrs. McCrae on the wooden sidewalk. Ernst knew her, and while they waited for the police car to pull up, he had a casual conversation with her. He volunteered that he had killed Pogmore.

There was more evidence. On the way to the Pogmore farm, Ernst asked the police to stop beside a field some sixteen kilometres (ten miles) north of Craigmyle. There he directed Constable Staley to the spot where he had hidden the murderous .32 rifle. At the Pogmore farm, his footprints matched those found outside the kitchen window. When he was removed to a cell in the Stettler police station, he wrote several letters to relatives in which he admitted the shooting.

There remained only the question of Mrs. Pogmore . . .

After being confronted with Emanuel Ernst's confession, Mrs. Pogmore gave a statement, allegeding that while she had planned the murder with him, at the last moment she had told him not to go through with it. During the short meeting with him on Sunday night, she felt that she had convinced him and assumed he was going back to Craigmyle. When she heard the shot a few minutes later, she realized he had "disobeyed her" and carried out the slaying.

She was arrested and conveyed to the cells at Stettler.

Ernst went on trial first, appearing before Mr. Justice Ewing and jury at Red Deer on Monday, December 7, 1936. His defence counsel, Mr. R. Fred Jackson of Edmonton, clearly laid out his plan of attack. He would not deny the murder, but would prove that because of the injuries caused by the formaldehyde, the thirty-six-year-old Russian had no comprehension of what he was doing.

The trial proceeded smoothly until the second day, when

evidence was given concerning the confession he had made to the police at the Craigmyle Hotel. One of the police witnesses stated that he thought someone had told Ernst to "come clean" or "come clear." Then Ernst made the statement. Although none of the other officers present recalled this, His Lordship took no chances and declared a mistrial since the jury had already heard this part of the Crown's case.

The second trial, which followed immediately upon the first, concluded on Saturday, December 12. Judge Ewing refused to allow the statement given to the police to be introduced, but conceded that the verbal statement made to Mrs. McCrae outside the hotel was voluntary. In speaking to the jury, Crown Prosecutor J.J. Frawley argued that there was ample evidence to prove that Ernst was guilty, and no indication of insanity. Conceding the murder, Emanuel's lawyer contended that the unfortunate accident with the formaldehyde had so weakened the accused's mind that he was not responsible for his actions. The jury, which had not been given any other examples to bolster the defence argument, found him guilty with no recommendation to mercy.

Christine Pogmore came to trial on December 15, also before Judge Ewing. Prosecutor Frawley tried to introduce several statements she had made to the police on the day of her arrest and later. Since these were made after she learned of Ernst's confession and were the result of that confession, which he had ruled inadmissible, His Lordship would not allow these to go to the jury.

The letters she had written to Ernst proved that a conspiracy to kill George Pogmore had existed at one time, but the critical point was: When did she abandon that scheme? Emanuel Ernst, the last and principal witness for the Crown, denied that she had told him to break off the plan on the Saturday before the murder. He contended that on Sunday evening, a few minutes before the shot was fired, she was still in favour of it. She made it clear that she wanted her husband dead, he went on, and on one occasion he had bought strychnine with which she could poison him.

Christine Pogmore took the stand, and while admitting that she had planned the murder of her husband, claimed that she had renounced the whole idea. Her version of the Saturday night meeting was supported by the recollections of her daughter Margaret, who testified that she had heard her mother telling Happy to "go away and stay away."

In his address to the jurors, defence counsel J.R. McClure argued strongly that his client was guilty of no more than wishing her husband dead and that she had clearly pulled out of any plan. What had followed was a vengeful act on the part of Ernst to get even, not only with her, but for his dismissal earlier by the victim.

The jury was in a catch-22 situation, for while conceding that she probably had changed her mind at the last minute, they believed that her prolonged counselling of Ernst to commit the murder had unleashed a force that she was unable to stop. She had misjudged her control over him, and once he had set his mind to shoot, he had carried it through despite her last-minute admonitions to desist. After two hours of deliberation, they returned a verdict of guilty but added a recommendation to mercy on those grounds.

Mr. Justice Ewing sentenced both to be hanged at Fort Saskatchewan prison on March 3, 1937.

The Alberta Court of Appeals dismissed both cases and Emanuel Ernst was executed at Fort Saskatchewan at the designated time. Christine Pogmore's sentence was commuted to life imprisonment on February 26 on the grounds that "It is possible that she did tell Ernst not to carry it through."

Mrs. Pogmore was confined in the Women's Prison at Kingston and remained there for thirteen years. She was granted a parole on March 23, 1950. Though she was then fifty-two years of age, she was still an attractive and trim-looking woman, and she later married again in Vancouver. She briefly visited her old home at Byemoor on several occasions, but on the death of her second husband she stopped coming. She died during a visit to relatives in the United States. Nothing remains today of the old house where the tragic drama was played out.

· · ·

Death by Gunshot

The majority of Canada's female killers were cold-blooded assassins who knew exactly what they were doing and who intended that their victims should die. They certainly did not expect them to sit up smiling after the attack. Of the thirty-five women who carried out the act of murder themselves or who were active participants in the slayings, eight chose guns as their weapons. The first recorded instance of a woman using a gun was Catherine Brown of Newfoundland.

Catherine Brown
Forgery and Murder

*L*IKE MOST CASES FROM COLONIAL TIMES, precise details are lacking and only fragmentary documents exist to provide information about the crime. In the instance of Catherine Brown, two records are extant. The first, the Calendar for the Court of Assize in General Gaol Delivery held at St. John's on Monday, the 20th day of August, 1804, contains the following list of activities of the Grand Jury:

Catherine Brown, murder, true bill, guilty. Let her be hanged by the neck.
Richard Nickells, murder, no bill.
Richard Nickells, forgery, true bill, guilty. Let him be hanged by the neck.
James Brown, forgery, true bill, guilty. Let him be hanged by the neck.

Signed: Thomas Tromlett, Chief Justice.

The James Brown listed had no connection with or relationship to Catherine Brown.

The second document is a death-warrant signed by His Excellency Sir Erasmus Gower, Governor of Newfoundland, and dated August 29, 1804. It is addressed to Henry Phillips, esq., High Sheriff:

> Whereas at a Court of Assizes and General Delivery holden at the Court House at St. John's in this Island daily from the twenty first to the twenty fifth day of August instance, Catherine Brown was in due form of law convicted of the wilful murder of her husband John Brown and was sentenced for the same to be hanged by the neck until she is Dead, I do, by virtue of His Majesty's Commission made letters Patent bearing date at Westminster the thirty first day of May in the Forty Fourth year of His Majesty's reign, hereby authorize and command you that on Saturday morning next the first day of September, between the hours of nine and twelve you cause execution to be publically done upon the said Catherine Brown according to the sentence aforesaid, by hanging her by the Neck until she is Dead and so doing this shall be your Warrant.

· · ·

Catherine Brown and her husband, John, lived in a house on Southside Road in St. John's. Among their close friends was a young man named Richard Nickells, a clerk in the firm of Thomas Row. Just how close a friend may be judged by the events that followed.

A forgery was perpetrated against the firm of Thomas Row in an amount less than $80. Forgery was a capital crime and the perpetrator could be hanged. Richard Nickells was later to tell the court that he had investigated the forgery and discovered that both Catherine Brown and her husband were implicated. Believing that he could take the blame for it and that his employer would not press charges but allow him to replace the money, he decided to confess. He told his masters that he was responsible and begged mercy. They opted to think the matter over.

While Nickells was following this dangerous course of action, Catherine Brown—for reasons known only to herself—undertook the murder of her helpmate. While visiting the home of a neighbour, George Whitten, she stole his muzzle-loading revolver. When he missed it, he reported it to the police, never suspecting Catherine.

Three days later, as she prepared to murder her husband, she discovered she had no gunpowder. So, she asked Hannah Whitten, George's sister, to lend her some, saying that her husband intended to shoot a troublesome dog.

That night, while her husband slept, she killed him, dropped the revolver beside him on the bed, set fire to the bedclothes and ran into the street crying: "John has shot himself, my God, help me."

When the fire was extinguished, John Brown was found with the pistol close to his hand.

Catherine Brown was not a very clever killer. The next day she confided to George Whitten that it was not suicide and confessed she had taken the revolver from his house and used it to dispatch her husband. When Whitten passed this new information along to the police, Catherine was arrested.

Searching for a motive, the police fastened upon the friendship between Catherine and young Richard Nickells, and chose to believe that it was much more serious than appeared. They laid a charge of murder against him, alleging that he had plotted with her to get rid of her husband.

As a result, the firm of Thomas Row evidently decided that Richard was a first-rate scoundrel and not the knight gallant he pretended to be and proceeded with a charge of forgery against him. When the Grand Jury met in late August, Nickells faced joint charges of murder and forgery, both of which carried the death penalty.

The Grand Jury found that the evidence against Richard was insufficient to support a charge of murder, but found him guilty on the count of forgery, despite his plea that he was only trying to protect Catherine Brown and her husband because they had been kind to him. They sentenced him to be hanged for forgery.

Catherine Brown was tried next, and on the basis of her confession to George Whitten, supported by the testimony of his sister Hannah that the accused had borrowed gunpowder from her on the evening of the murder, she was convicted after a short hearing.

When brought before Chief Justice Tromlett for sentence on August 29, Catherine Brown could give no reason why the sentence should not be carried out and was ordered to be hanged three days later. Richard Nickells made a last valiant attempt to save his life by repeating his story that he was merely trying to shield good friends. Though sentencing him to die, His Lordship promised to convey this information to Governor Gower, in whose hands lay the power of mercy.

The governor extended mercy to Richard Nickells and commuted his sentence to life imprisonment. At that time, this punishment carried a special meaning. St. John's did not have the facilities to house and care for long-term prisoners, and any person sentenced to life was placed on the next boat to the Caribbean Islands. If they returned to Newfoundland at any time in the future, they were liable to be hanged without trial.

There was no mercy in Governor Gower's heart for Catherine Brown, and on Saturday, September 1, 1804, she was hanged publicly in the market place outside the old wooden prison that stood just off Duckworth Street.

Thus, Catherine Brown became the first "gun-slinging Momma" to pay with her life.

. . .

Hilda Blake

The Elusive Tramp

*E*MILY HILDA BLAKE, twenty-one, had the unhappy distinction of being the only female ever hanged in "Friendly Manitoba," and she went to her death on the chilly morning of December 27, 1899, in the yard of the old prison on the eastern outskirts of Brandon. Her crime was the murder of Mrs. Mary Lane, mother of four, and while the motive was never officially released, it is not difficult to fathom what it was.

Hilda Blake, as she was commonly known, was born in Norfolk, England, in January 1878, the daughter of a county constable. Her parents died while she was young and she and her brother, Arthur, were raised by an older sister. When her sister married, Hilda and Arthur were placed in the Heckingham Workhouse until suitable accommodation could be found for them. The patron of the Workhouse was Sir Richard Beauchamp, upon whose estate her father had been a cottage tenant. He arranged for the two children to be shipped to Manitoba. It was a common occurrence in the 1890s for numbers of British children to be shipped to various parts of Canada, and about eighty or ninety children were sent to Manitoba each year. The most famous of these child-placement agencies was the Barnardo Ranch at Russell, Manitoba.

In May 1888, Hilda and Arthur were brought to Canada by Arthur Broadhurst, who served as their escort, and were delivered to the family of Arthur P. Stewart of Elkhorn, Manitoba, who had paid part of their expenses in exchange for their services. Mr. Broadhurst later remembered Hilda as "a quiet, well-behaved, and affectionate child and she seemed greatly to appreciate the little benefits." Hilda was then ten years old.

After several years in the quiet little community of Elkhorn, Hilda Blake branched out on her own and took employment as a maid. On July 15, 1898, she accepted a position as servant to Robert and Mary Lane at Brandon.

The normal tenor of life at the Lane household seemed to move smoothly over the next year. Mary Lane was an ardent church member and a favourite on their block. Her husband, Robert, was well positioned in the business world and treasurer of the influential gun club. He was on a first-name basis with those who counted. The four Lane children played easily with the other children in the neighbourhood. Hilda, though reserved and somewhat of a loner, seemed to fit in well with the family. Then on Wednesday, July 5, 1899, all that changed.

The first intimation of trouble came when two shots were heard coming from the Lane house. Moments later, Mary Lane, her clothes on fire, staggered out onto the sidewalk in full view of her children, who were playing in the front yard. Neighbours came running to the scene, and after putting out the fire noted that she was bleeding from an ugly wound in her back. While they were bending over her, Hilda Blake came limping from the house with a breathless tale.

While one man phoned for a doctor and the police, Hilda blurted out her story. She and Mrs. Lane had been hanging curtains in the living-room when a tramp came to the back door and asked for food. Mrs. Lane had told him to "be off." Hilda had her back turned to the man and did not see him shoot, but she heard the gun blasts and saw Mrs. Lane fall. She next saw the man running down the back lane in the direction of the CPR tracks.

The police arrived within minutes of the shooting—the station was only a block and a half from the Lane house—and immediately began to form posses to search for the stranger. Hilda was able to give them a very accurate description, stating that the man was about thirty, around five feet ten inches, dressed in new overalls, a dark coat, and a black slouch hat. He spoke broken English and carried a pack on his back. The two oldest Lane children, Wilson and Barton, said that they had also seen the man walking away. Mortally wounded, Mary Lane was unable to speak and died on the sidewalk within moments.

Armed with Hilda's description of the vagrant, the posses headed for the railway yards. A CPR employee, J. Murray, told them that he had seen a man who fit that portrait get off a freight train earlier and walk up Tenth Street; that would have taken him past the Lane home. A half-hour later, the transient was located by some grain sheds and taken into custody. By this time, word of Mrs. Lane's death had reached the townspeople and there were angry cries of "Lynch!" Fortunately, the police arrived in time and led the suspect away.

The hobo, whose name was Peter German, claimed that he lived at Stuartburn, Manitoba, a small village south of Winnipeg, and that he was on his way home. While he admitted calling on several homes in search of work in exchange for a meal, he denied that he had shot anyone. He had no weapons on him. He could not remember whether he had stopped at the Lane home or not.

Hilda Blake was brought to the police station but upon viewing the prisoner said that he was not the man who had shot Mrs. Lane. This message was quickly relayed to the manhunters and the search resumed. When the two young Lane boys were brought to the station, however, they readily identified Peter German as the man who had called at their house, but they could not remember whether they had seen him leaving just after the shots or some time before. They had been too busy playing.

Although several other transients were brought to the police station that evening and the following day, Hilda was unable to identify any of them.

Suspecting that the killer would have thrown away his gun as quickly as possible, Police Chief James Kirkaldy detailed several men to search the area behind the Lane dwelling. Two of them were engaged in scouring the lane when Hilda came out of the kitchen.

She asked them if they had looked under some lime casks that stood against the back fence, and when they said no, she went to the barrels. Tipping one up, she called to them. They discovered a box of .22 shells and a small .22 revolver wrapped in newspaper.

Assisting James Kirkaldy in his investigation was Detective John Foster, a member of the Manitoba Provincial Police and one of the most astute investigators on the frontier. He noted that according to Hilda Blake, Mrs. Lane had been standing on a sofa hanging curtains when the shots were fired. She had further placed the killer in the kitchen door, five or six feet away. The autopsy reports, however, showed that the fatal bullet had travelled in a parallel fashion, not upwards. Also, the gun muzzle had been so close to the victim's back that the powder had set her dress on fire. A second bullet had been found in the ceiling. After conducting several ballistic experiments, Foster became convinced that the tramp was a fabrication and he fixed his attention on Hilda.

At the inquest, held on Friday and Saturday, Blake repeated her story of the tramp, adding that after Mrs. Lane had been shot and ran outside, she had tried to follow her to help her but had tripped in the hallway and stunned herself. When she finally got to the front yard, neighbours had already arrived on the scene. Hilda could add no further information except to iterate that Mary Lane had been standing on the sofa when the bullets were fired, and that she had jumped down and run outside screaming.

While Hilda was on the witness stand, Detective Foster paid a hurried visit to her rooms. There he discovered a bottle of laudanum and a brooch wrapped in a torn scrap of newspaper. As a precautionary measure, he replaced the laudanum with a coloured wine. Back at the police station, he was able to match the torn fragment of newspaper with a section ripped out of the sheet that had been wrapped around the revolver. Convinced now that Hilda Blake was the killer, he reported his findings to Chief Kirkaldy.

Although the coroner's jury returned an open verdict, the police were so certain that they had their killer that they released Peter German, the transient, from custody on Saturday night. In a small gesture at amends, a collection was taken up on his behalf, and among those who contributed were some who had been screaming "Lynch" a few days before.

On Sunday, July 9, Chief Kirkaldy arrested Hilda Blake, brought her to the police station, and after warning her presented her with the evidence against her. Although she bore up well under initial questioning, within fifteen minutes she began to crack. Unknown to her, Detective Foster was in an adjacent room from which he could hear the questions and answers.

After reaffirming that her relationship with Mary Lane had always been good, Hilda stated that she had been planning suicide and had gone to Winnipeg on June 20 to purchase a gun. She had obtained a .22 revolver and some shells from Hingston, Smith Arms Co. This was readily confirmed later since the shells were an unusual brand. Her resolve had wavered on returning to Brandon and she kept putting off the final act. She had also bought some laudanum, but had been unable to take this either.

On Wednesday, the tramp had come to the back door asking for food and Mrs. Lane had been curt with him and turned him away empty-handed. Because of her own background, Hilda had identified with the man. She had then got the gun from its hiding place in her room, gone up to Mary Lane, kissed her, and shot her in the back. Mrs. Lane had swung around sharply, knocking her to the floor and jarring her elbow, which caused the second shot that ended harmlessly in the ceiling. Then Mrs. Lane had run out onto the street.

According to Kirkaldy, the young maid then said that she knew she had done wrong and wanted to be punished. She asked if he would kill her right there and get it over with. Kirkaldy said that wasn't possible. Her later behaviour seemed to bear out her desire to make amends with her own life.

A preliminary hearing on Monday, July 10, before Magistrate Campbell, heard overwhelming evidence of her guilt. Asked if she had anything to say on her behalf, she replied: "Yes, I want to tell you that I am guilty and I want the severest punishment you can inflict. That is all." She was committed to stand trial on November 14.

Incarcerated in the women's section of the Brandon Provincial Jail, Hilda was at first despondent and refused to eat, but as the days passed she took a new interest in life and began to write her autobiography. She was a great favourite with Warden Noxon and his wife, but although Rev. C.C. McLaurin visited her frequently, she was cool to his ministrations.

Knowing that she was penniless, several lawyers offered their services free of charge, but she rejected all their kindnesses, and when her trial opened before Chief Justice Killam, she went to court undefended. His Lordship offered to appoint someone to act for her, but she refused. Nevertheless, he adjourned court briefly and sent her into a side room with lawyer G.R. Coldwell. When they returned ten minutes later, she was still adamant.

The Clerk of the Court then asked: "Emily Hilda Blake, you stand charged with the murder of Mary Lane. Are you guilty or not guilty?"

"Guilty," was her reply.

As a precautionary measure, guilty pleas are seldom accepted in murder cases without the presentation of some corroborating evidence, but after conferring together with prosecutor Patterson, His Lordship decided that this would not be necessary. She was remanded over to the next day for sentence.

On Wednesday, November 15, Hilda Blake stood in the prisoner's box and heard herself sentenced to death. The execution was to take place on December 27, 1899. She received the news calmly, without the slightest trace of stress or emotion.

The case of Hilda Blake was a puzzling one for the agents of the Minister of Justice to unravel as they debated the issue of clemency. The most vexatious problem was that of motive. One theory was that being unable to carry out her own suicide, she wanted the state to kill her. Another rationale suggested that she was jealous of the attention given to the Lane children by Mary Lane and she sought revenge. A third possibility was that she wanted to dispose of the wife in order to marry Robert Lane.

Her behaviour in the death cell was peculiar. Towards the end of November, Warden Noxon discovered that one bar of her cell window had been sawed almost through and another was partially cut. Saying nothing to her, he secreted himself nearby that night and heard her begin to work on the bars, but she was doing it in a very half-hearted manner, almost as if she did not wish to free herself. When confronted, she first said that the hacksaw had been smuggled to her in a banana by a young male friend. Then she changed her story and accused her death-watch matron, Mrs. Emma Tripp, of bringing the saws into the prison.

When questioned, Mrs. Tripp confessed that she had taken the saws from her son's tool-box and brought them to Hilda. She tried to justify her actions by saying that she really did not think Hilda wanted to escape, but only wished to occupy her time. Her plea was to no avail, however, and on January 25, 1900, she was sentenced to two months in the same prison. A reporter at her trial noted: "It is the opinion that Mrs. Tripp was under the influence of Hilda Blake, whose superior will power was strong enough to command the woman now in jail."

As the day of her execution neared, Hilda told the only story that remotely contained a motive. She claimed that a young man had promised to marry her if she killed Mary Lane and said she had documentary evidence to back this up. However, she either could not or would not direct the police to this evidence.

The famous executioner John Robert Radclive spent Christmas Day aboard a train, arriving at Brandon in the evening. He spent December 26 at the prison, awaiting news. The indecision of the authorities was so intense that the final death warrant was not signed until December 26, the day before the hanging. It was almost as if the Governor-General was hoping for some conclusive piece of information one way or the other. When the decision was telegraphed to Brandon, the final preparations were made.

When morning broke, a solemn procession of sleighs snaked through the misty haze that enveloped the city and stopped before the prison door. The coroner's jury, several reporters, and two friends invited by Hilda were the only outsiders in attendance when she was led from her cell to the foot of the sixteen steps leading to the platform. She delayed her ascent as long as possible, and several times Radclive had to urge her forward, gently but firmly. Before the hood was lowered, she scanned the spectators, as if hoping to see a particular person. She went to her death with calmness and dignity.

Hilda Blake carried her secrets to the lonely grave in the northeast corner of the prison yard. Police Chief James Kirkaldy never released her autobiography, nor did he reveal the contents of the last letter she wrote. Beyond saying that she had written a letter to someone in Brandon forgiving him for something, Kirkaldy would release no information. His cohort in the affair, Detective John Foster, was equally tight-lipped. They were obviously protecting someone.

· · ·

Jennie Hawkes

Pistol Packin' Momma

*T*HE CASES OF JENNIE HAWKES of Wetaskiwin, Alberta, and Grapena Shulman of Calder, Saskatchewan, had many similarities, and had they killed their husbands in a later, more sophisticated era, they would probably never have been convicted of murder. The attitude towards women who kill the men who abuse them has advanced a long way since those grim early days, as evidenced by the acquittal of Jane Hurshman at Liverpool, Nova Scotia, in November 1982. After years of sexual and physical abuse, she killed Billy Stafford with a shotgun and was charged with first-degree murder. Courtroom spectators applauded the jury after they found her not guilty.

Jennie Hawkes was apparently born around 1860 in the United States, but where and when is not known. The first official record comes in 1882, when she married a rancher in Montana by the name of Washington Hawkes, a number of years her junior. Although no children were born to them, they adopted a young girl who eventually married a man named William Rosser; her life would be closely linked with theirs. Jennie and Washington resided in Montana for thirty-two years before moving to Alberta in 1914, lured by the offer of cheap homesteads in the Canadian West.

The promise of bargain land brought an influx of American farmers into central Alberta from the western United States, and many of these settled around Lewisville. The village, which no longer exists, was about thirty-two kilometres (twenty miles) from Wetaskiwin on the Calgary-Edmonton Railway. In addition to Washington and Jennie, the Rosser boys, David and William, and the Hawkes's daughter moved as well, settling within a mile of the Hawkes homestead. Their presence persuaded other Americans to take up land nearby, creating one of the few strictly American settlements in western Canada.

Washington Hawkes had done well ranching in Montana and he quickly erected a substantial house and outbuildings on his farm. In keeping with his ambitious nature, he took another quarter-section of land at a place called Buck Lake.

Henry E. Stoley, another American, arrived in the district at the same time, bringing with him his wife, Rosella, twenty-eight, and three children aged eleven, nine, and eight. He was one of those affable, easy-going men who seem to survive with little ambition and few financial resources. His family was never broke but often badly bent. Rosella was just the opposite. She throbbed with the desire to better her position in life and grabbed any opportunity to pull herself upwards. Sometimes she was not too particular about what she grabbed.

Almost from her first meeting with Washington Hawkes, she found a kindred soul; Hawkes liked women and she liked aspiring men. She made no secret of her attraction for him and Hawkes returned her interest. On Christmas Day, 1914, without consulting his wife, he invited the Stoley family to share his residence.

To allow privacy for the two families, Washington Hawkes divided the ground floor of the house by erecting a partition between the front and rear rooms. He occupied the front section with his wife and his twice-widowed mother, Mrs. Martha Long, seventy-nine. The five Stoleys set up house-keeping in the two rooms at the back. If Henry Stoley was delighted with, and trusting of, this new arrangement, Jennie Hawkes was downright suspicious.

Over the next two months, there was a growing intimacy between Washington Hawkes and young Rosella Stoley, causing Jennie to eavesdrop on them at every opportunity. She would later testify that in addition to proof positive of sexual intimacy, she overheard them plotting to get rid of her by having her confined in a mental hospital. If they succeeded, their next venture was to engineer the demise of Henry Stoley "by an accident." That would clear the way for their marriage.

Jennie's suspicions were well founded. Washington began to take household articles such as dishes, chairs—even the cook stove—and move them into the back section of the house under the pretence of "helping those poor Stoleys." When Jennie protested, he threatened to have her "put away." In late February 1915, he announced that he was moving in with the Stoley family and she could fend as best she knew how.

The ultimatum finally came on March 2, when he told her that he was going to his homestead at Buck Lake, and when he returned she had better be out of the house. He had no further need for her and his plans for the future did not include her. Then he left.

Jennie Hawkes took refuge with her married daughter, Mrs. William Rosser, who lived a mile away. She brooded, but by Saturday, March 13, she announced that since there did not appear to be anything she could do, she was reconciled to the loss of her husband and home. There were some personal, treasured items that she wanted to retrieve. The day being warm, she decided to walk home and left just before one in the afternoon. She had not gone far before she was overtaken by David Rosser driving a sleigh, and she accepted a ride with him.

On reaching her farm, she visited with her mother-in-law, Mrs. Long, who still occupied the front portion of the house. David Rosser continued on to the barns to make some repairs to the team harness.

The Stoleys, who were in the kitchen, saw the rig arrive. Henry put on his hat and coat and joined David Rosser at the barn. His wife, in the meantime, went and eavesdropped at the partition that divided the ground floor. She could hear Jennie and Mrs. Long talking, and realizing that Jennie was gathering articles to take with her, immediately called out, ordering Jennie to leave things alone. Everything now belonged to her, she bragged, and Jennie had no right to remove anything. Her challenge triggered off a terrible sequence of events.

Because Washington was absent at his homestead so often, Jennie had borrowed a .32 revolver from David Rosser for protection and kept it in a cupboard. She now got it.

Two of the Stoley children were playing in the yard, and as Jennie marched out of the house and came around the corner towards the rear door with the gun in her hand, she shouted at them to get out of the way: "Look out, you little devils, or I'll shoot you!"

The third child, Elsie Stoley, eleven, was sitting at the kitchen table, but Jennie ignored her as she tramped through the kitchen and planted herself in front of the bedroom door behind which Rosella was lurking. She blindly fired six shots at the closed door, five of which penetrated and the sixth ended up in the ceiling.

Henry Stoley and David Rosser, who had seen her come around the corner of the house with the gun and a terrible look on her face, reached the kitchen just as the last shot was fired. They found her standing with the revolver dangling from her hand. David removed it gently and sat her on a chair. She kept saying that Rosella was trying to take her husband away from her.

When they opened the bedroom door, they found Mrs. Stoley lying on the floor. Of the six shots, one had struck her in the right arm, one in the right hip, and one in the head. She was unconscious, but not dead. A doctor was called and he advised Stoley to take her to the hospital in Wetaskiwin as quickly as possible and he would meet them there.

Jennie Hawkes appeared to be in a coma nearly as profound as that of her victim. She made no objection when David Rosser put her in his sleigh and drove her to her daughter's home. There she worked around the house in a mechanical fashion until midnight, at which point Sergeant Michel of the Royal North-West Mounted Police arrived and placed her under arrest. Taken first to the detachment at Wetaskiwin, she gave a disjointed, rambling statement that had little to do with the shooting. She related that she had been talking to Mrs. Stoley through the partition when she heard a shot from behind her. The next thing she remembered was lying on the Stoley's kitchen floor. She went outside and found David ready to drive home and she got a ride with him to her daughter's. Later, someone told her that Rosella had been shot.

Jennie's aim had been blind but the havoc wreaked was devastating. Rosella Stoley was in a state of paralysis. Dr. Roberts hesitated to operate until the following day, and then only dared remove the slugs from her arm and hip. Before attempting to extract the bullet from her brain, he consulted with two other physicians, who agreed that it would be too risky until she had regained some strength. They waited. Instead of rallying, however, Rosella weakened and died two days later, on March 15.

It was no surprise that a coroner's jury found that she had been shot to death by Jennie Hawkes.

· · ·

Mr. Justice William Ives approached the trial with some misgivings. Given the ingredient of provocation and because there was a strong American element in the district, he realized that a verdict of justifiable homicide was entirely possible. His fears were groundless, however, and the whole trial was played in *sotto voce*. W.H. O'Dell presented only five witnesses for the Crown in addition to the medical testimony, and defence lawyer W.J. Loggie confined his efforts to placing Jennie Hawkes on the stand. She told of her fears that her husband and Mrs. Stoley were plotting to dispose of her and Henry Stoley so that they could marry. Washington Hawkes was conspicuous by his absence. The evidence and the addresses to the jury occupied only two days, after which His Lordship summed up strongly, but kindly, against her, reminding the jury that regardless of the aggravation, she had intended to kill the victim.

After taking only an hour and twenty minutes to consider the evidence, the jurors returned with a verdict of guilty and—as was expected—a strong recommendation to mercy. His Lordship then sentenced her to be hanged at Fort Macleod on December 29.

The defence did not enter an appeal, preferring to leave the matter of clemency for officialdom in Ottawa. Considering the case, the Cabinet felt that the slaying smacked more of manslaughter than murder and on December 13 the Governor-General altered the death sentence to ten years in the penitentiary.

At that time, all female federal prisoners were taken first to the closest penitentiary to be fingerprinted, photographed, and interviewed just as a male prisoner would be. From there they were conveyed to Kingston Penitentiary in Ontario. In Jennie's case, the nearest federal prison was the old penitentiary on Government Road in Edmonton.

Not considering it necessary to mount a full detail for her, Inspector J.S. Piper of the RNWMP undertook to personally escort Mrs. Hawkes from Fort Macleod to the Edmonton prison. In his memoirs, written in 1928, he outlined an interesting sidelight to the story.

> It was a very peculiar circumstance, but I can vouch for the truth of it. While we were passing through the Wetaskiwin district (by train) Mrs. Hawkes pointed to some farm buildings and stated that these had been her former home. At almost the identical moment, the woman's husband was working with a gasoline engine in the neighbourhood when it exploded, killing him instantly.

· · ·

After four and a half years of her ten-year sentence had been served, the prison doctor at Kingston reported that Jennie was in very poor health and that further confinement would likely be fatal. Combining this with another report that stated: "Mrs. Hawkes has the promise of a home and every comfort with her daughter," the

Governor-General again exercised the Royal Prerogative of Mercy and granted her a pardon on July 31, 1920. She returned to the home of her daughter, Mrs. William Rosser, at Lewisville, where she died shortly afterwards.

· · ·

Elizabeth Coward
Cabin Fever

*T*HOUGH THEY WERE BOTH only run-of-the-mill, average citizens with no distinguishing marks, when Elizabeth Coward killed her husband, James, in a remote section of British Columbia, the echoes of her deed nearly brought down a government.

Elizabeth Coward, née Shaffer, was born of Italian parents in New York City in 1881. Her family moved to a mining community in Colorado, and in 1894, at the age of thirteen, she married a man named Dell. He was killed accidentally six months later and shortly after his death, a daughter, Rose Dell, was born.

A year later, Elizabeth re-married, this time to a man named Calibris. They operated boarding-houses in various parts of the United States over the next sixteen years, and brought four children into the world. In 1911, they separated, with Mr. Calibris taking two of the children and Elizabeth keeping the boarding-house and the two youngest. Later, they obtained a divorce. Rose Dell remained with her mother and the two young Calibris children.

The next chapter of Elizabeth Coward's colourful life began with James Coward's arrival at her boarding-house. Separated from his own wife and two children, he did not have any assets and had been a drifter all his life. Nevertheless, Elizabeth found herself attracted to him. At this time, she was thirty-four, a short, dark-featured woman of vivacious bearing. As Judge Murphy later observed at her trial: "She is intelligent, but an awful liar." Considering her upbringing, this characterization was probably accurate.

In the spring of 1915, James Coward persuaded Elizabeth to sell her boarding-house and move to a homestead in central British Columbia, "the land of opportunity." They left their assorted children with welfare agencies and, without benefit of marriage, arrived at Fort St. James in mid-June. Elizabeth wanted her oldest daughter, Rose Dell, to accompany her but Rose was working as a waitress in San Francisco and did not want to leave her job.

At Fort St. James, after outfitting themselves with a grubstake and equipment for their homestead, the Cowards settled on a holding about sixteen kilometres (ten miles) from town. A friendly neighbour, John Roberts, gave them the use of a small cabin while they were clearing land and erecting a shelter.

Life in the backwoods was not the existence to which Elizabeth was accustomed, and she quickly became lonely and depressed. In addition, with her life-savings exhausted by travel expenses and the purchase of equipment, she suddenly realized she was entirely at the mercy of her husband's whims. Should he decide to desert her as he had abandoned his own wife and children, she would be destitute. She finally persuaded her daughter, Rose Dell, to join her for company, and the nineteen-year-old arrived at Fort St. James on July 9. With her arrival, James moved out of the cabin and took up sleeping quarters in a wagon sheltered under a tent.

As sometimes happens when city folk are transplanted to the wilderness, Elizabeth developed a thousand fears. One of these concerned Jimmie Ahoul, a man who for a whole dollar had transported Rose Dell's trunk from Fort St. James to the homestead. After that, he stopped by the house from time to time on business, but each appearance alarmed Elizabeth. She was sure he had evil designs upon her and consequently borrowed a .32 revolver from their neighbour John Roberts.

On the afternoon of Monday, September 6, 1915, James Coward walked into Fort St. James to transact some business. During his absence, Elizabeth and Rose visited with two women—Florence Whitehouse and Lusetta McInnes—who occupied a cabin some 180 metres (200 yards) from their home. Elizabeth confided that she was afraid because "that Indian" had visited again; she was also worried that her husband would not return from town. She suspected he was planning to desert her, just as he had left his current wife.

However, Jim Coward came home about six o'clock that evening, had supper with them, and went to his wagon-tent to sleep.

About nine-thirty, Florence Whitehouse and Lusetta McInnes

heard a single shot from the direction of the Coward cabin. Some fifteen minutes later, Elizabeth and Rose arrived, breathless and apparently frightened. Rose, who did all the talking, said that she had just gotten into bed and her mother was kneeling in prayer beside her when they heard a shot outside. Startled, they had dressed and gone out, expecting to find Elizabeth's husband prowling around the yard investigating the source of the gunshot. When they did not, their fears increased. Approaching the wagon, they had found everything quiet there but were afraid to lift the tent flap and peer inside.

Whitehouse and McInnes accompanied them back to the cabin and searched the yard with the aid of lanterns. They went to the tent-covered wagon and called to Coward but there was no answer. Since they were afraid that a killer might be lurking in the woods, they fired a shotgun into the air, hoping to attract the attention of John Roberts, who lived about a mile away. That failing, they went to the Whitehouse cabin and stayed inside until dawn.

In the morning, the four women went to the wagon and when Coward still did not respond to shouts, they lifted the flap that covered the box. Coward was dead. He had apparently committed suicide by shooting himself in the nose. Badly shaken, they walked to the Roberts cabin and told him the news.

Roberts checked for himself to make sure that Coward was dead. When Rose and Elizabeth declared that they were frightened to remain alone on the homestead, he hitched up a wagon and drove them to town, where they found shelter with friends.

Constable Rupert Raynor of the British Columbia Provincial Police was the first on the scene, and he was joined by Chief of Police William Dunwoody. What first appeared to be a simple suicide took on a more ugly slant when, on removing the body from the wagon box, they failed to find a gun. If Coward had killed himself inside the wagon while lying down, the gun should be beside him.

Over the next five days, the two men made several trips to the Coward homestead to gather information and attempt to locate the weapon. They were unsuccessful.

On Friday, September 10, a coroner's jury returned an open verdict in the death of the Californian, and his wallet was turned over to Mrs. Coward. Finally, furnished with the means of leaving the district, she announced that she and her daughter Rose would be heading south. They planned to visit the cabin on Monday and pick up their belongings. It would be their first trip back to the site of "the suicide."

Though they had been unsuccessful in locating the murder weapon, Constable Raynor and Chief Dunwoody decided to make one last inspection of the farmyard and went to the homestead on Sunday, September 12. While searching the area around the house, Constable Raynor noticed a wooden washtub at one corner of the cabin. Upending it, he saw that the dirt beneath had been disturbed. He scraped the topsoil away and found a loaded .32 revolver. One shell had been fired.

The next day, the policemen arrived at the Coward place before the two women and concealed themselves. At first, the women's conduct appeared normal, but then Elizabeth went furtively to the washtub at the corner of the house and peered under it. She immediately set it down and returned to the cabin. A few minutes later, she emerged again and after looking around to assure herself that she was unobserved, she went to the tub and began to scrape away the dirt beneath it. At that point, Raynor and Dunwoody made their presence known and placed both women under arrest.

A preliminary hearing held before Magistrate J.P. Hooson at Fort St. John committed the pair for trial. There being no suitable prison quarters in the district, they had to be escorted all the way south to Kamloops to await their appearance.

At that time, all major trials in the central district of the province were held at Clinton, and since the accused were in prison at Kamloops and the witnesses were all in the vicinity of Fort St. John, the authorities were faced with a problem. In the end, they decided it was less expensive to bring the prisoners up to Clinton than to transport all the witnesses down to Kamloops. Elizabeth and Rose went on trial at the Fall Assizes before Mr. Justice J.C. Murphy on October 6. Seventeen Crown witnesses wove a powerful net of circumstantial evidence against the pair. William A. Scott of Kamloops, who had been appointed by the court to defend the prisoners, placed both women on the stand to testify on their own behalf. Elizabeth Coward still maintained that the shooting must have been done by Jimmie Ahoul, while her daughter testified that her mother could not have done it since they were together when they heard the shot.

Though the evidence was far from conclusive, Elizabeth's strange behaviour at the washtub told heavily against her and the jury took only an hour and a half to convict her but appended no recommendation to mercy. Rose Dell was acquitted. Sentencing Elizabeth to be hanged on December 23 at Kamloops, His Lordship remarked that he felt the verdict was a just one and that she should expect no mercy for the cold-blooded killing.

A lengthy petition was sent to Ottawa begging clemency on the grounds that she "was under the stress of having moved from the congestion of a large city slum to the wilds of British Columbia and that this unhinged her mind." Much more formidable was the British Columbia cabinet's powerful opposition to her execution. It advised the Minister of Justice that no woman in the history of the province had ever been hanged and there was enormous objection to having this pattern broken. It was said, in fact, that several members were prepared to resign if the sentence were carried out.

In an effort to avoid a confrontation with the British Columbia government, Mr. Charles Doherty, Minister of Justice, sent a telegram to Dr. J.G. McKay, New Westminster psychiatrist, asking him to examine the woman.

Dr. McKay visited Elizabeth at Kamloops on the weekend of December 11 and reported that he "found no reason for supposing that she was mentally abnormal in any way that would excuse the crime for which she was sentenced."

Unable to avert the execution on the grounds of insanity, but not wishing to affront the western government, Ottawa passed an Order in Council on December 20, stating diplomatically:

> Considering the views of the Attorney General of British Columbia as to the expediency in the interests of justice in carrying out the extreme penalty of the law in the case of the accused, who is a woman, and in the face of public feelings as expressed in numerous petitions, it was thought that the infliction of the death penalty would be unduly harsh.

The Governor-General commuted her sentence to life imprisonment.

After serving just over six years of her sentence, Elizabeth Coward was deported to the United States on March 29, 1922, into the custody of a married daughter in San Francisco.

. . .

Grapena Shulman

The Calder Tyrant

*I*F EVER A MAN ASKED TO BE MURDERED, it was
Alex Shulman of Calder, Saskatchewan, and if ever
a woman talked herself into a death sentence, it was his wife,
Grapena. Their terrible "madness for two" lasted for nearly ten
years before the crash of a rifle bullet destroyed both their lives.

Alex Shulman was an aggressive psychopath with a lust for
women and a contempt for every human being but himself. The only
unusual thing about his death was that someone had not scuttled his
ship years before. An Austrian by birth, he had migrated to Canada
around 1908 and established a homestead near Calder, some fifty-
five kilometres (thirty-four miles) east of Yorkton, Saskatchewan. In
1910 he married an Austrian girl named Grapena, sometimes called
Frafrena, and over the next ten years she bore him five children, one
of whom died at an early age.

Grapena Shulman was simply a chattel for her husband and he
treated her as he would one of the cows on his farm. He worked her
hard in the fields and beat her at home. To show his supreme
contempt for his passive little woman, he would bring other women
into the house and have intercourse with them in front of her. She
bore this patiently, seeing no way out until a neighbour persuaded
her to go to the police. With some encouragement, she left her
husband and obtained a court injunction against him. Using his
psychopathic charms, however, he persuaded her that all would be
well if she returned to him, and as is so often the case where
husbands beat wives, she believed his protestations of repentance
and went back to the farm.

The only hired men who could survive on the Shulman farm
were passive types with latent masochistic traits similar to Grapena's.
Such a man was Frank Rutka, who came with his wife to live with
them in the fall of 1918. Despite the fact that Alex Shulman quickly
seduced the winsome Mrs. Rutka and bragged about it to his wife,
Frank Rutka bided his time and went meekly about his chores.

Nevertheless, a rumour spread through the district that he had bought a rifle and was teaching Grapena Shulman how to use it. It was a closely knit community, where people guarded their secrets from outsiders and preferred to have as little contact with the police as possible. Neighbours merely noted events and watched from the sidelines.

Regardless of his faults, Alex Shulman was a hard worker and a shrewd businessman. At the time of his death, he had built up a herd of 150 head of cattle and 60 horses, and his fanatical penchant for neatness kept his farmyard and buildings immaculate. His propensity for violence had not abated, however, and on the afternoon of Thursday, September 19, he beat his wife again. As she ran screaming from the farmhouse, he took a shot at her with a rifle, but missed. She hid in the woods surrounding the farm until late that night.

According to Mrs. Shulman's first account, she waited until her husband was asleep and returned to the farmhouse. Getting into the bedroom through an open window, she removed her rifle from a cache under the floor where she had kept it for a month. She declared that as she was crawling back out the window, the rifle discharged and the bullet struck her husband. Seeing that he was dead, she hurried to the home of some neighbours and told them that her husband was trying to kill her. She stayed with them for the rest of the night.

The body of Alex Shulman was found early next morning by his six-year-old son. Relatives were called and someone sent for the police and a doctor. If the children had heard the early morning shot, they said nothing; they had long ago learned to mind their own business.

Corporal Wrogan of the Saskatchewan Provincial Police arrived at the farm ten kilometres (six miles) south of Calder that morning to begin the investigation. He found the deceased lying on the bed with a Winchester rifle beside him. On the floor nearby was an expended shell. The bullet, which had entered his head behind the left ear, exiting through the right eye, was found in the pillow. Death had been instantaneous. The lack of powder burns ruled out suicide, and it was later estimated that the bullet had been fired from the bedroom doorway, about two metres (six feet) away. Medical evidence placed the time of death at around five-thirty that morning.

Though he spoke the language of the district, Corporal Wrogan had difficulty unearthing the facts of the case. Indeed, one of the first people he interviewed shocked him with one of his responses. Asked if there had been trouble at the Shulman farm, the neighbour replied that Shulman had threatened to kill Grapena the same way Christian Dressler had killed his wife, Winnie.

This being the first he had heard of such an incident, Corporal Wrogan was puzzled. He checked it out. He discovered that a couple of weeks earlier, on September 3, a man named Christian Dressler had taken his wife into the garden and executed her with a shotgun in front of their children. He had then turned the weapon on himself. The doctor who attended easily determined that it was murder and suicide and unsuccessfully tried to locate a coroner. When neighbours asked what they should do with the two bodies, he advised burial and filed death certificates listing the above causes of death. No investigation followed and the children were taken by relatives. It was an indication of how isolated the area around Yorkton was in 1918.

As Corporal Wrogan continued his inquiry into the Shulman case, he learned that public opinion had already passed judgement. The common belief was that Mrs. Shulman and Frank Rutka had "executed" Alex for his behaviour towards her and his callous seduction of Mrs. Rutka. While there was a good deal of sympathy for the woman, Rutka was looked upon as the instigator of the crime. In the eyes of the community, it was justifiable homicide. Wrogan had a job to do, however, and reluctantly arrested both Rutka and Shulman and held them for murder. A coroner's jury agreed with him and found both people culpable.

Following the preliminary hearing on October 3, when both suspects were committed for trial, Grapena Shulman began a series of "confessions" that eventually brought her to the death cell. Had she stuck to her original story, she might well have gone free. Speaking to her mother in the presence of Constable Harrick, who knew their language, she said she had kept a gun hidden in the house for a month. On the Thursday, after her husband had beaten her and taken a shot at her, she went to Rutka and asked him what she should do. She contended that Rutka had advised her to shoot him but to wait till he, Rutka, was asleep. If she failed to kill him, she was to awaken Rutka and he would finish the job. She had then gone and shot her husband from the bedroom door. The rest of her story was the same.

In the days that followed, while she waited trial, Mrs. Shulman vacillated in her versions, sometimes claiming that her husband's death had been accidental and at others readily admitting her guilt and declaring that she had planned to kill him. By the time she came to trial at Yorkton in mid-January 1919, she had settled upon a version that contained elements of both.

Mr. Justice MacDonald was on the bench when Grapena was brought to trial on January 16, 1919. W.J. Graham conducted the prosecution, while Messrs. McPhee and O'Regan acted for the defence. Frank Rutka's trial was scheduled to follow hers.

Grapena was her own worst enemy when she took the stand to defend her cause. She hesitantly explained that she and Rutka had planned for some time to kill her husband, and that he had purchased the rifle for her and taught her how to use it. The plot had climaxed on the afternoon of September 19, when her husband beat her and tried to kill her. She had gone to Frank Rutka and they had decided to act that night. She had returned to her own bedroom separate from her husband's. Rutka came later and sent her into Alex's bedroom to make sure he was asleep, but before she reached it, she head a shot. She entered to find Rutka leaning through the window with a rifle in his hands. He had fired into the air; she could smell the powder. He then handed her the weapon, ordering her to shoot her husband. She pointed the Winchester blindly and pulled the trigger. Still following his instructions, she laid the rifle beside her husband's body, while Frank Rutka tossed in the shell casing from his bullet.

The story was to be that she had gone into the bedroom and that her husband had shot at her. The shell case would bear this out. Failing to kill her, he had turned the weapon on himself and committed suicide. She was not sure, she said, but she thought her husband was already dead when she shot at him.

The other confessions she had made since the murder were admitted into evidence as well and the jurors were left to sort out what truth they could. These, plus ample testimony from witnesses who described the ten years of hell she had endured at the hands of her psychopathic husband, formed the bulk of the evidence the jurors took to their deliberations.

When they returned, it was apparent that they had a most unpleasant duty to perform, as none looked in her direction. Visibly affected, the foreman read the guilty verdict in a voice choked with emotion, then immediately slumped into his seat and buried his face in his hands.

His own voice tense with the drama of the situation, His Lordship sentenced her to be hanged at Regina on April 22, 1919. The first woman to be so sentenced in Saskatchewan, Grapena Shulman calmly accepted her fate when it was translated for her.

Frank Rutka's trial should have begun the following day, January 18, but his counsel, J.A. Patrick, moved that the hearing be delayed to the next sitting of the court, contending that the emotional nature of Mrs. Shulman's trial would preclude his client from having a fair and unprejudiced hearing. His Lordship agreed, remarking that a jury could not fail to have been influenced against the prisoner Rutka.

No one who had listened to the tale of brutality and terror that had unfolded in the Yorkton courtroom believed that Ottawa would allow the death sentence to be carried out. Ten days before her date with the executioner, word was received at Regina that her sentence had been commuted to twelve years of imprisonment.

The day before this decision was reached, Frank Rutka went on trial at Yorkton, charged with being an accomplice in the death of Alex Shulman. Though public opinion was still strongly against him, there was no evidence beyond the confused and sometimes contradictory statements of Grapena Shulman. The jury found him not guilty and he was released from custody.

Mrs. Shulman served five years of her twelve-year sentence before being granted a parole on April 14, 1924.

· · ·

Sarah Jackson
The Last Christmas Present

*T*HE LITTLE TOWN OF SWAN RIVER, Alberta, on the Edmonton-Dunvegan Railway, settled down to enjoy another Christmas Day after an evening of visiting and cordiality. There was a lot of goodwill towards fellow creatures, except in one small cabin on the edge of town. For Sarah Jackson, December

25, 1919, was a day of deadly resolve. When darkness crept over the village, she took a shotgun, stood over her husband's bed, and blasted him into the next world.

Born Sarah Stevenson at Orangeville, Ontario, in 1885, friends called her Sadie. She apparently had a child out of wedlock some time around 1908, for when she came west that year she brought with her a child, Dora. Like many unattached young women in the West, she existed by living common-law with several men. She eventually married a Fred Baldwin in 1913, but their union was short-lived. He enlisted in the army, went overseas, and was killed. In 1915, at Wainwright, she married Hugh Jackson, a specialized railway worker living at Swan River whose skills took him to various sections of track. She moved there with him, taking her four children by previous unions. Their family was soon swollen by the addition of a fifth child, a girl.

The alliance appeared to benefit both for the first two years. Jackson was a devoted husband and a kind father to the children, even though his work frequently kept him away from home for extended periods of time. They were not affluent, but they were never in real want either. Their living quarters consisted of a rough shanty in winter and a tent in warm weather, and in this respect they were no different from the vast majority of their neighbours who lived in isolation along the railway siding.

There were no secrets in Swan River and it was not long before most people realized that Sarah Jackson liked the company of men. Rumour had it that she entertained male visitors while her husband was away, and Jackson could not help but hear about this. He was a proud man and these rumours hurt him, but he did not physically abuse her. Instead, when he had too much to drink, he would threaten to kill her and the five children.

· · ·

Hugh Jackson had been working at a town some distance north of Swan River in the fall of 1919 and was not expected home for Christmas. When he returned unexpectedly he found a young Native man, Zerma Courtrielle, occupying his side of the bed. Flying into a rage, he ordered his wife's new lover out. This awakened all the old animosities and during the next few days the Jackson cabin was filled with drinking, quarrelling, and his oft-repeated threats to wipe out his unfaithful wife and all the kids. This unrest continued all through December 24 and into Christmas Day.

Sarah Jackson took his threats seriously, and although it was not clear when she first decided to kill him before he killed her, on Christmas Day she confided in her fifteen-year-old daughter, Dora, that she would kill him that night in his sleep. The only weapon she could think of was a hammer. She might need help . . .

The weapon problem solved itself. Later that evening, Hugh Jackson heard noises at his corrals, and thinking that someone was trying to steal his stock, he took his shotgun and went outside. Discovering it was only some stray cows feeding on his haystack, he fired a couple of rounds to scare them off and returned to the cabin. Not satisfied with that, he reloaded the weapon in his wife's presence and waved it at her while repeating his drunken threats to kill them all. Then he set the gun down, toppled into bed, and fell asleep.

Sarah Jackson waited until she was certain that everyone was asleep before she put her plan into action. Afraid that the hammer might not be effective, she picked up the shotgun. Hugh was lying on his side facing the wall. She put the muzzle close to the back of his head and fired. The shot killed him instantly.

The noise awakened the children, but only Dora realized what had happened. Together with her mother she soothed the four young ones back to sleep, leaving them unaware that the man they called Daddy was dead.

Sarah and Dora wrapped Hugh Jackson in a horse-blanket and dragged him through the snow to the stable. Putting his body in a corner and covering it with hay, they returned to the cabin to clean up the mess on the bed. When she explained to the children the next morning that "Daddy has gone away again," the youngsters stoically accepted his departure as they had done many times before.

Sarah's lover, Zerma Courtrielle, was living with a neighbour, Joe Sounds, and the next afternoon Sarah went to visit him. She told him what she had done and that the body was in the stable, but she needed his help to dispose of it. At first he refused, realizing that because of his relationship with her he might be suspected, but she applied considerable pressure and he finally agreed. She had worked it all out; she and her daughter would go to a district dance that night as if nothing was wrong; he would take the corpse from the stable and put it in the lake.

The women conducted themselves so normally at the dance that no suspicion arose when they gave out the story that Hugh Jackson had gone back to his job in northern Alberta. When they got home and checked the barn, however, they found the body still under the hay. Zerma had chickened out.

Sarah visited her twenty-year-old boyfriend at the Joe Sounds farm the next day, the 27th, and applied more pressure. He said he was sorry, he could not do the job alone, but he would help her. Keeping his word, he arrived at their farm around midnight. The three of them wrapped cords around the horse-blanket to hold it shut and weighted the bundle with railway irons. Loading it onto his sleigh, they drove to a nearby lake, and after chopping a hole through the ice, slid the body into the dark, frigid water.

The routine at the Jackson household quickly returned to normal, with Sarah continuing to give out the story that Hugh had left on Boxing Day to his job on the railway in the north. No one was surprised when Zerma Courtrielle moved back in with her to look after the stock and attend to other marital duties.

Nevertheless, there were whispers. They started when someone remarked that he had been at the railway siding when the north freight pulled through on Boxing Day and he had not seen Hugh Jackson catching it. Nobody could remember Hugh having purchased a ticket either. There were only two trains a week, each with a single passenger coach attached. Comings and goings by rail, whether by ticket or otherwise, were rare and usually everyone knew who was going, why, and where.

.   .   .

The break in the case did not come until May 31, 1920. An early thaw had broken up much of the lake ice and Joe Sounds went out in his boat to do some fishing. Chunks of ice had already begun to move downstream through a small creek that led from the main body of water, and as he worked his way towards the middle of the lake, he caught sight of a dark object floating on the surface. Unable to approach it because of the ice, he went home and enlisted the help of Zerma Courtrielle, and with the aid of an axe broke a path through the surface ice until they reached the thing. It proved to be the frozen body of a man wrapped in a horse-blanket. Recognizing the shroud, Zerma realized that Hugh Jackson had surfaced and said nothing, but helped Joe tow the bundle close to shore.

Joe Sounds was an intelligent man despite his lack of formal education, and he had his suspicions. The population of Swan River was not very large and there was only one man unaccounted for in the village—Hugh Jackson. Well aware that his young companion, Courtrielle, was sleeping with Jackson's wife, and having no desire to get directly mixed up in something this close to home, he decided to tell a neighbour, Ron Bishop, that there was a body on the lakeshore. He knew the news would eventually come to the ears of the authorities.

The closest thing to authority at the siding was Mr. Pierce, the stationmaster. When he learned that a body had been pulled to shore and tethered, he sent a telegram to the Alberta Provincial Police at Edmonton.

Inspector W.F.W. Hancock and Constable Bissell came up by car on Wednesday, June 2, set up headquarters in the Swan River restaurant, and began gathering information. Even before they finished their first cup of coffee they had picked up the ugly rumour that the body might be that of Hugh Jackson, who might have met with foul play. Joe Sounds reluctantly took them to the spot where he had anchored the cadaver, but the corpse was gone.

While Inspector Hancock was organizing a party to drag the lake bottom near where Joe Sounds had moored the carcass, Sounds sent a message to the Jackson place that he wanted to talk to young Zerma. He quickly got the full story of the murder and the attempted disposal of the body through the ice. After some inner debate, he decided to inform the police. Inspector Hancock asked to be taken to the Jackson cabin and requested that Joe come along as interpreter. Leaving the police car in town, they went out in Joe's wagon and found Sarah living in the tent to which she habitually moved for the summer months.

Faced with Zerma's confession of his part in originally disposing of the body, Sarah admitted that when Zerma told her the body had been found, she had persuaded him to help her take it from the shore and move it beneath a bridge over the river that flowed from the lake. They had hoped that the spring flood would carry it away. Sounds took Inspector Hancock to the bridge and they found the body snagged on a sunken tree a short distance downstream.

When questioned, Sarah Jackson made a partial confession, but claimed that Hugh had tried to kill her and that in self-defence she had used the shotgun. Getting the stories of both Dora and Zerma, Inspector Hancock felt that they would make better witnesses than accomplices and he decided not to prosecute them. After assuring himself that Dora and Zerma would take care of the children, he arrested Sarah and escorted her to the women's section of the Fort Saskatchewan Jail.

. . .

Veteran prosecutor Edward Bowen Cogswell presented the case at the Fall Assizes to Mr. Justice Walsh and jury. There was little doubt as to the outcome. Dora, who was the Crown's chief witness, wove an inescapable net of guilt around her mother. On behalf of the defence, Mr. H.H. Robertson pleaded the dual excuses of insanity and self-defence, but the jury chose to believe that it had been a cold-blooded murder inspired by sex and possibly fear. They found her guilty on September 29, 1920, and she was ordered to be hanged on December 21.

The Minister of Justice was Charles Doherty, a Montreal lawyer and judge who had gone into federal politics and gained a formidable reputation on both the national and international scene. On assuming the post in 1911, he brought with him an aversion to executing women—no matter how heinous their crimes—and respited the ten women whose cases came across his desk before that of Sarah Jackson demanded his attention. It was no surprise then that on December 4, 1920, he announced that the sentence against Sarah Jackson had been altered to life imprisonment.

After serving fourteen years of her term, she was paroled on May 2, 1934, and returned to the northland. Her freedom, however, was short-lived and she had to be taken to the hospital in Edmonton, where she died on December 26, 1935, almost sixteen years to the day after she murdered her husband.

. . .

Florence Lassandro

He's Dead and I'm Alive

S HE WAS BORN IN 1900, the daughter of an Italian
railway worker in the coal mining town of Fernie,
British Columbia. Her name was Florence Constansa, and Fernie
was a cluster of shacks and false-fronted stores along the tracks of
the newly built CPR through the Crowsnest Pass. A lovely, spirited
girl with a yen for adventure and a nose for excitement, she grew to
womanhood in an era when the dreaded words Black Hand Society
(precursor of the Italian Mafia) were only whispered, and when most
men and a considerable number of women carried guns. Violence
in one form or another was often only a step away.

Full prohibition came to Alberta on April 1, 1918, and Florence
soon found the excitement of rumrunning a magnet that drew her
deeper and deeper into the demon rum controversy. Her interest
came partly from design and partly through marriage.

Rumrunners ran fast cars through the Pass, carrying liquor to
the thirsty on both sides of the American border. The king was
Emilio Picariello, a forty-seven-year-old Sicilian who owned the
Alberta Hotel in Blairmore. Affectionately known as Emperor Pic,
he had connections that led north to Edmonton, west to Fernie, east
to Medicine Hat, and even dipped south into Montana and Idaho.
Among his employees was a young mechanic, Charles Lassandro,
who kept the vehicles in A-one running condition. Florence's marriage to him gained her entry into the world of illegal liquor. She
became a favourite of Emperor Pic, and one of her delights was to
ride as a passenger in the liquor cars. She believed that the police
would not fire on them if there was a woman in the auto, although
she herself habitually carried a .38 revolver in her purse.

On the afternoon of September 21, 1922, Sergeant Scott of the
Alberta Provincial Police raided the Alberta Hotel at Blairmore.
Steve Picariello, Emilio's son, was about to deposit a carload of
liquor, but seeing the police, managed to escape and head west. As
he passed through Coleman, Steve saw Constable Stephen Lawson

step into the roadway, but he ignored the signal to stop and sped past.

Constable Lawson fired several shots at the vehicle, one of which wounded Steve in the hand. When young Picariello did not stop, Lawson and a fellow officer took off after him in a police car but had to abandon the chase when it suffered a flat tire.

There were unwritten rules to the constant game of search and pursuit surrounding illicit liquor, and one was that no violence would be used on either side. Constable Lawson broke that gentleman's agreement, and from that breach stemmed the deadly drama that claimed three lives.

The business relationship between Emperor Pic and the police worked well. When the police needed liquor for a party, they talked to Emilio. When he needed a favour, it was often forthcoming. When one of his cargos was confiscated, he took his loss with grace and without grumbling. Constable Lawson's actions angered him. That evening, not having heard from his son and fearing that he might be lying wounded somewhere, he drove to Coleman to confront the officer. Florence Lassandro insisted on accompanying him.

The Coleman detachment of the APP was located in a small cottage on a side-street of Coleman and was occupied by Stephen Lawson, his wife, and five children. Picariello and Lassandro arrived there just before seven o'clock. When they stopped in front of the cottage, Lawson came out to their car.

Constable Lawson was an Englishman, born at Brixton on June 8, 1880. Coming to Canada in 1904, he had ranched near Macleod for three years before joining the town police. When World War I began, he left his job as chief and served with distinction overseas. He went on to become chief of police at Fernie and was there when the bitter prohibition war began. On March 12, 1922, six months before his death, he joined the Alberta Provincial Police and was stationed at Coleman. A stickler for rules, he did not subscribe to the no-violence rule, believing that his job was to stop the liquor trade—period!

Constable Lawson advanced to the Picariello car and stood with one foot on the running-board while he talked with Emperor Pic. When the liquor king berated him for shooting at his son, Lawson merely replied that it was his job. Picariello then demanded that Lawson come with him to Fernie and help locate his son. Lawson refused. Pic pulled a gun and waved it at the officer to enforce his demand.

Steve Lawson was a brave man and the threatening gun did not frighten him. Grabbing Picariello around the neck, he tried to get the weapon, and in the ensuing struggle the revolver went off twice but both shots expended themselves harmlessly.

There were several people on the street, among them nine-year-old Pearl Lawson. Watching in terror as Florence Lassandro took a gun from her purse and fired, she saw her father stagger back from the car, turn, and start towards the house. A moment later, Lassandro's gun exploded again and her father fell. As she said later: "Father fell and the big car ran away."

Onlookers came running and carried Steve Lawson into the Miners' Hospital next door to the police station, but before doctors could assist him, he died of two gunshot wounds.

Officers soon arrived in Coleman and began sorting out the conflicting eyewitness stories. They were able to identify one assailant as Emperor Picariello but no one knew the woman. A search of his apartment at the Alberta Hotel failed to locate him, and since it was late in the evening a full manhunt was postponed to the following day.

With dawn, patrols of APP officers began scouring the Italian district at the north end of Blairmore. About three in the afternoon, Constables E. Clarke and C. Tuttin, RCMP, and Constable Joe Bradner, APP, saw a man climbing a hill back of town. Pursuing and overtaking him, they discovered it was Picariello. Questioned about the woman who had accompanied him, he said he guessed they would find out soon enough anyway and identified her as Florence Lassandro, twenty-two.

When Sergeant James Scott went to the Lassandro house to question her, she expressed no surprise. "He's dead and I'm alive and that is all there is to it," she told him. A .38 revolver was found in her room and ballistics linked it to the murder slugs. She admitted it was her gun.

That evening she made a voluntary statement in which she said that there had been no intention to kill Lawson. They were trying to locate Steve Picariello and suspected the police were holding him. When the men started to struggle for Picariello's gun and she saw the muzzle swing towards her, she fired in panic, fearing for her life.

The couple were held in the provincial jail at Lethbridge until they appeared for their preliminary hearing before Magistrate Gresham at Coleman on October 2. Twenty-nine Crown witnesses appeared, but no defence was offered and they were committed to stand trial.

Since both were popular figures in the Crowsnest Pass, Attorney General J.E. Brownlee moved the trial to Calgary, where it opened on Monday, November 22. Mr. Justice W.L. Walsh was on the bench, with the Attorney General himself conducting the prosecution. J. McKinley Cameron, noted Calgary criminal lawyer, appeared for the accused.

The Crown presented an airtight case with several actual eye-witnesses. One of the most powerful pieces of evidence against the woman was the statement she had given to Sergeant James Scott on the night of her arrest, in which she had admitted shooting the policeman once in the car and again while he was moving away.

The trial concluded on Saturday afternoon, December 2, with Mr. Cameron having submitted neither witnesses nor evidence for the defence. Attorney General Brownlee pointed out in his address to the jurors that there was no question that Mrs. Lassandro had shot Constable Lawson; the only issue was whether she intended to kill him. Her plea of self-defence might be plausible, he contended, except for the second shot. Lawson had been moving away—no menace to her—when that shot was fired. As for Emilio Picariello, two witnesses testified that they heard him shouting at his companion to shoot. That made him equally culpable.

Nevertheless, the jury took almost four hours to reach its decision, returning to the courtroom at eight in the evening. When they rendered their verdict of guilty, they did not recommend mercy for either. In sentencing both prisoners to be executed at Fort Saskatchewan prison on February 21, 1923, His Lordship hinted that because of past government policy, Mrs. Lassandro might expect a commutation of sentence. He held out no such hope for Emilio Picariello, however, and suggested that he prepare himself for the supreme penalty.

· · ·

J. McKinley Cameron launched a series of appeals that resulted in the cancellation of the original execution date and a new date being fixed for May 2. The Supreme Court of Canada finally rejected the last appeal, leaving only one avenue of clemency open.

The case had attracted dominion-wide attention, not only because of the notoriety of the rumrunning angle, but because a young and beautiful woman was involved. Yet, strangely, the majority of petitions received by the Department of Justice prayed that both hangings be carried out. In a desperate, last-minute bid to escape the noose, Florence Lassandro tried to throw the fault on her accomplice. She had only taken the blame for firing the fatal shots, she protested, because the police advised her that, being a woman, she would not be hanged. The trial evidence had clearly shown, however, that she had fired twice, and her "confession" was ignored.

When the final word was received in Edmonton, Sheriff John Rae found himself the object of intense pressure from the newspapers. No woman had been executed in Canada since 1899, when Cordelia Viau had died in Montreal and Hilda Blake had been hanged at Brandon. Fearing the impact of a blunder in this glare of publicity, he wanted no mistakes. First he tried to engage Arthur Bartholemew English, alias Arthur Ellis, the most experienced hangman in Canada, but that worthy had gone into semiretirement on a fruit farm in the Okanagan. In desperation, he advertised, and was astonished to receive dozens of applications. He finally settled for a man named Wakefield, who had gained some fame as a perfectionist. Cordoning off a special section of the prison yard, Rae had an enclosed gallows constructed in this area.

There was a last-minute hope that the Minister of Justice, Sir Lomer Gouin, would still commute the death sentence imposed on Florence Lassandro, but the final decision was reached the day before the scheduled execution, and her death-warrant was issued.

Emilio Picariello was fortunate that the new scaffold had been erected a few feet from his cell so he had not far to walk. He went to his death bravely at 5:00 in the morning and life was pronounced gone within ten minutes.

Florence was housed in the Women's Prison, and when her time came she was subjected to a long walk across the prison yard before reaching the men's quarters and climbing the stairs to the second floor, where entry was made to the scaffold from a window. Confident to the very end that she would be spared, she seemed suddenly to realize as she stood on the trap that the end was at hand. "Why do you hang me when I didn't do anything?" she cried, staring about her like a trapped beast. "Is there no one here who has any pity?"

Undeterred from his ugly task by her piteous cries, Hangman

Wakefield fixed the noose and hood with expert hands and sent her crashing through the trapdoor. She was pronounced dead at 5:51 AM, the fifth woman to be executed since Confederation.

Florence Lassandro was the only woman hanged in the province of Alberta, and in all fairness it must be said that her death was the result of the hysteria brought on by the violent conflict over prohibition, rather than any real necessity for her death.

. . .

Lina Voisine

I Decided to Kill My Husband

*W*HILE *MARGUERITE PITRE* had the unhappy distinction of being the last woman hanged in Canada, twenty-six-year-old Lina Voisine was the last to have the dread sentence: "You shall be hanged by the neck until you are dead" pronounced against her, for although the death penalty was not abolished until 1976, fate decreed that no other woman would face the rope for the next twenty-two years. She exhausted every avenue of appeal until all that remained was the Royal Prerogative of Mercy.

She was born September 15, 1928, in a backwoods area of New Brunswick, and grew to womanhood knowing nothing but poverty and hardship. Unable to attend school, she matured without the benefits of reading or writing. At age fifteen on July 26, 1943, she married a man eight years her senior who was also uneducated and illiterate. Her husband, Joseph Claude, while possessing some skills as a meat cutter, was unable to provide an adequate income for his family and they were always on the brink of desperation. This of itself might not have been unbearable, but to his neglect he added physical abuse, and Lina was frequently the target of his frustrated fists. To supplement their scanty income, he operated a modest bootlegging business.

This activity brought a variety of men to their home and one of these, Rosario Gauvin, took an interest in her plight. Ripening into something more serious, the liaison continued for some time, giving Lina a glimpse of a light at the end of her dismal tunnel and a chance to escape from her private hell, but that hope exploded with unexpected suddenness on the evening of November 3, 1954, when Gauvin told her that he had another girlfriend and that he was planning to marry her.

At this time, Lina and Joseph were living in a small, two-level house situated on a side-road some four kilometres (two and a half miles) from a main highway. With them were five children ranging in age from three to nine. Their nearest neighbour was Leonard Desjardins, a farmer whose house was a mere thirty metres (thirty-three yards) from theirs across the road. Three nights after she received the devastating news from her lover, Lina Voisine attended church with the Desjardins family, returning back with them about nine-thirty in the evening and walking across the road to her own house.

A few minutes later, she came back to the Desjardins home with her youngest child in her arms. She was crying, saying that her husband had shot himself. "If I had not gone to mass, this would not have happened," she announced. She told Mrs. Desjardins that shortly after she arrived home, she had heard a shot. She had gone upstairs and found her husband lying on the bed.

Though no one in the Desjardins home had heard a shot, Desjardins went at once. He found Joseph alive, lying on the bed with a rifle beside him. It was one that Desjardins had lent him a few days earlier to shoot a horse. Joseph told him that he had shot himself and said that his arm was paralysed. Desjardins phoned for the parish priest and the police, and both arrived within minutes.

Father Fidele Poitras comforted the dying man as best he could until an ambulance arrived. When asked who shot him, Joseph said: "No one." He made no further statement and died within half an hour of admittance to the hospital.

Since the gunshot wound, which entered Joseph's back near the left shoulder, could not have been self-inflicted, a murder investigation was launched by RCMP Corporals J.R. Lapointe and Maurice Pelletier. Their attention first focussed on Lina's alleged boyfriend, Rosario Gauvin, twenty-seven, who worked in a garage. When he was able to provide an adequate alibi for the time of the murder, the police then concentrated on the wife.

Interviewed the next day, Lina, who had taken refuge in the

home of Mrs. Aldea Desjardins, maintained that her husband had shot himself, but also made a curious statement: "You know that I am going to die by the rope." Seeing that she was distraught and upset, suffering from severe shock, they removed her to the hospital for rest and recuperation.

While she was there, a coroner's inquest found her responsible for the murder of her husband, and on Monday, November 8, she was formally charged by Corporal J.R. Lapointe. The following day, she allegedly made a statement in the presence of Corporal Pelletier and Constable J.A. Frenette, which she signed with her X.

Her preliminary opened on November 24 before Magistrate A.M. Chamberland, and while he decided that the confession was not admissible, there was sufficient other evidence to bind her over. He committed her for trial.

.   .   .

On April 12, 1955, Lina Voisine went to trial before Mr. Justice J.E. Michnaud, and Crown Prosecutor Albany Robichaud presented twenty-seven witnesses over the next nine days. In view of Joseph Claude's statement that no one had shot him, it was vital that the Crown be allowed to enter the defendant's two confessions; the outcome of the trial hinged on His Lordship's attitude to them, and there was an intense debate on whether they might be given to the jury.

Lina had made her first statement on the afternoon of November 6, the day after the murder, when Corporal Lapointe interrogated her in the Desjardins's kitchen. He had anticipated that her answers might lead to the incrimination of her boyfriend, but when he pointed out that her husband's wound did not suggest suicide, Lina had responded: "You wish to place a rope around my neck." Later he had asked: "Is it on coming back from the church you decided to do it?" She had replied: "Yes."

The second admission, made three days later, was more detailed:

> While coming back from mass, I decided to kill my husband. I was at an end and could not stand it longer. I arrived at the home of Leonard Desjardins, and I thought of it still. I then returned to my house. I went and found the gun in another room and the cartridges in a drawer. I took the first cartridge on which I put

my hand. I did not have any difficulty putting it in the gun. I went upstairs and my children and husband were sleeping. My husband slept at the back of the bed near the wall. I went to the bed and placed the gun 7 or 8 inches from my husband. My husband had his face turned towards the wall and I fired. There was an explosion. I threw the gun on the bed and I took my baby and I returned to the home of Madame Desjardins. My husband did not speak. My girl got up. I was sick. I am quarrelling all the time. I was maltreated, injured and I was becoming mad, I think.

When His Lordship decreed that these statements could be given to the jurors, the outcome of the trial was assured.

Mr. W. Pichette called no witnesses for the woman, but in his address to the jury held out the possibility that, despite her alleged confessions, Joseph Claude had killed himself. He also drew attention to the evidence of several prosecution witnesses, who testified that Claude had been seen to strike his wife on several occasions and that the home was not a good one for the children, who were always cold and hungry.

The jurors were sympathetic towards the pathetic young woman in the box and would gladly have returned a verdict of manslaughter had not the evidence of premeditation been so strong against her. They returned a guilty verdict on April 23, 1955, but recommended mercy, and in passing sentence, His Lordship announced that he would also be recommending her to executive clemency. She was to be hanged on June 28, 1955.

Officials granted a respite to November 9 in order that her case might be taken to the Court of Appeals. When this body upheld the findings of the lower court, an application was made to the Supreme Court of Canada, which decided that there was no legal ground on which to hear the case and refused the application. Mr. Pichette then turned his full efforts towards obtaining commutation of sentence; his pleas were rewarded on October 26, when an Order in Council changed the sentence to life imprisonment. She was taken to the Women's Penitentiary at Kingston.

After serving seven years, she was interviewed by members of the recently appointed National Parole Board and granted a parole. She was released to the city of Kingston on June 25, 1962.

· · ·

Child Victims

Modern Canadian criminal law recognizes three types of culpable homicide. These are murder, which includes first- and second-degree offences depending upon the amount of premeditation and malice aforethought; manslaughter, which usually denotes the absence of premeditation; and infanticide, which is the slaying of a newborn child by its mother. Prior to 1948, infanticide was classed as common murder, but it was always clearly recognized that the killing of a newborn child did not carry with it the same stigma as when the child had reached some degree of physical maturity. Of the thirteen cases presented in this study, five would today be classed as infanticide, while eight would fall into the category of murder of a child. Three of the latter–Minnie McGee, Hope Young, and Marie Anne Houde–have already been dealt with in previous chapters.

The question of what constituted physical maturity was one that jurists and the dispensers of executive clemency clearly did not wish to address, for fear of setting standards. And it is interesting to note that while the ages of the children concerned here ranged from a few hours to fourteen years, not one of the thirteen women convicted was executed. Some of these slayings were extremely brutal, reflecting the fact that generations up to the very recent past regarded children as chattels and subject to the whims of their parents. Child protection legislation, in fact, is a relatively new area of the law.

Marie McCabe

More Sinned Against

*I*N COLONIAL TIMES and up to 1914, the killing of a new child by its mother was not a newsworthy event, and it would take a prodigious amount of research to come up with even fragmentary statistics on the subject. A prime example was Betsy Williams. Reverend J. Douglas Borthwick's *History of Montreal Prisons* mentions her briefly, indicating that on April 16, 1840, she was found guilty of the murder of her child and condemned to be hanged. She was later respited and her sentence commuted. Though appalling to contemporary readers, the matter was apparently so incidental that there was not even any mention of it in the newspapers of the day. Our history abounds in such passing references to the subject.

The same year, the *Toronto Globe* titillated the readers of its May 5 edition by informing them that Mary Huffman and her father, Philip, had been sentenced to be hanged at Windsor, Ontario, on May 5, 1840, for "having procured the death of an infant known to be the child of Mary Huffman who was supposed to have been living in incest with her father. The evidence was conclusive and a verdict of guilty was rendered with a recommendation for the unfortunate woman." The issue was left there and attempts to follow it up are thwarted by the fact that all court records and newspaper files for the early years of Windsor's history were destroyed by fire. The ultimate fate of Mary and Philip Huffman remains a mystery.

The first instance where adequate records are still available is that of Marie McCabe, of Hamilton. Marie was a winsome young Irish lass of eighteen, brown-haired, grey-eyed, and slender. Born in Dublin in May 1865, she was one of nine children of an ironmonger. When she was six her mother died, and almost immediately thereafter her father was injured in an industrial accident that cost him his sight. Marie and the other children were put in a Catholic convent, but over the next few years sickness and plague claimed the lives of all except Marie and an older sister.

When she was fifteen, an opportunity came for her to come to Canada under the auspices of a charitable organization, and she landed at Quebec City on September 8, 1880. A position as a maid had been found for her in Hamilton, Ontario, and she went directly from the port of entry to her new home.

Her early employment history was spotty, for she was an independent lass "who would brook no guff from anyone," as one employer described her. She had no difficulty obtaining new jobs, and in the spring of 1882 found herself working as a chambermaid at the Mansion Hotel in the city. Though not a pretty girl, she was a lively, adventurous character, and caught the eye of a local businessman who frequented the establishment. She became pregnant.

When Marie's condition became obvious, the hotel fired her. She sought assistance from the city welfare officials and private charity sources without success, and her life was a hard one until one woman took her into her home and maintained her until the child was born. She gave birth to a baby boy on November 5, 1882, in the General Hospital.

On her release from confinement, she sought financial assistance from the father of her child, but he rebuffed her. She again appealed to local charities, but she now had the reputation of a dissolute woman and there was little assistance to be had. It was at this desperate juncture of her life that she came into contact with Mrs. Ann Foster, wife of James Foster, at 182 Hughson Street. A childless couple, the Fosters struck a vague agreement with her whereby the Fosters would support her and her child until he reached the age of one, at which time the Fosters would adopt him. Marie would be paid one dollar a month and her keep for duties as a maid.

The relationship between Marie and Ann Foster was tempestuous, and on several occasions Mrs. Foster put her and the child out of the house. With nowhere else to go and with financial assistance denied, Marie always managed to return to the Foster home to endure another bout of uncertainty and emotional abuse. She was an outcast among girls her own age, who apparently rebuked her for her evil ways.

Her quiet desperation came to a climax on the night of March 7, 1883. She had just been "kicked out again" by Mrs. Foster and had made another fruitless round of the welfare agencies in search of a way out of her predicament. Towards nine in the evening, having no other resource, she returned to the house on Hughson Street. As she walked into the back yard, she caught sight of an old, unused cistern. On sudden impulse, she uncovered it and threw her four-month-old child into it. Then she covered it. She explained the child's absence by saying that she had boarded him out. Mrs. Foster, whose enthusiasm for adoption had waxed hot and cold over the months, accepted her story and took her back as a house servant.

Now unencumbered by a child, Marie had no difficulty finding more suitable employment, and after a fortnight at the Foster home she left and took a position as chambermaid at the Victoria Hotel.

The infant's body was not discovered until August 1. Attracted to the cistern by a bad odour, Mrs. Foster and her new maid uncovered the corpse. Constable John Knox happened to be passing at that moment and he was alerted. When he removed the child from the vat, Mrs. Foster was able to identify him from the clothing she had purchased for him. Constable Knox took the remains to the local hospital.

Taken into custody at the Victoria Hotel, Marie readily confessed that the child was hers and that she had thrown him into the cistern. She stated that as she returned to the Foster home that evening, she knew that her troubles with Mrs. Foster would only start again as long as she had the child. There seemed no other solution. She had gotten rid of her baby.

The coroner's inquest held that evening under Dr. White returned a verdict naming the mother. The boy's body had been in the water so long that it was impossible to determine the true cause of death, but it was believed to have been from drowning.

From the beginning, public sentiment was on the side of the young Irish girl. The editor of the *Hamilton Spectator*, while not condoning the crime, did much to arouse support by printing her woeful story and keeping the issue alive before his readers. He boldly printed details of Marie's attempts to get assistance and of the treatment she received at the Foster home. When there was no rebuttal from either the Fosters or the charities in the city, readers were left to draw their own conclusions as to the truth of her tale.

In his editorial on August 3, the editor turned his scorn on the father: "If the law cannot reach him, he should be made to feel that the people of this city have no sickly sentiment to waste upon such as he."

Marie McCabe made no attempt to escape punishment for what she termed "a bad thing," and when she was brought before a magistrate on August 7 for preliminary hearing, she readily admitted her guilt. The only witnesses called were Dr. White, coroner, and Chief of Police Stewart. She was committed to stand trial at the Fall Assizes.

On October 13, the Grand Jury returned a true bill against her and she was arraigned before Mr. Justice Morrison five days later. Without counsel, Marie again pleaded guilty and her plea was accepted. No jury was called.

Before passing sentence, His Lordship asked the young woman to repeat her story in full, and during her narration he made copious notes on vital points. That concluded, he asked that she be brought out of the prisoner's box to stand close to his bench while he ordered her execution. He spoke in such soft tones that only she could hear him. After promising to forward his recommendation, with reasons, to the Department of Justice, he sentenced her to be hanged on December 18, 1883. She was then led away, sobbing.

Though Marie had lacked support and understanding when she went her rounds begging for assistance for herself and her child, that help now poured in from all sides. Her case was taken before a special session of the next Grand Jury, and in an unprecedented move, that panel of citizens sent an extra petition to the Secretary of State. Local women began to visit her in prison, taking small gifts of food and comforting her with their presence. The newspaper continued to campaign for commutation of sentence and maintained its barrage of contempt for the father of the child "whose name is well known to this source." However, the putative father never came to the girl's assistance.

There was little doubt that a commutation would be forthcoming, and on November 10 the Minister of Justice sent a reassuring telegram to Sheriff McKellar at Hamilton. He advised that her case had been brought before the Privy Council that afternoon and they had all concurred that she should be recommended to the Governor-General for clemency. While the matter rested entirely with His Excellency, there seemed no reason why he might not follow the recommendation. Fulfilling the telegram's promise, the Governor-General signed an Order in Council on November 16. Unexpectedly, the term was fixed at fourteen years in lieu of life. Sheriff McKellar delivered the message to her that night.

Interviewed the following day by a reporter, Marie was asked: "Do you think the sentences is too long?"

"No, I do not. I did a bad deed, and I deserve punishment for it." Later in the press conference she remarked with a touch of nostalgia: "My young life was spent in a convent. I little thought at that time that I would ever be sentenced to be hung, or be sent to the penitentiary for fourteen years."

Charitable organizations in Hamilton maintained considerable pressure on the Department of Justice over the next few years, and after she had served just over five and a half years, executive clemency was again extended to her. In a letter to the Governor-General dated May 1, 1889, the Minister wrote: "It further appears that several benevolent ladies are willing to provide for her if she should be released and it is therefore recommended that she be released." His Excellency concurred on May 5 and Marie McCabe was released into the hands of her new-found friends in Hamilton.

· · ·

Annie Robinson
He Should Be Hanged, Twice

*P*ROBABLY NO OTHER CASE in the history of Ontario evoked as much public sympathy and compassion for one accused and so much hatred for the other as did that of Annie Robinson, sentenced to death in 1909 for the murder of her grandchildren. Not only were petitions for mercy forwarded from all parts of the province, but newspaper editorials from far and wide joined in the clamour for executive clemency. And yet, when the tumult and fury died, there were those more familiar with the dynamics of similar cases who wondered whether justice had really been served when the final penalties had been assessed.

The pathetic affair began to unfold in July 1909, when Reverend Dunlop, Methodist minister at Warren, Ontario, sixty-nine kilometres (forty-three miles) west of North Bay, wrote a letter to J.J. Kelso, Superintendent of Child Welfare in Toronto. Rev. Dunlop outlined his concerns by saying that a man named James Robinson, about fifty, lived on a farm near the village with his wife and ten children. They were all hard workers and their farm was prosperous. In March of the previous year, however, the oldest girl, Jessie, had given birth to a child and no one had seen the infant since. Her younger sister Ellen had also mothered a child in March 1908 and it had never been seen either.

Superintendent Kelso responded by saying that his department would look into the matter. It never did.

When no investigation was undertaken by the provincial Child Welfare agency, the local authorities decided to check into the matter. Their concern was spurred by a report that Jessie had given birth to another baby on August 4. Magistrate E.A. Wright and Dr. Dixon approached James Robinson on August 7 and asked if the rumour was true. Robinson boldly invited them to come to the farm and see for themselves.

Arriving at the Robinson farm on August 9, the two men spoke with Annie Robinson, James's wife and grandmother of the reputed child. She confirmed that a child had been born to Jessie, but said that it had died and been buried. She directed them to a spot behind the barn, where her oldest boy, John, twenty, dug up a small coffin. The infant inside was taken away and examined by Drs. Wilson and Dixon, who confirmed that the child had died of natural causes.

The mystery of the other two children was still unsolved, however, and when Magistrate Wright learned that James Robinson had suddenly disappeared, he became suspicious. Obtaining a search warrant, he returned to the farm later that day, August 9, in company with Constable Boyd of the Ontario Provincial Police. When they began to question Annie about the babies supposedly born in March 1908, she broke down and gave a written statement directing them to another spot in the farmyard where two tiny coffins, placed one on top of the other, were unearthed.

After questioning Annie Robinson and her two eldest daughters, Jessie and Ellen, the investigators were able to put together a rough framework. In 1906, Jessie, then sixteen, had given birth to a child who was still living. The same year, on June 7, Ellen, fifteen, had given birth to a child that had either died or been murdered; its body was one of those found on the farm.

On March 7, 1908, Jessie had given birth to another child. According to Mrs. Annie Robinson:

A baby was born to my daughter Jessie on March 7 last . . . When my husband came in from the field on March 7, I told him the baby was born. I don't remember what he said. I know he was the father of the babies. An hour after Jessie's baby was born, I smothered it between two mattresses.

James Robinson had fashioned a wooden box for the remains and buried it in a back field.

Ellen, then seventeen, gave birth to another child on March 23, 1908. Related Mrs. Robinson: "My husband was present when the second baby was born. I smothered it also. My husband put the bodies in the field."

The two girls confirmed her story and admitted incest with their father. The situation had been going on for nearly five years and also included another young daughter, Maggie. The sexual encounters had started before the children reached their fourteenth birthdays. Annie Robinson had given no hint to her own relatives or neighbours of what was secretly going on under their roof.

Mrs. Robinson was taken into custody and held without bail while a search was instituted for her husband. In their absence, her brother, Reverend James Matheson, moved onto the farm to care for the children and tend to the numerous chores. When interviewed, he expressed astonishment that such conditions could have existed at his sister's farm without his knowledge.

James Robinson did not return to the farm until September 13. He told his brother-in-law that he was tired of hiding and wanted to give himself up and was on his way to Sudbury for this purpose but had stopped at the farm to see how his family was faring. Matheson was suspicious of his true intentions, however, and watched him closely. The next morning, Robinson tried to make a break for it and sped off across the fields. Matheson overtook him and after a struggle managed to subdue him. Taken to Warren, Robinson appeared before Magistrate Wright and was committed to stand trial on several counts of incest and rape. The following day, he was lodged in the jail at Sudbury.

In the days that elapsed between Annie Robinson's preliminary hearing and trial, there was a ground-swell of sympathy on her behalf. She was depicted as a submissive woman, completely under her husband's thumb, who had committed the murders at his urging. Described as a good mother, a warm person, and a devout churchgoer, she was seen merely as a tool of her lust-ridden, diabolical husband. Consequently, when a jury was empanelled, their sympathies were strong in her favour.

The Fall Assizes opened at Sudbury on Monday, September 20, 1909, with Mr. Justice Magee on the bench. A special prosecutor, A.E.H. Creswicke, was brought in from Barrie, since the local solicitors wished to distance themselves from the messy case. The Grand Jury returned true bills against Annie Robinson for the murder of Jessie's child on March 7, 1908, and for that of Ellen's baby on March 23. It indicted James Robinson on three counts of incest and rape.

Annie Robinson was first tried for the murder of Jessie's child. This was the strongest case against her, relying on her own admission that she had killed the infant while her husband was at work. The jurors retired at 4:20 and came back with a verdict of not guilty, supporting their finding by claiming that she was not responsible for her actions at the time of the crime. Mr. Justice Magee explained that this was not an acceptable verdict and outlined the law as it pertained to insanity.

After a second deliberation, the jury returned to the courtroom with the same verdict and the same line of reasoning, clearly expressing the general feelings of the public, regardless of the law. His Lordship again explained the definition of legal insanity to them. Retiring a third time, the jury eventually brought in a verdict of guilty with a strong recommendation to mercy.

The next day, September 22, Annie Robinson was brought back to court to face the charge of murdering the child born to her daughter Ellen. Though her own evidence and that of one of her daughters strongly suggested that she had been pressured into this by her husband, she was found guilty. Sentence was deferred to the last day of the court calendar.

As a result of the evidence given at this trial, a further true bill was returned against James Robinson, charging him with being an accessory to this murder. Mr. B. Kessock, who was defending Robinson, asked that the trial be set over to the next session of court in order that his client's sanity might be ascertained. Mr. Justice Magee granted an adjournment, but only until October 26, at which time he would return to Sudbury to hold a special sitting.

At the close of the Assizes on Friday, September 24, Annie Robinson was returned to court to hear her sentence. Moved by the weight of his sad duty, His Lordship openly expressed the wish that the task had not fallen to him. While acknowledging the strong recommendations in her favour, he added that from his viewpoint he could hold out no hope of executive clemency. He then sentenced her to be hanged at Sudbury on November 24.

Scarcely had the date been set than a strong campaign was launched for leniency on her behalf. Spearheaded by the editors of the *Sudbury Journal,* who ran off several hundred copies of a petition, the movement was not simply for a commutation of sentence but for a full pardon. The drive caught fire when other newspapers across the province took up the cause, and hundreds of petitions took shape. In its October 7 issue, the *Sudbury Journal* noted that "the petitions are being signed by almost every person to whom presented."

The *Toronto Star* summarized the out-of-town feelings when it wrote: "The general opinion seems to be . . . that her husband should be hanged slowly, painfully, and twice."

Nevertheless, there were many people who could not forget that the incest in the Robinson home had gone on for at least five years and that Annie Robinson had been aware of it. They found it difficult to accept that she had done nothing to protect her children. Many of these were wives and mothers. While they did not concur with the death penalty, they felt that some punishment should be meted out.

The trial of James Robinson as an accessory to the murder of the second child took place on October 28 and 29 at Sudbury before Mr. Justice Magee. Because of the lurid nature of the testimony, HisLordship imposed a publication ban. The evidence against the man was not strong, and in his summation to the jury the learned jurist leaned in the man's favour.

While the jury was in seclusion, the Crown prosecutor and defence attorney struck a deal in which the prisoner would plead guilty to the lesser charges against him. This was acceptable to His Lordship, and before the jurors returned, he sentenced James Robinson to twenty-eight years for incest with the youngest daughter and to fourteen years for each of the two older girls. All sentences were to run concurrently.

When the jurors returned a verdict of not guilty to the charge of being an accessory, the Crown indicated that it would not appeal and would be satisfied with the other sentences. There were many who felt that the twenty-eight years, considering that Robinson was then over fifty, were tantamount to a life sentence and that justice had been served.

On November 8, Annie Robinson's death sentence was commuted to ten years in the penitentiary at Kingston, but that was not the final act of the drama. Fifteen months later, on February 25, 1911, she was paroled. She left Kingston on March 3 to return to her now fatherless family.

. . .

Mary Doolan
The Headless Infant

*T*HE DISCOVERY OF THE HEADLESS BODY of a baby at the Narrows at the north end of Lake Simcoe in Ontario, launched one of the most painstaking investigations by the Ontario Provincial Police in the history of their organization. In the end, it was patient, door-to-door footslogging that resulted in the solution.

The body was found on July 22, 1910, by Frank Utley, a fisherman. An autopsy on the badly decomposed remains indicated that the child had been about three months old at the time of its death and that it had probably died as the result of strangulation. The absence of water in the lungs showed that it had been dead before being placed in the lake. There were no pathological findings to suggest that it had died of natural causes and, in the absence of the head, which could have revealed wounds, the assumption was that it had been murdered.

Since the water in Lake Simcoe flowed north through the Severn River and eventually into Georgian Bay, the main focus of investigation centred around towns to the south of present-day Orillia. Fortunately for the investigators, the district around the Narrows was sparsely populated at that time, and they struck pay-dirt in the little village of Hawkstone.

Noah Cotton, a track worker on the local railway, remembered that he had seen a young woman walking along the tracks in March. He was able to pinpoint the day—March 25—because it was Good

Friday. Since it was miserable and cold and the young woman was carrying both a suitcase and a baby, he had invited her to his home to escape the inclement weather and she had stayed the night. His wife recalled the young girl, who had given her name as Mary Doolan, and told police that the girl had said she was on her way to Orillia. The next day, Noah Cotton had taken the lass to the train station at Hawkstone. He and his wife were able to supply the detectives with a description of "Mary Doolan" and the infant, which was believed to have been about three months old.

Townspeople at Hawkstone vaguely remembered seeing a young woman of this description around Easter, but none were certain of the exact day. One thought that he had seen her near a railway bridge north of town at that time. The local station master, however, was a much more precise source of information. He told the police that Noah Cotton had brought a woman to the station on Saturday. She had a suitcase and a baby with her. He saw her again on Easter Sunday, March 27. She was carrying a suitcase but there was no child with her. She had purchased a train ticket to Orillia—the only one he sold that day.

• • •

Believing that Mary Doolan either lived at Orillia or had friends there, the Ontario Provincial Police concentrated their efforts in that town and came up with a Mrs. Thomas McNulty, wife of the local poolhall operator. For some reason, Mrs. McNulty seemed pleased that the police were looking for Mary Doolan and informed them that her husband knew such a person. Where his wife was quite co-operative, however, Thomas McNulty struck the investigators as just the opposite. Admitting that he had known a woman by that name and that she resembled the description given by Cotton, he reluctantly gave them an address in Toronto where he believed she lived.

The address proved to be a boarding-house operated by a Mrs. Lavoie, and Mary Doolan was indeed living there. She was a pretty young woman of twenty-four, quiet and passive. Almost from the first questions, she broke down and told a pitiful story.

She had been born on a farm near Uptergrove, a small town on the north shore of Lake Simcoe a short distance east of Orillia. While still a teenager, she had made the acquaintance of Thomas McNulty, who owned a tavern in her village. He had been quite attracted to her and when their friendship ripened into intimacy, she had become his mistress. A child had been born to them in 1907 and McNulty had supplied her with money to go to Buffalo, New York, where she had left the child on a doorstep with twenty-five dollars and had returned to Uptergrove. The relationship resumed and continued even after McNulty moved to Orillia and opened a poolhall. She told the detectives that she thought Mrs. McNulty knew about the relationship, for she had several quarrels with the older woman.

When she became pregnant again in the fall of 1909, Thomas McNulty brought her to Orillia. He made a crude room for her on the upper floor of a stable behind the Great Central Hotel, where he visited her and brought her food. While he kept promising to marry her as soon as he had enough money, he also continuously reminded her that the support of his wife and two children prevented him from putting aside money.

Although she managed to keep her presence in the stable a secret throughout the winter, she suffered badly from the cold and drafty hideaway. She was afraid to venture out lest she be seen and her hiding place discovered. As her child grew within her, she became afraid of the continuing hardship of her cramped quarters and began demanding that he supply her with a better room. Finally, after four months in her veritable prison, he bought her a train ticket to Toronto and installed her in the boarding-house with Mrs. Lavoie.

Mary Doolan told the detectives that her baby had been born at Mrs. Lavoie's on March 10, 1910, and that she had written to McNulty to advise of its birth. He had never visited her. Later, she wrote to him again, asking what she should do with the baby. The next part of her voluntary statement sent a chill through the case-hardened investigators. Already touched by the narrative of her ordeal in the tiny room over the stable, they listened numbly as she described the next events.

Thomas McNulty had written back with detailed instructions on the disposal of the child. She was to take it to the Narrows at the head of Lake Simcoe and throw it into the water. The current, he assured her, would carry it to Georgian Bay, where it would never be recovered. He even mentioned a specific railway bridge suitable for the purpose. Following his instructions in the letter, she had burned it so that no incriminating evidence remained.

She went on to relate that she had taken the train to Hawkstone on Friday, March 25, and had been on her way to the bridge when she met Noah Cotton. When he left her at the station the next day, she had waited until night and under cover of darkness had made her way to the bridge described in McNulty's letter. Thinking death by drowning might be too painful, she had strangled the child before casting its body into the river. Then she bought a ticket to Orillia, and from there to Toronto, to await word from her lover that it was safe to join him. She was still waiting for his reply when the detectives arrived.

From their observations of her passive nature, the police were willing to accept her story. They questioned McNulty at his poolhall in Orillia, but he denied fathering her child, contending that Mary was a promiscuous young woman who was easy prey for any aggressive young man. Not surprisingly, Mrs. McNulty strongly supported her husband. Although McNulty admitted that he had given Mary money, he claimed it had been only out of pity and denied that he had kept her hidden in the stable behind the Great Central Hotel. Her story of the letter, he said, was pure fantasy, and he challenged the police to supply proof.

Realizing they had only Mary Doolan's word, the police made a thorough search of the stable and quickly located the boarded-up cubby-hole on the top floor. Further inspection showed that it had been occupied for some time, and confirming her presence were one or two discarded articles of her clothing. After conferring with the Attorney General's Department, they got a warrant for McNulty and took him into custody.

Mary Doolan was defended by Messrs. Robinette and Todhope, a firm that was to become famous for its criminal lawyers in later years. Her trial opened before Mr. Justice Britton at Barrie on September 27, and it was apparent from the beginning that the defence hoped to prove that she was merely McNulty's tool, blindly carrying out his instructions when she murdered her child and disposed of its body. No attempt was made to deny the offence, and the full focus was upon exposing all details of her unfortunate plight in the hope of future clemency. The jury had no difficulty bringing in a verdict of guilty or adding an unusually strong recommendation.

Thomas McNulty, whose lawyers—Creswick and Mulchy—fought to have him tried separately, was placed on trial as soon as Mary's case was complete. She was the chief witness against him, and though she collapsed from strain under vigorous cross-examination, she recovered and continued to weave a network of guilt around him. A strong attempt by his lawyers to prove that she was a woman of loose morals was not allowed by His Lordship, and they had to fall back on Mrs. McNulty's evidence. She painted an entirely different picture of young Mary, depicting her as a woman who had pursued her husband for years, tempting him with her pretty young face and body. If he had weakened and yielded to her charms, it was not his fault. She was the instigator. Thomas was not only a good father, she vowed, but a wonderful husband.

When the jurors retired at five o'clock on the afternoon of September 29, their main problem was the credibility of Doolan's statement about the mysterious letter of instructions. After three hours of deliberation, they gave their answer: guilty. Their only expression of uncertainty came when they unexpectedly recommended him to executive clemency as well.

On September 30, the pair were brought back to the old courtroom at Barrie for sentencing. On receiving the news that she would be hanged on December 14, Mary Doolan uttered a piercing shriek and collapsed on the floor. When she had been removed, His Lordship turned to the other prisoner. After stating that he fully agreed with the verdict, he suggested that McNulty should not count too heavily upon the recommendation to mercy and then imposed the same sentence on the wretched man.

It was no surprise when word was received on December 12 that His Excellency the Governor-General, Earl Grey, had commuted Mary Doolan's sentence. The Department of Justice fully believed that "she was in a desperate and forlorn plight" and completely under the domination of Thomas McNulty. What was unexpected was that the same mercy was shown to her accomplice. Pointing out that the only real evidence against him was the alleged letter supposedly written to the distraught mother, the Order in Council held that discretion dictated clemency. Both received life sentences.

On December 24, 1913, Mary Doolan was pardoned and sent home. She married and took up residence in the neighbourhood of her parental home near Orillia. Two years later, on December 24, 1915, Thomas McNulty was also pardoned at the urgent request of his wife, who said that she was unable to cope without him. His release was conditional upon no return to Orillia and no contact with Mary Doolan.

·   ·   ·

Catherine Hawyrluyk

Too Young to Die

*A*T EIGHTEEN YEARS OF AGE, Catherine Hawyrluyk was one of the youngest women in Canada to hear the solemn death phrases. In addition to this dubious distinction, she also presented the jury with a story that was, to say the least, difficult to understand, let alone believe.

Born in Poland in 1896, Catherine was sent to Canada by her parents at the age of ten to live with an uncle, John Prezemsky, at Sudbury, Ontario. Prezemsky at that time lived in a mining community known as Old Smelter Camp at Copper Cliff. This had started with the discovery of nickel and copper in the 1880s. Old Smelter Camp stood between the present mine buildings and Lake Kelly to the south. It was populated by ethnic groups from central Europe and consisted of a cluster of crude shacks with outdoor plumbing and roads that were mere trails. Life was rough and ready.

While staying at her uncle's house, Catherine became pregnant. Although the date of conception appears to have been sometime in October 1913, the father was unnamed. Towards Christmas, Catherine met a young man named Anton Hawyrluyk, a miner, and after a whirlwind courtship of two weeks, she married him. She later claimed that this was to give her child "a good name."

Catherine was not a large girl, physically, and it was not long before the women of the district knew that she was with child. They evidently said nothing. First children come any time; the rest take nine months. The husband, Anton, maintained later that he knew nothing of this pregnancy. By the time Catherine was nine months along, she must have been large indeed, considering her tiny frame.

On the morning of July 22, 1914, a neighbour lady happened to notice Catherine moving about the yard and saw that her physical condition had changed in a manner that suggested a child had been born. She went over to congratulate the young mother, only to be met with a flat denial that any child had arrived. The woman would have none of this nonsense and with motherly solicitation ordered Catherine to bed while she sent for the doctor.

Dr. Bennett, Copper Cliff's only physician, visited the shack around noon, and with the aid of interpretation from the friendly neighbour, he questioned Catherine. When she still denied that she had given birth, he suspected that the child had been stillborn and that she was trying to conceal a miscarriage. He reported his observations to the town policeman, Chief Clark.

As part of his job, Chief Clark had picked up a smattering of several languages, and among these was Polish. Questioning Catherine sternly, he gained from her an admission that two children had been born during the night, both dead at birth. Wishing to conceal their arrival from her husband, who was not their father, she had taken them out in the night and dropped them into the river that flowed from Kelly Lake. She did not know that this was wrong.

Chief Clark searched the shallow stream, found nothing, and became convinced that her story was not true.

When challenged, Catherine admitted that she had not put them in the river but had burned their tiny bodies in the stove. A quick sifting of the stove's ashes proved this story to be a fabrication also, and the policeman returned to his questions. Finally, Catherine admitted that on discovering that the children were dead, she had carried them to the bank of Kelly Lake and buried them. At his urging, she led him to a spot half a mile from her home. There the twins were found beneath an inch of soil, covered with flat rocks.

Mrs. Hawyrluyk was taken to Sudbury hospital to receive medical attention and the children were removed to Dr. Bennett's office. A thorough examination revealed that they were a boy and a girl, both perfectly formed. A more sinister finding was that both had lived after birth, and death had come either through strangulation or suffocation. He relayed his results to Chief Clark and the young woman was placed under arrest.

Interviewed at his place of work, Anton expressed astonishment that his wife had given birth. He said he had returned from work on Tuesday night to find everything in order. When he awoke Wednesday morning, his wife was already up and had prepared his breakfast; she seemed to be her usual cheerful self. He had then gone off to work and knew nothing of the affair until the police came to question him.

It seemed incredible to Chief Clark that Anton not only knew nothing of his wife's pregnancy, but also did not notice the changed condition of her body from Tuesday night to Wednesday morning. Suspecting that he had helped both with the birth of the twins and with their burial, Chief Clark arrested him and lodged him in the city jail. When Catherine was released from hospital, Clark clapped her in there with him.

There was a good deal of sympathy in the community for the young mother, and the coroner's jury expressed this when they returned an open verdict: "We find that these two babies met their deaths at the hands of a person or persons unknown."

The Attorney General himself found it hard to believe that this frail young woman had given birth to two children in the middle of the night and had carried them half a mile to bury them before returning to her cabin to prepare breakfast for her husband. Nevertheless, the evidence at her preliminary hearing on July 27 was sufficient to set her forward to stand trial before a higher court. Her husband was released.

Catherine made only one change in her story in the following weeks. She told her uncle, John Prezemsky, during one of his visits to the jail, that a young miner named Frank Fendrick had helped her dispose of the children. This "confession," however, was made only after extreme pressure from her uncle for a logical explanation. Chief Clark checked on the young man, only to find that he had been working at the mill when the children were born and had not left the shop.

Catherine Hawyrluyk was brought to trial before Mr. Justice Latchford on October 22, charged only with the death of the male child. Strangely, no women attended as spectators. Completely surrounded by men, little Catherine huddled in a corner of the prisoner's box, scarcely able to see over its rim, and listened to the voice of the interpreter, who translated the proceedings for her. Mr. Peter White, prosecutor, presented the case with the air of a man who was performing an unpleasant task and whose sympathies were entirely with the accused. Nevertheless, his case was strong, and under the law as it existed at that time, murder had been done.

Defence attorney J.A. Mulligan did not attempt to deny the crime, but sought to introduce testimony by an expert witness that Mrs. Hawyrluyk might have been suffering from pubertine insanity, a common reaction among young women immediately after the birth of their first child. His Lordship refused to accept this evidence, suggesting that there were other avenues open for dealing with diminished responsibility. The jury took only ninety minutes to return a verdict and added a strong recommendation to mercy based on the age of the accused.

Mr. Justice Latchford announced that he fully concurred with their findings and recommendation. Noting that the Governor-General could not only commute death sentences to life imprisonment but could alter any life sentence to a lesser term, he promised to press for the lightest possible punishment under the circumstances.

The young woman was sentenced to be hanged on January 27, 1915, but on January 14 this was changed to life in Kingston Penitentiary. After serving less than four years, she was granted a parole on March 2, 1918. Unable to return to her husband for obvious reasons, she was taken by a religious organization and re-established in a new city to begin life over again.

.   .   .

Viola Thompson
The Death of a Baby

*T*HE PHRASE "OPEN AND SHUT" is often applied in describing certain criminal cases where all the evidence points to one inevitable conclusion. In some respects, the case of Viola Thompson of Elm Tree, Ontario, fell within that category. It had no national newsworthy significance and even the local paper devoted only a few column inches to its coverage. Indeed, the only people concerned were those who had to be involved, such as the judge, the jurors, and the Department of Justice. There was a murder; there was a trial; there was a death sentence commuted to life imprisonment, and a subsequent parole. Everything moved so mechanically that it seemed almost unreal.

No one, not even the officials who eventually held Viola Thompson's life in their hands, made any attempt to fathom or understand the woman herself or her background. Her biography was unimportant. It was known that she was thirty-five years of age, that she was married to a James Thompson, and that she was separated from him and living with her mother. The only facts that seemed important to officialdom were that she had found herself with an unwanted infant, and faced with an apparently insoluble dilemma, she had murdered the child. In addition, it was politically repugnant at that time to execute a woman.

On February 13, 1919, Mrs. Thompson checked into the hospital at Kingston, Ontario, about eighty kilometres (fifty miles) from her hometown. She used her maiden name, Lovica Woodcock. Three days later, she gave birth to a baby boy, and because of minor complications she remained in the hospital until Friday, February 28. As she was checking out, there was some problem with the baby's clothing, and a friendly nurse, Kathleen Nichols, made some emergency sewing repairs to his nightie.

To return to her mother's home at Elm Tree, Viola would logically have taken a train north from Kingston to Sharbot Lake, which was situated on the rail line between Peterborough and Ottawa. At Sharbot Lake, she would have caught a westbound train and would have gotten off at Kennebec Junction, some twenty kilometres (twelve miles) down the line. From there she could have reached home by walking or by horse and sleigh.

Edward Chapman, conductor on the westbound train from Ottawa to Peterborough, recalled that she boarded his train at Sharbot Lake at 2:58 on the morning of Saturday, March 1. She was alone, with no suitcase or other baggage. He remembered her in particular because when he let her off at Kennebec Junction in the middle of the night there was no one there to meet her.

Later that morning, W.J. Paquette, fireman of a local freight shunting at Sharbot Lake, noticed a bundle lying beside the track about 500 metres (550 yards) from the station. Stepping down from the cab, he picked it up and found that it was a dead baby. A rag had been thrust into his mouth and was held in place by a cloth wrapped around his face. He replaced the body where he had found it and notified the police.

After a local coroner's jury sat briefly on the death, the dead infant was turned over to Inspector A.B. Boyd of the Ontario Provincial Police on March 4. He took the body to the hospital at Queen's University in Kingston, where Dr. Walter Connell determined that the child was two weeks old and that he had died of asphyxiation. Based on the child's navel, he ventured an opinion that it had either been born in a hospital or with a qualified medical person present at birth.

Nurses from nearby hospitals were invited to the forensic lab at the university to view the body, and among these were Alma Frost and Kathleen Nichols, both of whom worked at the Kingston General Hospital. Although Miss Frost was reasonably sure that the child belonged to "Lovica Woodcock," she was not certain. Kathleen Nichols remembered fixing the child's nightgown, however, and she positively identified her sewing handiwork. She reported that "Lovica Woodcock" had given her home address as Elm Tree and had left the hospital with her baby on Friday afternoon, February 28.

Inspector Boyd shifted his focus to Sharbot Lake, where the baby was found. When he got Conductor Edward Chapman's story, he was sure he had the sequence of events: Lovica Woodcock had left the General Hospital in Kingston on Friday afternoon, taking the train to Sharbot Lake; there, while waiting for her connection to Kennebec Junction, she had murdered her baby and laid him beside the tracks in the darkness; then she had boarded the westbound passenger train at 2:58 and had gotten off at the junction. He dispatched a constable to Elm Tree to question the woman, and if necessary, arrest her.

Viola Thompson was tracked down on March 10 at a farm near Arden. She told the arresting officer that when she reached the station in Kingston on Friday evening, she met a woman from Toronto who had taken a great interest in the baby. When this woman learned that she did not really want to keep her child, she offered to take him and give him a good home.

Mrs. Thompson had left the railway station to get something to eat, entrusting her baby to the woman. When she returned, both were gone. She was not alarmed, however, for the woman had given her an address in Toronto. Viola had then caught the westbound train from Kingston (not the north train that passed through Sharbot Lake), and after a roundabout trip had arrived at Kennebec Junction. From there, she had walked home. Before leaving to take the job at Arden, she had given the woman's name and address to her mother.

Her story was such an obvious fabrication that the constable arrested her and delivered her to Inspector Boyd at Kingston. That worthy did a perfunctory check of her "alibi," and when he discovered that the train she claimed to have taken did not stop at Kennebec Junction, he closed the investigation and turned his material over to the Crown prosecutor.

. . .

Mrs. Thompson came before Mr. Justice Lennox and jury at Kingston on September 27, 1919. The Crown's case, as presented by Peter Wright, had only to show that she had left the hospital with her baby on Friday; that she had boarded the train at Sharbot Lake at 2:58 the next morning with no baby; and that the baby had been found murdered beside the tracks later the same morning.

Trying to show that she was not mentally responsible, her lawyer, Mr. Rigney, placed Dr. Richardson, physician at the local prison, on the stand. Richardson testified that Viola was both mentally deficient and insane at the time the crime was committed. While he admitted that he was not "an expert in problems of the mind," he felt that his observations based on her conduct at the jail were accurate.

The Crown countered with Dr. W.K. Ross, Superintendent of the Rockford Mental Hospital, and another specialist, Dr. A.W. Richards. They both testified that the accused was mentally defective, but there was no evidence of psychosis.

The entire proceedings took only one day, and at 5:05 the jury retired to consider their verdict. They returned to announce that they were having trouble reaching a decision. Their main problem was, who had seen the child and mother together? The only evidence before them was that Viola was supposed to have left the hospital with the child, but no one saw them together after that. His Lordship explained that the mother and infant were jointly in the hospital. The mother was seen boarding the train at Sharbot Lake alone. The child was found murdered at that spot, therefore . . . .

Some of the jurors took offence—whether at his words or his attitude is not known—and heated barbs flew across the courtroom. They wanted more evidence and he said they had enough. The debate ended when the judge suggested testily that another set of jurors would have no problem with this evidence and wondered why they even raised the issue. That was the evidence; take it or leave it. His annoyance with them equalled their displeasure with him and the Crown's case. Nevertheless, they went into seclusion again, and after ten minutes returned with a verdict of guilty, though they softened it with a recommendation to mercy.

His Lordship's sympathies were clearly with the prisoner, for he was visibly affected when he passed sentence. Remarking that he was sure there had been no miscarriage of justice and that he was confident the prisoner had known what she was doing, he ordered her to be executed at Kingston on December 17, 1919. In a kindly effort to ease the harshness of the sentence, he tried to assure her "that it has not been the custom in Canada to inflict the supreme penalty on women."

His comforting words were based on the fact that no woman had been hanged during the past twenty years, since Hilda Blake went to her death in 1899. The next eleven women condemned had all had their sentences respited. His reassuring message, however, seemed to fall on uncomprehending ears, for Viola Thompson received her sentence without a glimmer of expression. When it was over, she walked from the courtroom with the air of a woman who had just returned from shopping.

Though one extensive petition was forwarded to Ottawa asking for commutation, the main thrust came from numerous letters written by friends and neighbours of the condemned woman. These pointed out that her problem arose from the fact that she had been forced to escape from her home to avoid the abuse of her husband, James. From this had resulted her pregnancy and ultimate troubles. James Thompson himself wrote to the Governor-General, shouldering much of the blame for her predicament and asking him to be merciful.

Viola Thompson's sentence was changed to life on December 4, 1919, and after spending just over six years behind bars, she was discharged on parole on February 10, 1926. A year later she wrote to the Department of Justice stating that she had been offered a job in the United States and was seeking permission to accept it. This was granted—effectively cancelling her parole—but with the condition that if she returned to Canada, the parole would be reinstated. That action closed the sad file.

· · ·

Mary Paulette

A Northern Tragedy

*T*HE LAST WOMAN to be sentenced to death for child murder was Mrs. Mary Paulette of Fort Smith, Northwest Territories. She was born in 1928, the daughter of Mr. and Mrs. Jeremy Tourangeau. She was believed to be one-half or three-quarters Native. As a teenager in Fort Smith, she acquired a reputation for honesty and integrity, and was noted for the excellence of her intelligence. By womanhood, she had developed into a slender, gracious, and beautiful young woman who was sought after by the unattached men in the community.

At age eighteen, she married Magloire Paulette, a special constable with the Royal Canadian Mounted Police, and their first child, Lloyd, was born on May 19, 1947. Unfortunately, her husband was a troubled young man, and in June 1948, he took his own life. Mary then went to live with her parents, where a second child, John, was born on December 4, 1948.

Mary was not a promiscuous young woman and the relationships she formed were meant to be lasting. She became intimate with a young man stationed at Fort Smith and by him had a child out of wedlock in 1950. Because he was unable to marry her or set up living quarters with her, she was forced to keep the child with her at her parents' home. This was said to have created problems with her mother. Confidential police reports say that she was threatened with expulsion from home if she had another illegitimate child.

In the fall of 1950, Mary again found herself pregnant by the same young man, and to complicate matters, he was suddenly transferred from Fort Smith, leaving her to find her own solution. Being of delicate build, it was not long before her condition became apparent.

On May 15, 1951, RCMP Corporal Betts met her on the streets of Fort Smith, and seeing that she was no longer pregnant, he automatically asked how her new baby was. To his surprise, she denied that she had been with child or had given birth. When he pressed her, she volunteered to be examined by Dr. W.M. McFee.

At this juncture, Corporal Betts consulted with his superior, Sergeant George Abrahams, a long-time acquaintance of Mary Paulette who kept a fatherly watch over her. He decided that, for her own protection and medical health, she should see Dr. McFee.

When the doctor confirmed that Mary had borne a child within the past week, Sergeant Abrahams had a talk with her. Faced with the medical evidence, she acknowledged the birth, saying that on May 10 she had been in the outdoor privy behind her house when the "baby slipped out and fell into the hole." She had been afraid and had covered it with sand, saying nothing to anyone about it.

After obtaining a search warrant, the police removed the body of a female child from the privy. An autopsy revealed that she had been born alive and was full term. Death had been caused by paper wadded into her mouth. Faced with this information, Mary gave another statement to Sergeant Abrahams in which she said that she had been home alone with her children on May 10, and when she felt labour pains coming on, she had gone to the outdoor toilet and there the baby had been born. Afraid to take her back to the house for fear of incurring her mother's wrath, she had stuffed paper in her mouth, placed the body in the hole, and covered it with sand. She expressed a great deal of remorse, saying that she wished she had kept it regardless of the consequences. At that point, he reluctantly charged her with the murder of her baby.

Following a preliminary hearing before Magistrate L.H. Phinney on June 25, Mrs. Paulette was committed to stand trial and Mr. D.J. Hagel was appointed by the court to represent her. Trial was set for September 19, 1951. Her mother, who testified at the preliminary, maintained that Mary's pregnancy was "all a surprise to me" and denied any suggestion that she had threatened to throw her daughter out of the house if she brought home another child.

The law regarding child murder had been changed in 1948 to provide that if it could be shown that the mother's mind had been disturbed by the birth of the child, the homicide might be classified as infanticide. In other parts of Canada, this new provision had been used several times and the charge had been reduced from murder to infanticide. The sentences meted out were also less severe, measured sometimes in months rather than years. As in regular charges of murder, however, the assumption was that the accused was sane at the time of the crime unless the defence could show otherwise.

Electing to be tried without jury, Mary Paulette's trial for murder opened before Stipendary Magistrate J.F. Gibben at Fort Smith on September 19, and was heard by him alone. The fact of the child's death was uncontested, as was Mary's responsibility for it. Defence counsel Hagel intended to prove that her mind had been disturbed at the time and she should have been charged with the lesser crime of infanticide.

In his report to the Minister of Justice, Magistrate Gibben remarked that no evidence had been presented to suggest that her mind was disturbed. Those who saw her immediately before the murder and shortly after it, failed to comment upon any change to her behaviour. Thus, he had rejected the plea of infanticide and had found her guilty of murder. With reluctance, on September 20, he had sentenced her to be executed at Fort Smith on February 15 of the following year.

If her lawyer's inexperience left something to be desired in her defence, Mary Paulette had other supporters. Crown Prosecutor John Parker wrote to the Commissioner of the Northwest Territories on September 24, 1951: "My feeling is that although this is a case of murder under the law, it is, in spirit, a case of infanticide." In a belated effort to gather evidence as to whether her mind might have been unsettled at the time of the crime, he arranged for Dr. F.S. Lawson, Superintendent of the Mental Hospital at North Battleford, Saskatchewan, to examine her. Dr. Lawson was only able to say that he could find no evidence that this might have been the case.

As anticipated, a commutation of sentence was issued on January 25, 1952, but in lieu of a short prison term, she was ordered to serve life in Kingston.

One of the hazards facing Native people confined to prison or mental hospitals in the first half of this century was tuberculosis. The transition from absolute freedom to close confinement with its psychological trauma was highly conducive to the onset of the social disease. Within a year, Mary Paulette fell victim to the scourge and weakened rapidly. In 1953, she was given a temporary parole to allow her to be moved to a sanatorium. On June 21, 1954, this conditional release was altered to full parole, which would become effective when she was well enough to be discharged from the sanatorium and return to the North.

· · ·

Elizabeth Tilford's husband, Tyrell, suspected she was planning to poison him when the local druggist delivered a package of arsenic to the house. But he continued to eat the meals she prepared and eventually died. Elizabeth was hanged for the crime in Woodstock, Ontario, in 1935. NATIONAL ARCHIVES OF CANADA/C143483

The death cells in Westmorland County Jail, Dorchester, New Brunswick. Carmello Marablito died of a heart attack in one of these cells before her execution for the murder of her husband in 1918 could be carried out. ARNOLD'S STUDIO, MONCTON, NB

Hangman Arthur Ellis, Canada's most famous executioner, hanged or assisted at the executions of more than six hundred people around the world. The macabre bungled hanging of Tomasina Sarao at Montreal's Bordeaux Jail on March 29, 1935, ended his career. ESTATE OF ALEX EDMISON

The old Prison of Quebec, where Marie Cloutier and Achille Grondin awaited execution at Montreal's Bordeaux Jail for the murder of Marie's husband, Vilmond, in 1938. Hoping to disguise the effects of the arsenic she used to poison him, Marie insisted on a first-class embalming for her beloved spouse. BIBLIOTHÈQUE DE MONTRÉAL

The home of William Hamilton, near Hamiota, Manitoba, where housekeeper Teenie Maloney killed her employer's aged mother, Mary, in 1916. COLLECTION OF THE AUTHOR

Gallows at Deer Lodge Penitentiary in Montana. In the early days, a gallows was not a permanent structure in most prisons, but was taken apart, moved, and reassembled in lock-ups throughout a county as the need arose. COLLECTION OF THE AUTHOR

The front entrance to the Fort Saskatchewan Jail northeast of Edmonton. Dina Dranchuk was held here briefly in 1934 to await execution for the hatchet murder of her husband. When her sentence was commuted she was sent to Kingston—the first prisoner admitted to the new Prison for Women—but her mental condition deteriorated rapidly and she was transferred to the Kingston Psychiatric Hospital, where she remained for forty-three years. COURTESY FORT SASKATCHEWAN HISTORICAL MUSEUM

The side door to the men's prison at the Fort Saskatchewan Jail. Florence Lassandro made the long walk across the prison yard from the women's quarters and went through this entrance to reach the scaffold where she was hanged in 1923 for the murder of Constable Stephen Lawson in Coleman, Alberta. COLLECTION OF THE AUTHOR

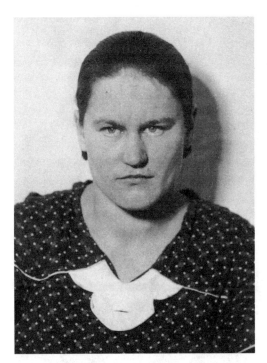

Mary Cowan, who convinced her seventeen-year-old lover, Allan, to murder her husband, who also happened to be Allan's brother. NATIONAL ARCHIVES OF CANADA/C143484

The prison at Renfrew, Ontario, where Mary Cowan was held pending her trial for the murder of her husband, Albert, in 1935. COLLECTION OF THE AUTHOR

Florence Lassandro, a young woman caught up in the excitement of rumrunning who paid with her life because she panicked in a confrontation with police. COURTESY ESTATE OF CARMEN PICARIELLO

Florence Lassandro shot Constable Stephen Lawson in front of this house in Coleman, Alberta, in 1922. Lawson's nine-year-old daughter, Pearl, was a witness. COLLECTION OF THE AUTHOR

Emilio Picariello, affectionately known as Emperor Pic, was a rumrunner during prohibition days in southern Alberta. He was hanged at the Fort Saskatchewan prison for his part in the death of Constable Lawson. COURTESY ESTATE OF CARMEN PICARIELLO

Charles Lassandro, left, Florence's husband, and Emilio Picariello with a pet bear. COURTESY ESTATE OF CARMEN PICARIELLO

John Russell Foster in 1893, one of the most astute criminal investigators on the frontier. His evidence was instrumental in the convictions of Hilda Blake and Teenie Maloney. COURTESY BRANDON POLICE DEPARTMENT

The jail at Brandon, Manitoba, where Hilda Blake went to her death on a chilly December morning in 1899 for the murder of her employer's wife, Mary Lane. COURTESY MANITOBA ARCHIVES

Pot-Pourri

There are some cases that contain features which set them apart from the usual classification by method or motive and which seem to merit singular treatment. In statistical tables, they are often lumped into a category called "Other." The six instances covered here fall naturally into this grouping. Each had something special.

Mary Aylward

They Held Two Trials

A TWENTY-THREE-YEAR-OLD COLLEEN by the name of Mary Aylward earned the unhappy distinction of being the first woman in Canada to be hanged jointly with her husband. The event took place at Belleville, Ontario, on the chilly morning of Monday, December 8, 1862.

Mary, who was Irish, had arrived in New York with her brother, and on his death had obtained work as a maid, an occupation that took her to various parts of the state, one of which was Poughkeepsie. There she met Richard Aylward, a fine-looking Irishman who had arrived in the United States around 1850 as a lad of fourteen. His family had settled near Poughkeepsie. Richard and Mary were married on August 15, 1855, and later moved to Belleville, Ontario, where they took up farming. Three girls were born to them, and at the time of their parents' deaths, the children ranged from seven years to sixteen months.

The Aylward farm was adjacent to that of a man named William Munro, and for some reason animosity developed between them.

There were frequent disagreements that grew into bitter quarrelling, and the friction climaxed on the afternoon of Monday, May 19,
1862, when William Munro and his son rode into the Aylward
farmyard armed with pistols.

Seeing their armed approach, Richard Aylward ran into his
cabin and emerged with a rifle. His wife, who had been working in
her garden, came to stand beside him with a scythe in her hands.
The truth of what happened next was obscured by conflicting
testimony at the trial, but it is clear that Aylward shot both William
Munro and his son. In defence of her husband, Mary also attacked
the older man with the scythe, inflicting severe wounds. When
William Munro died of his injuries, Richard and Mary were charged
with murder. The son survived to become the chief Crown witness.

The trial was held at Belleville on October 21, 1862, and the
medical evidence showed that William Munro might have survived
the bullet wound, as his son had, but the combined effects of the
gunshot and the scythe damage had brought about his death. His
son testified that Richard had shot his father without warning and
then turned the gun on him. Mrs. Aylward had used her weapon
while his father was lying on the ground. Richard told the court that
he had not fired his rifle until the pair reached for their revolvers.
His wife corroborated his story, adding that she had only been trying
to defend her husband against two armed men.

The Munro family had long been resident in the community and
had many friends, some of whom were on the jury. In contrast, the
Aylwards were newcomers and had the reputation of being both
stubborn and hotheaded. Despite the fact that the Munros were
clearly the intruders, the jury returned verdicts of guilty against both
husband and wife. These were tempered, however, with strong pleas
for mercy.

In contrast to the earlier colonial system, where executions had
followed hard upon the heels of conviction, the judicial system had
moved by the 1860s to the practice of setting a period of six weeks
between the two, in order to allow a full and unhurried review of the
facts by agents of the Canadian government. This move had been
necessitated by the spread of settlement into the remote areas of
Ontario and Quebec, which often presented communication problems. Hence, the Aylwards' date was set for December 6, 1862.

There were few in Belleville and district who believed that the
couple would be put to death, and they readily signed the petitions

begging for clemency. These were forwarded to Ottawa, which had become the new capital of Canada on December 31, 1857. Unfortunately, petitions signed by friends of the Munros were also sent, asking for no interference.

When word was received that no mercy would be shown, direct appeals were made to Governor-General Viscount Charles Stanley Monck, an Irishman born in Templemore, Tipperary, in 1819 and appointed as Governor-General in 1861. It was hoped that he might find it in his heart to extend compassion to two fellow countrymen, especially when one was a woman, but it was not to be. Viscount Monck refused to intercede.

There had been only two executions in Belleville previously and both of these had been public. George Barnhard had gone to his death in the summer of 1854 for the murder of a man named Dafoe—also the result of two neighbours quarrelling. The last had been Samuel Rock, hanged on June 12, 1859, for the murder of Robert Dickie during a burglary.

Richard and Mary were housed in cells in the basement of the courthouse, and during the first week of December their ears were constantly assailed by the noise of the erection of their scaffold. A platform about five feet by nine feet was built out from a large window on the second floor of the east side of the building. Above the two trapdoors were two steel hooks positioned in a beam about three feet apart. The work was finished Saturday night, December 6, and all during Sunday curious people drove by in sleighs and cutters to survey the structure.

Monday morning dawned clear and cold, but despite the sub-zero temperature, some five thousand people from the district gathered in silence outside the courthouse. Although the execution had been scheduled for ten o'clock, there was an hour delay caused by Reverend Mr. Brennen, a tireless worker on their behalf, who had sent a last-minute telegram to Ottawa. This proved vain, and at eleven o'clock, a white-hooded hangman stepped through the window onto the platform. Imported from Toronto, he had spent the entire weekend hidden in the building. He was followed by Richard Aylward, his hands manacled behind him and a rope dangling from his neck. Behind him came the Reverend Mr. Brennen and then Mary Aylward, also handcuffed and with the deadly rope already around her throat. The local sheriff and other members of the execution party stepped out to take positions near the window.

Both white-faced prisoners conducted themselves with great forti-
tude during the recitation of a short prayer by the minister, and both
protested quietly that they had only been defending themselves against
the Munros. With that, the executioner fixed their ropes to the two
steel hooks, lowered the white County Kerchiefs over their faces, and
pulled the lever. The executions were clean and both died instantly.

That was not the end of it, for there were two trials in the case
of Richard and Mary Aylward. The first had been conducted in the
duly constituted court of law and its decision had been "guilty." The
second was held in a court of public opinion, conducted by Reverend Mr. Brennen from his pulpit that afternoon. With the coffins of
the condemned before him, Brennen launched into an impassioned
review of the facts. Pointing out that two men armed with pistols had
gone to the Aylward farm on May 19, he contended that Richard had
fired to protect his life and that of his wife. Mary had attacked only
when she feared for her husband. Much that was common knowledge, but which was not permitted into evidence, went to show that
the Munros had gone to the farm with deadly intent, and Reverend
Brennen was not averse to bringing this into the open.

Long before he finished his scathing denunciation of the local
authorities and the government, most of his audience were crying
openly. In concluding his sermon, Reverend Brennen declared that
in the eyes of the church, the man and woman were not murderers
and therefore would be buried in sacred ground.

Late that cold December afternoon, Mary and Richard Aylward
were interred in the local cemetery, the first husband and wife to
suffer the supreme penalty side by side.

· · ·

Phoebe Campbell
A Merciful View

ONE OF THE INTERESTING FACTS about
Canada's female killers is that of the forty-two
accomplices who were indicted with them, all were male. Apparently

the first instance of two women participating in a murder did not come until September 5, 1986, when Marilyn Arneson, thirty-four, and Donna Turner, thirty-seven, killed Marlene Collins, thirty-four, at Toronto. They pleaded guilty to second-degree murder on December 19, 1987, and were sentenced by Mr. Justice John O'Driscoll to life imprisonment.

Of the forty-two male accomplices, twenty-six were hanged for their crimes. In seven instances, the man was hanged while the woman was reprieved. Of the remaining sixteen, five were banished for life; six received life sentences; three were acquitted; and one was sentenced to twenty years. The fate of the forty-second man, Philip Huffman, is unknown.

Thomas Coyle was one of the lucky ones. He walked from the courtroom a free man.

The facts behind most murders seldom come out in court, even when a confession is advanced. The detailed explanation of the crime and motive, so dear to the hearts of fictional detectives, is seldom important in reaching a decision in real life. The Crown may suggest a motive, but need not prove it. All that is necessary is to show beyond a reasonable doubt that murder was committed and that the accused is the only person who could logically be guilty. Such was the case in the death of George Campbell at his farm near London, Ontario, on the night of July 15, 1871.

Neighbours were first alerted around midnight, and those who arrived at the scene were told by Mrs. Campbell that two black men had broken into their home and murdered her husband. Entering the bedroom, they discovered the farmer lying on his back near the door. His throat had been cut and his head bore other cuts and bruises. A pistol, butcher knife, and axe were found on the floor of the room, and although the revolver did not seem to have been discharged, both the knife and the butt of the axe were covered with blood.

The man assigned to the case was Detective Harry Phair of the London police force. A native of Armagh, Ireland, he had arrived in Canada as a boy, and after an apprenticeship as a shoemaker, had joined the London police force around 1862. His ability as an investigator was so marked that he quickly rose through the ranks to become a detective. In later years, he was to gain a certain notoriety for his work in the famous Donnelly case in Lucan, Ontario. He died on October 19, 1892, after being shot by two men he was trying to arrest.

His first move on arriving at the Campbell farmstead was to organize a search for "the two black men," but this proved futile. No one remembered seeing these two people either before or after the incident. More significant to Phair was the fact that both the knife and axe belonged to the Campbell farm; the knife was normally kept in a kitchen drawer. After taking a detailed statement from Mrs. Phoebe Campbell, the twenty-three-year-old widow, he concentrated on the pistol.

The revolver had never been fired—the firing pin was defective—but it was of such an unusual design that it was easily traced to a man in St. Marys, a few miles north of London. This man, William Robert Taylor, told detectives that he had sold the weapon only a short time before to a young Irishman. He remembered only that the lad, about twenty, had been quite rustic looking and had a face that was fresh and almost beardless.

In his conversation with neighbours, Detective Harry Phair learned that the Campbell marriage had never been a happy one, despite the presence of two children, one of whom was still at the breast. George Campbell, some years older than his wife, was a rough, harsh man, who was extremely jealous of her. At different times, Phoebe had told neighbour women that he had beaten her for suspected trysts with a young neighbour boy, Thomas Coyle.

Checking into these rumours, Phair learned that Thomas Coyle, twenty, was a hired hand on the farm of Joseph McWain, a short distance from the Campbell place. McWain was Phoebe Campbell's father. On questioning the youth, Phair noted that he bore a striking resemblance to the description of the lad who had purchased the pistol from William Taylor at St. Marys. He arranged for the dealer to come to London secretly, but while Taylor was unable to say positively that Coyle was the customer, he admitted that the lad looked like the buyer. On the basis of this, Phair arrested Coyle as a probable accessory to the murder.

Failure to locate any trace of the two black men led Detective Phair to conclude that they were nonexistent. He then centred his attention directly on Phoebe Campbell, with Thomas Coyle as a possible accomplice. At the inquest and later the preliminary hearing, however, three lads who shared a bedroom with Coyle on the McWain farm presented strong evidence that he had not left the room on the night of the murder. Thus, when Phoebe Campbell went on trial at London on April 6, 1872, she stood alone in the dock.

Though Mrs. Campbell stuck steadfastly to her story that her husband had been killed by the two men who had fled when they heard her coming downstairs from the upper floor, the jury failed to believe her. Detective Phair's carefully woven circumstantial case was too strong. The only surprising element of the trial, considering that the defence had managed to introduce ample evidence that Phoebe's husband had abused her frequently, was that the jurors did not recommend mercy. Mr. Justice Thomas Galt sentenced her to be hanged on June 20, 1872. Thomas Coyle, who had been held in prison as a potential material witness, was set free.

· · ·

Detective Phair was not totally convinced that Phoebe Campbell had murdered her husband alone, for he had not been able to explain the presence of the revolver in the bedroom. Though he questioned her several times, he received contradictory answers. First, she would insist that the two black men had killed him; then she would accuse Thomas Coyle, and once she even tried to implicate a cousin, John McWain. There was nothing Phair could use officially until May 20, when Phoebe Campbell called for paper and pen and wrote an eight-page narrative detailing Coyle's part in the slaying. This confession was forwarded to the Attorney General for action.

Phoebe alleged that two months before the murder she had confided to Thomas Coyle that her husband was very bad to her. Coyle sympathized with her and suggested that he could "do away with him" if she would later marry him. Nothing was done at that time, and although they later considered poisoning him, they eventually settled for shooting. On the strength of this, Coyle went to St. Marys and purchased a revolver. The murder was to take place on the night of Friday, July 15.

On that evening, George Campbell read his Bible as usual and chatted with Phoebe for a while before he retired. She sat up and sewed some clothing. Some time after eleven, she heard the signal outside and went out to find Coyle waiting for her with the revolver. They debated who should fire the shot. She was afraid she would miss, so Coyle agreed to do it. When they went into her husband's bedroom, however, the gun would not fire. Coyle then went outside and returned with the axe, striking the victim with the blunt end.

George Campbell was stunned but managed to grapple with his assailant. The two men struggled, but Coyle got the upper hand. He then ordered her to bring him a knife from the kitchen, and when she did so, he took it and cut Campbell's throat.

Phoebe's accusation related that after Thomas Coyle had washed his hands and checked his clothing for blood, he had returned to the McWain farm and had slipped unnoticed into the bedroom he shared with the other hired hands. She had waited for awhile before running into the road to give the alarm and tell her story of the two black attackers.

Though there was sufficient material in the confession to justify the arrest of Thomas Coyle, Detective Phair was still not sure he knew the full story. One part still bothered him. The medical testimony indicated that Campbell's throat had been cut some time after he had been struck the fatal blows on the head—probably after he was dead—since very little blood had come from the neck wound. Phoebe nevertheless stuck to her story that her husband had been alive when his throat was cut. Phair had no other course but to arrest Coyle.

He lodged the man in the London police cells, putting him in a cubicle not too far from the woman, hoping that they would talk when they thought they could not be overheard.

Mrs. Campbell now reverted to her erratic pattern of accusing the two black men, her cousin John McWain, and Thomas Coyle, without supplying further details to back up any of her versions. As the day of her execution neared, however, she became resigned and seemed even to anticipate the act, expressing herself as happy to meet her fate and spending her time singing and praying.

No closer to solving the enigma of Thomas Coyle and the revolver, Phair arranged to have a reporter from the *Toronto Globe* placed in a cell adjacent to that of Coyle. Two days before the execution, he persuaded the warden to allow Mrs. Campbell to visit with her alleged accomplice. The reporter, Nickols, an accomplished shorthand recorder, was later to claim that he had written down some damaging admissions from the resulting conversation between Mrs. Campbell and Coyle.

The services of a professional hangman from Toronto were secured for the hanging, and since the gallows had been erected in the open prison yard and could be seen from neighbouring buildings, the back of it was boarded up to shield Phoebe from prying eyes. She left her cell shortly after eight o'clock, June 20, 1872, and walked with a steady step to her doom. Clutching in her hand an embroidered handkerchief, she knelt on the trap; the rope was fixed and she dropped through the opening. The execution was flawless, and when her body was examined, she was still holding the handkerchief in her fingers. She was buried later that afternoon in the prison yard.

On October 2, 1872, Thomas Coyle was finally charged with being an accessory to the fact of murder and came to trial before Chief Justice John Hagarty on October 7.

Mr. Kenneth McKenzie for the Crown had bad luck with his witnesses. William Taylor, the man who had sold the revolver, could not positively identify Coyle as the youth who had bought it. The star witness, reporter Nickols, confessed that he had lost the notebook in which he claimed to have recorded incriminating statements made by Coyle during the compassionate meeting with Mrs. Campbell; his testimony had to be given from memory. Unfortunately, his memory was not that strong, and defence counsel David Glass easily weakened most of the statements he was able to remember. By the time the Crown had finished its presentation, however, it appeared that enough material had been introduced to secure a conviction.

Defence lawyer David Glass presented the jurors with a picture of Coyle as a naive young man who was being pursued by an older woman. He had rejected her advances, and her accusation against him was the direct result of her anger at being rebuffed. To strengthen this point, he introduced a surprise witness, Mary Springstead. In July 1871, she had shared a cell with Phoebe Campbell and once took a letter from her to Coyle. He had refused to accept or read it, saying he did not want to have anything to do with her. David Glass also brought out the fact that when Detective Phair arranged the interview between the two in Coyle's cell, the lad had objected and again stated that he wanted no part of her.

The testimony of the three farmhands who shared Coyle's bedroom with him on the night of the murder was expected to be a strong point in the defence case, but under stern cross-examination by Prosecutor McKenzie they grudgingly admitted that it would have been possible for him to slip out of the attic and return without their knowledge.

When all the evidence was in and both lawyers had completed their pleas to the jurors, it seemed evident that there were only two questions for the jury to decide. Had Thomas Coyle purchased the revolver found in the murdered man's bedroom, and had he been there when murder was done? In his charge to the jury, Chief Justice Hagarty seemed to lean in favour of the prisoner.

The jury returned after less than an hour's deliberation and delivered a verdict of not guilty. After thanking them for their patience, Chief Justice Hagarty turned to the prisoner. While he had earlier given the impression that he would agree with such a decision, he now remarked that the jurors "had taken a merciful view of the case." He then discharged Coyle.

. . .

Elizabeth Workman
Something's Wrong with Jim

*I*N THE MALE-DOMINATED SOCIETY of the eighteenth and nineteenth centuries, the killing of a husband by his wife was considered to be the second-worst crime a human being could commit, treason being the first. Indeed, the fact that for some years it was classified as petit treason sheds grim light on the relationship of men to women. Husbands literally owned their wives and any rebellion against their authority was viewed gravely. A prime example of this was the May 14, 1733, execution of Marie-Josephte Corrieaue at Quebec City for the murder of her second husband. Her body was then displayed in an iron cage at Pointe Levy as a warning to other wives.

This was the official view and explains why, in some instances, Ministers of the Crown ignored the recommendations of the jurors and carried out the supreme penalty. Male authority had to be maintained. Gradually, the belief grew that women were the weaker sex—"more to be pitied than censured"—and wherever possible male jurors recommended mercy for them. That it did not always work was illustrated in the case of Elizabeth Workman of Mooretown, Ontario.

James Workman had earned his living as a labourer for a number of years in the picturesque little village of Mooretown, two jumps and a rollover south of Sarnia on the banks of the St. Clair

River, which flows from Lake Huron into Lake St. Clair. He was a large, raw-boned man with a reputation for quarrelling and a fondness for liquor. He had originally married a local girl and by her had a daughter and son. On her death, he had married Elizabeth, a woman much younger than himself.

As is so often the case when opposites attract, the new Mrs. Workman was a small woman of delicate features and gentle manner. She quickly earned recognition as a good mother to the two Workman children, a hard worker, and a devout church member.

James Workman was in his late fifties when he married Elizabeth, and while the marriage held promise in the beginning, it soon deteriorated. His ability to work decreased with age, and over the next six years he became sullen and irritable, and turned more and more to drinking. What few friends the family possessed were gradually driven away by his attitude and drinking. He became so abusive to his wife and children that the eldest left home and sought sanctuary with a lady at the opposite end of town. On several occasions, he beat his wife so badly that she also had to escape from him. Typically, however, she always returned home.

By the fall of 1872, the situation had begun to change. Tired of taking abuse, Elizabeth turned on the tyrannical old man, waiting until drink had sotted his brain and diminished his physical powers and then beating him. It was then often difficult to determine whether it was a case of husband beating wife or wife beating husband. Their home was a constant battleground of quarrelling and physical violence.

About October 1, 1872, a new element entered the picture. A black man by the name of Samuel Butler arrived in the village and opened a barber-shop a short distance from the Workman residence. Elizabeth Workman, who supplemented the family income by scrubbing and cleaning for homes and businesses in town, soon added the barber-shop to her janitorial services. Samuel Butler was a free-and-easy, outgoing man who loved whisky and company. Within a week, he had become a frequent visitor at the Workman home, always bringing a bottle of whisky with him. Though tongues clacked furiously in the village, there was no evidence to indicate that the Workmans and Butler were anything more than drinking buddies.

James Workman was a jealous husband. On Tuesday, October 22, he turned up at the barber-shop while she was working and demanded that she return home. She refused and the argument became heated. It ended with Butler seizing the older man by the collar and tossing him outside. Beyond a few scrapes from the gravel roadway, Workman was uninjured and picked himself up and disappeared, muttering dire threats and curses.

The Workmans occupied the ground floor of a small, two-storey house on the outskirts of the village. Their living quarters consisted of two rooms—a bedroom where they slept with the seven-year-old boy, and a kitchen that served all other purposes. On the second floor, David and Sarah Patterson lived in similar quarters. There was little sound-proofing between the two establishments, and the Pattersons had long endured the muffled sounds of shouting and blows coming from beneath them. They had listened with sardonic amusement over the months as the wife beating turned to husband bashing.

On the forenoon of Friday, October 25, Sarah Patterson heard the familiar sounds of a family argument rising from the ground floor; this was followed by the dull thud of several blows. The house was quiet until about two in the afternoon, when there was a repetition of the affair. This time she heard Elizabeth ask her husband if he had had enough. Mrs. Patterson's version of these spats was later confirmed by the young Workman lad, who said that his mother had beaten his father with a mop handle.

Several more blows were heard during the course of the day, but by nightfall all was quiet. David Patterson was later to attest that during the night he heard moaning coming from the bedroom below theirs. Unfortunately, David had a habit of mixing times and days and his recollections were not always reliable. Probably more accurate was his wife's statement that she heard James and Elizabeth talking rationally during the night.

On Saturday morning the arguments resumed, and once more the sounds of wood on flesh carried through the house.

Then all was quiet.

. . .

About three o'clock, David Patterson was working in the yard when Elizabeth Workman approached him. She said: "Something's wrong with Jim," and asked him to take a look. Patterson entered the bedroom and found Workman lying on his back. His face was a mass of blood and bruises. Without touching him, he sent the boy upstairs to call Mrs. Patterson.

Sarah, who was not as squeamish as her husband, checked the old man thoroughly and announced that he was dead. Mr. Patterson then ran out of the house hysterically screaming that murder had been done. Within a short space of time, neighbours came running and began to parade through the bedroom to view the corpse for themselves. This sightseeing did not end until Dr. Campbell, the local coroner, arrived and put a stop to it.

After a cursory examination of the body showed several massive bruises on the head and upper portion of the body, Dr. Campbell dispatched messengers to locate Dr. Oliver and the village constable.

Elizabeth freely admitted that she had beaten her husband with a mop the day before, but claimed that she had struck him no harder than usual. When the volunteer village policeman arrived, she was placed under arrest.

A hastily convened coroner's jury heard medical testimony that evening. James Workman had died of "haemorrhage of the brain," resulting from two specific wounds. These were cuts, rather than blows from a blunt instrument, and appeared to have been inflicted by an iron weapon. In Dr. Oliver's opinion, a mop handle could not have inflicted such injuries.

The inquest continued on Sunday, when David Patterson gave evidence that added a dramatic twist to the affair. He stated that about four o'clock on Saturday morning he had heard a noise outside, and on looking out from the upstairs bedroom window had seen Sam Butler, the barber, leaving the house. About two hours later, he had seen Butler return. The barber had remained in the house for some time and taken his leave around eight in the morning.

At the conclusion of the inquest, the jury found "that the deceased, James Workman, came to his death by excessive violent abuse, and then the evidence indicates us to believe that the said abuse was inflicted by Mrs. Workman, the wife of the deceased, or by Samuel Butler, or by both."

A warrant was issued for the arrest of Samuel Butler and he was taken into custody later that evening. Both suspects were transported to Sarnia and lodged in the county prison.

The two accused were brought to trial at Sarnia on March 21, 1873, before Mr. Justice Adam Wilson, later Sir Adam Wilson. A strict authoritarian, he had been born in Edinburgh, Scotland, in 1814, and after coming to Canada in 1830 had enjoyed a career in business before embarking upon politics and law. Raised to the bench in 1863, he was famous for his harsh judgements and unyielding attitude towards offenders.

The evidence against Elizabeth Workman was uncontested, and there was little question that hers was the hand that had struck the blows. The only outstanding issue was whether she intended to kill her husband. The case against her alleged accomplice, Samuel Butler, was not so clear-cut. From the very moment of his arrest he steadfastly denied that he had been in the house on Friday evening and Saturday morning. Elizabeth Workman corroborated this. There remained against him only the testimony of David Patterson.

Under the pressing examination of defence counsel, Mr. Mackenzie, David Patterson suddenly remembered that it was Friday morning, not Saturday, when he had seen the barber leave the Workman residence. At the conclusion of the prosecution's case, Judge Wilson ordered Samuel Butler to be discharged as there was no evidence against him.

In his charge to the jury, Mr. Justice Wilson seemed to sense that a feeling existed among them that they wished to return a verdict of lesser severity, for he summed up very strongly against her. Dwelling upon the prolonged nature of the beatings, he hinted that their only purpose had been to cause severe injury and that the accused had been reckless of the consequences of that injury. He closed by saying that James Workman's death was either murder or nothing.

Given these instructions, it was not surprising that the jury returned a verdict of guilty against the unfortunate woman, but they tempered their judgement by appending a strong recommendation to mercy.

It seemed that the Department of Justice officials were of the same opinion as His Lordship, for they ignored all pleas for clemency. The execution was set for May 19, 1873. A large number of petitions had been forwarded to Ottawa by defence counsel A.J. Mackenzie, however, and a respite of thirty days was given in order that they might be examined. This raised the hopes of the people of Sarnia that the sentence would be commuted to life, but it was not to be, and as time passed and no word was received from the capital, hope turned to alarm. Efforts were redoubled.

Finally, on June 11, a telegram was received from Prime Minister Sir John A. Macdonald, saying that he would be in Montreal the following day—as would the Governor-General, the Earl of

Dufferin—and would hear any further representations at that time. The Sarnia City Council, horrified at the prospect of hanging a woman in their town, met hurriedly and delegated Messrs. Mackenzie and Rae to carry a last plea to the government. In this petition, signed by the city council and members of the jury, attention was drawn to the fact that two years previously, a man named William Horton had been sentenced to hang at Sarnia for the shooting death of a man named Robinson, and his sentence had been altered to life. It was hoped that this example would be duplicated in the case of Mrs. Workman, a much more worthy subject. What the delegates did not know was that William Horton's sentence had been respited not from mercy but because of strong evidence that he was mentally ill.

The delegation sped to Montreal via the Grand Trunk Railway and met with His Excellency and the Prime Minister. Although they felt that their interviews had been productive, hardly had they arrived back in Sarnia when word came that their appeals had been denied and the execution would take place on June 19 as ordered.

Prior to 1869, executions were public spectacles carried on outside the prison walls. The law was changed that year to decree that all future hangings would take place inside the prison. The intent was not to make executions private, but merely to better control the audiences. Since all prison yards were small, the spectators could be more effectively supervised, and it was hoped by this means to avoid the violent riots and disturbances of the past. A hanging was still a public affair; once the event moved inside the prison walls, provisions were made to issue invitations to the public. These black-bordered cards could be obtained simply by applying to the local sheriff. As the day of Elizabeth Workman's death drew near, only a few applied for tickets.

The scaffold, erected in a rear section of Sarnia's prison yard, had a grave dug directly beneath it. A rough wooden coffin was placed in the excavation so she would literally drop into her own bier.

Mrs. Workman and the hangman were the calmest people in attendance as she stepped onto the trap carrying a handkerchief and some white flowers in her right hand. The executioner, imported from Toronto, wore no mask but had blackened his face to conceal his identity. At a gesture from the county sheriff, whose name had been on the petitions begging for mercy, the hangman pulled the lever and she dropped to her death. She died instantly of a broken neck. After hanging for twenty minutes, her body was viewed by a coroner's jury and then lowered into the coffin. Dirt was shovelled over it.

. . .

Alice Davis

The Coffin on the Move

*C*ONTRARY TO POPULAR OPINION, most killers make no effort to conceal the body of their victim. They leave it in plain view. The case of Alice and Arthur Davis, of Toronto, was remarkable not for the nature of the murder, but for the manner in which the guilty pair tried to cloak their act. Had the reason not been so tragic, their efforts would have qualified as high comedy.

The crazy sequence of events began on the morning of Saturday, July 31, 1875, when a man known as Dr. Arthur Paul Davis approached William Fraser, carpenter, and asked him to saw some boards to make a box. This box would be two by two by six feet. Fraser offered to put the box together, but Dr. Davis assured him that this would not be necessary. The carpenter met his customer's specifications and delivered the boards to the Davis home at 33 Scott Street that afternoon.

Later the same day, Mrs. Alice Davis went to the livery stable of a man named Dunning and asked him to bring a horse and buggy around to the doctor's office at No. 4 Exchange Lane. The outfit would be returned later in the day. He dropped the horse and rig at the rendezvous about five in the afternoon.

. . .

Toronto at this stage of its development had a two-tier system of policing its streets at night. In addition to the regular constables, a cadre of night-watchmen made routine tours of the business section, checking doors and windows and keeping an eye out for unusual happenings.

Towards eleven o'clock, one of the latter, Robert Campbell, saw a horse and buggy standing in front of the Davis home on Scott Street. On his next circuit, he saw a man and woman carrying an oblong box from the house to the buggy. The woman was Alice Davis. The box looked like a coffin. His suspicions aroused, he kept in the shadows, and when the couple drove off, he followed the buggy to the end of the street. When the rig turned north towards Bloor Street, he broke off contact and went to look for a policeman.

Constable McClelland also found the circumstances peculiar and went directly to the Central Police Station, where he reported his observations to Detective Henry Reburn. Reburn assured him that there was nothing unusual about coffins being transported at night, adding that some undertakers did this in order to protect the sensibilities of passers-by. Usually such caskets were destined for a smaller town or village and were taken to the Great Western station for shipment by rail the next day. It was a quiet night, however, and he decided to check on this particular one.

Arriving at the Great Western station, Detective Henry Reburn and Constable McClelland learned that no coffin had been left there, nor was any expected. Puzzled, they returned to the police station. Out of curiosity, Detective Reburn checked the register of doctors in Toronto and failed to find the name of Dr. Davis, resident at 33 Scott Street. There was an Arthur Davis there, but he was not listed as a physician. He then drove with McClelland to the Davis home and noted a light in an upstairs window, but due to the lateness of the hour he did not announce his presence but returned to the police station.

In the meantime, the horse and buggy with its oblong box had been seen by another night-watchman. Charles Elliott was patrolling along Wellington Street shortly after midnight when he saw the rig approaching. He stopped it and chatted with the two occupants on the front seat. The woman, later identified as Alice Davis, informed him that they were delivering the coffin to a small village north of the city. His curiosity allayed, he stepped aside and allowed them to proceed.

About an hour later, Mrs. Davis appeared at the livery stable and returned the horse and buggy. She apologized for being so late—it was then nearly two o'clock—but said that her errands had taken much longer than anticipated. After receiving his fee, Mr. Dunning drove her first to the doctor's clinic at No. 4 Exchange Lane, but the windows being dark, he drove her on to 33 Scott Street and left her there.

· · ·

Dawn broke cold and misty over Toronto the next morning, Sunday, August 1, and Charles Lovell kept his head down as he hurried along Bloor Street to his place of employment. By pure chance, he happened to stop and look around as he came opposite a small park. His eye was attracted to some new upturned dirt a few feet back from the roadway, and as he investigated he saw the yellowish colour of new pine lumber beneath the sods. Brushing the dirt aside, he saw what looked like a coffin, but he jerked his hand away when it touched what appeared to be blood around one of the cracks between two boards.

A police constable, John Albert, was called and he took charge of the spot. He had passed the park the evening before and the box had not been there. With the assistance of another officer, John Hendry, he carried the coffin to the Mantel Hotel, a short distance away. Opening it, they found the nearly naked body of a young woman inside. The sweet smell of putrescence assailed their nostrils and they hastily closed the coffin.

After a doctor gave his opinion that the young woman had died as the result of a bungled abortion, the corpse was removed to the Dead House, where several persons identified it as the remains of Jane Vaughn Gilmour.

Jane Gilmour, a twenty-three-year-old Scottish lass, had come to Canada three years previously with her father, John Gilmour. She had earned a living as a live-in maid with several Toronto families, among them John Clements, a former alderman. She had left his place on July 6 and had last been seen alive at Union Station on the afternoon of July 24, a week before her body was discovered.

Detective Henry Reburn was placed in charge of the case, and scarcely had the discovery of the coffin on Bloor Street been reported when he had suspects in mind. Waiting only for medical confirmation that murder had been committed, he went to the home of "Dr." Arthur Davis on Scott Street and questioned the couple. Both Arthur and his wife denied all knowledge of the coffin or the woman inside. Nevertheless, Reburn placed them under arrest and began a painstaking door-to-door inquiry in the district.

Throughout that Sunday and the following Monday, teams of police scoured the area, and their efforts were rewarded with several significant finds. A wooden barrel behind the Whyte Saloon contained articles of clothing identified as belonging to Jane Gilmour, and a small satchel holding some of her personal items and jewels was also located. These were familiar items to Mrs. John Clements, in whose home Jane had worked. The Davis home on Scott Street yielded more articles of clothing along with a bloodstained mattress, while a search of the clinic at No. 4 Exchange Lane turned up medicine and surgical instruments normally used in abortions.

By interviewing dozens of people, Detective Reburn was able to find the man who had cut the lumber, the watchman who had seen the coffin in the buggy, and the livery man who had supplied the vehicle. The rig was traced turning onto Bloor Street, but it was assumed that something or someone had intruded on the killers as they were burying the body and forced them to flee before the task was completed. Questioning a Mrs. Maria Anderson, who owned a boarding-house whose windows overlooked the Davis residence, Reburn learned that Jane Gilmour had been seen entering the house on Saturday, July 24. Mrs. Anderson had also seen other young women going there and had long suspected that the Davis pair were operating an abortion clinic.

The man and woman were brought to trial in Toronto on October 13, 1875, before Mr. Justice Joseph Morrison. The event attracted a good deal of attention, but for the most part, the courtroom seats were occupied by women. Mr. MacKenzie, for the Crown, easily proved that Arthur Davis was practising medicine without a licence, and that he had brought about Jane Gilmour's death through a terrible mistake in procedure. Even under the best of conditions in 1875, abortions were tricky. Mr. MacKenzie traced the actions of the accused from the construction of the coffin to its discovery in the park. The defence offered no witnesses or evidence to offset the damning chain of circumstance.

There was little sympathy for Arthur and Alice Davis among the jurors, and after only an hour and a half of deliberation on Saturday evening, October 16, they found them guilty. When they were sentenced to be hanged on December 8, 1875, it was the first time in the history of Toronto that a woman had been thus condemned. The gentlemen of the press adopted a more favourable attitude, and while they evoked little sympathy for the man, they presented her as the dupe of her husband: "It is a woman's ambition to marry well, and she, as a farmer's daughter from the state of New York, no doubt thought she was doing well to marry Dr. Davis," wrote one reporter.

Though the jury did not recommend mercy in either instance, the government took a more lenient view of the crime, and on November 30 issued an Order in Council commuting both sentences to life imprisonment. After serving only five years, Alice Davis was deported from Kingston Penitentiary in 1881 and returned to her native New York. Her husband served a few more years before being released with the strong suggestion that he take his talents elsewhere.

. . .

Teenie Maloney
The Benefit of the Doubt

W*ARWARA MALONEY* was a tiny woman, standing less than five feet in height and tipping the scales at under a hundred pounds, but within that miniature frame she packed enormous energy and could work seemingly endless hours without tiring. Born in Austria in 1880, she came to Canada with her family before the turn of the century and settled in the prairie West. Like many immigrants from central Europe, her father changed his Austrian name to avoid the prejudices so prevalent in the early days, and became known as Maloney. Likewise, Warwara dropped her Christian name and took that of Teenie.

Teenie Maloney was a frugal woman who saved every penny she earned as a maid at various farms in southwest Manitoba, and by the time she was twenty-five she had put away a sizeable dowry. She was, in the parlance of the frontier, "a good catch." On November 1, 1906, at the age of twenty-six, she married a man named Tomin and they purchased a farm. It is not known whether this was her first marriage or not. In 1908, her husband deserted her and was never heard from again, and after a suitable period, she obtained a divorce. In the meantime, she continued to run the farm with the assistance of various hired men. In 1910, she rented her land and took employment with William G. Hamilton of Hamiota, Manitoba.

The Hamiltons were among the earliest pioneers of the farming district northwest of Brandon, having homesteaded two kilometres (one mile) east of Hamiota in the 1880s. After the death of her husband Thomas on January 21, 1911, Mary Hamilton had continued to reside on the property but turned the management over to her eldest son, William, who was unmarried. Though she was then eighty years of age, Mary Hamilton took an active part in household chores and resented her son spending money on a helper. She had a sharp tongue and let her son know that she did not like Teenie.

After two years of trying to cope with Mary Hamilton, Teenie left and took employment at Shoal Lake, a farming community to the north. When the old lady became ill, however, William sought out Teenie and persuaded her to return as his housekeeper and to take care of his mother. That was in late 1912.

The exact relationship between Teenie and William remains a bit of a mystery. They were both strong, silent people who never discussed personal affairs with friends or relatives. It is known that from January 1913 to March 1916 he did not pay her wages and owed her a considerable sum. In addition, in 1914 she sold her farm for eight hundred dollars and loaned him the money at 8 percent interest. The loan and interest came due on December 31, 1915, but he was unable to repay her. By March 1916, his total indebtedness to her amounted to just over fourteen hundred dollars.

On the other hand, the association between Mary Hamilton and Teenie Maloney was well known. Mrs. Hamilton still did not like Teenie and was constantly after William to "get rid of that woman." Nevertheless, according to the independent testimony of the two hired men, Teenie was both kindly and tolerant towards her employer's mother.

On the morning of Tuesday, March 21, 1916, things appeared normal on the Hamilton farm. After breakfast the two hired men—Constantine Schmidt and Philip Kaler—left for work and William Hamilton prepared for a trip to Hamiota. Just as he was leaving, Mary Hamilton asked him in Teenie's presence when he was going to fire her. He gave her an evasive answer, as always, and left.

Teenie Maloney is the only source of information on the events of the next few hours. She said Mary announced that she was going to make dinner for the family. Accordingly, Teenie left her in the kitchen and went to her room on the upper floor, where she was making a quilt. She came downstairs just before eleven o'clock and discovered that the meal had not been prepared, and assuming that Mrs. Hamilton had gone back to bed, she bustled about making dinner.

When the hired men came in for their noon meal, they found Teenie to be her usual, capable self. They noticed a scratch on her nose that had not been there at breakfast, but she explained that she had been chopping wood and a piece had flown up and struck her in the face.

William Hamilton returned from Hamiota about one o'clock and Teenie served his dinner in the kitchen. When he had finished, she asked him if he would start a gas generator in the cellar; she had never mastered the art of firing it to supply electricity.

Reaching the bottom of the cellar stairs, William discovered his mother lying there dead. Her face was covered with ugly bruises and cuts and there was a good deal of blood on the upper portions of her dress. At first glance, she appeared to have fallen downstairs. Dr. Hudson was called from the village, but after inspecting the body and the wooden construction of the stairwell, he reached the conclusion that not all the wounds had been caused by the fall. Some were much too severe.

After a more thorough examination of the body in his office, Dr. Hudson was convinced that Mary Hamilton had been murdered, and he conveyed his suspicions to Constable J.A. Stewart of the Manitoba Provincial Police in town. In turn, Constable Stewart telephoned to Brandon and talked with ace criminal investigator John R. Foster, who immediately left by car for Hamiota.

Detective Foster, then in his thirty-fifth year as an investigator for the force, had gained considerable acclaim over the years. Talking with Teenie Maloney, he learned that she had heard no loud noises while she was in her room sewing. Likewise, the two hired men had not seen anyone about the farm premises during the time Mary Hamilton was presumed to have been murdered. As a precautionary measure, Foster checked in Hamiota and learned that William Hamilton had an alibi for the time of his mother's death, which was assumed to have taken place between ten and eleven that morning.

On March 18, a coroner's jury returned a verdict that Mary had met her death at the hands of a person or persons unknown.

After reviewing the known facts, Detective Foster decided to hold Teenie Maloney in the local lock-up as a material witness, and once she was out of the house he concentrated on an inch-by-inch search of the ground floor. Although he did not locate any possible weapons, he found a place near the dining-room table where bloodstains appeared to have been washed away. There were more spots in the archway between the dining-room and the kitchen, and still more near the kitchen table. All had been washed thoroughly, but some residue remained in the cracks of the wooden flooring. He took sample scrapings of these to Dr. Gordon Bell, pathologist at the hospital in Brandon, along with some articles of the maid's clothing.

Dr. Bell was only able to state that the samples were blood, but could not identify them as human blood.

Believing that Teenie Maloney had attacked Mrs. Hamilton in the dining-room and that the assault had continued in the kitchen, Detective Foster arrested her and charged her with murder. She was brought before Magistrates Raymer and Anderson at Hamiota on March 24, and sufficient evidence was presented to warrant having her held for trial. Taking the stand in her own defence, she stoutly denied that she had anything to do with a murder, claiming that Mrs. Hamilton must have fallen downstairs by herself.

The evidence presented at her trial, which opened before His Lordship Mr. Galt at Minnedosa, Manitoba, on November 27, 1916, was purely circumstantial. The Crown suggested that the two had quarrelled and Teenie had attacked. After throwing the body in the cellar, she had cleaned the floors and either disposed of her weapon or cleaned it thoroughly. There was a subtle hint that Teenie had hopes of becoming Mrs. William Hamilton and that only the old woman stood in the way. That might account for the savagery of the attack. Evidence suggested that the only way Teenie would get her money out of Hamilton was through marriage or a lawsuit.

Mr. Justice Galt, who followed William Hamilton's evidence very carefully, later speculated that William might have "suggested" to Teenie that only the old woman stood in the way of their marriage.

Messrs. Buckingham and St. John, who appeared for the prisoner, placed her on the stand and meticulously led her through the story she had told in the beginning and which she was to maintain to the end. She had left Mrs. Hamilton in the kitchen, gone upstairs to do some sewing, and had heard nothing until she came down to find dinner unprepared. That was all she knew about the matter. Detective Foster had already testified that he had conducted some experiments on noise and was unable to say whether noises downstairs could be heard by the woman if her bedroom door was closed.

The trial wound up on November 30. The jury took two hours to conclude that the only logical suspect was Teenie Maloney. Although their verdict was guilty, they expressed their continuing uncertainty by adding an unusually strong recommendation to mercy. They might have found for manslaughter had the killer not thrown the body down the stairs and cleaned up afterwards to conceal the manner in which the death had occurred.

Mr. Justice Galt sentenced her to be hanged at Minnedosa on February 21, 1917. In a detailed report to the Minister of Justice, His Lordship wrote:

> It seems almost incredible that under the circumstances disclosed in the evidence, the prisoner could have suddenly changed from a competent and useful human being into a cruel and savage murderess and that after accomplishing such a prolonged attack upon a comparatively helpless old lady [Mrs. Hamilton was eighty-five] she could revert once more in the short space of an hour or less to her usual every day behaviour."

The whole tenor of his report, while it leaned to her guilt, strongly suggested a commutation of sentence. In a mild understatement, he remarked that it was improbable that Teenie Maloney would ever collect the money owed her.

In response to His Lordship's remarks and their own scrutiny of the trial evidence, the agents of the Minister of Justice recommended to Cabinet that the death sentence be commuted to fifteen years of imprisonment. On February 15, 1917, the Governor-General issued an Order in Council carrying out this suggestion. The reason given for Executive Clemency was that "The condemned woman was given benefit of doubt as to her guilt."

After serving just over seven years of that sentence, Teenie Maloney was given a Ticket of Leave, or parole, and on January 26, 1924, was released to Toronto under the auspices of a prisoners' aid society.

. . .

Carmello Marablito

No Apparent Motive

*T*HE ONLY UNCONTESTED FACT about the death of Peter Marablito near Stellarton, Nova Scotia, on June 27, 1917, was that he had been murdered. Beyond that, the case was a mass of innuendoes, suppositions, and conjectures. Even after twelve good men and true found two people guilty of the slaying, His Lordship, Mr. Justice B. Russell, was so concerned about a miscarriage of justice that he wrote to both the Minister of Justice and the Secretary of State recommending commutations of both sentences lest an innocent person suffer the supreme penalty of the law.

The mystery began in the early morning hours of June 28, 1917. Harold Hanes and his brother, Fred, were on their way to work along a little-used path to the MacGregor Pit Mine at Evansville, near Stellarton, when they came across the body of a man lying beside the trail. It was then about six-twenty. The man was lying on his back with a coat wrapped around his head. His chest and neck were bare. There were two deep cuts on his neck, one of which had almost severed his head from his body, leaving only a thin strip of flesh at the nape of his neck to keep the two together. The second cut was shallower and had not severed the spine. Surprisingly, despite the severity of the wounds, there was little blood on the ground around him. A revolver was found close to his left hand, but an examination revealed that it had not been discharged.

They reported their grisly find to Constable George Davidson, who in turn notified Chief Watters. After absorbing the impact of their report, Watters assigned veteran detective Peter Owen Carroll to investigate the crime.

The victim was quickly identified as Peter Marablito, forty-five, a miner who worked the morning shift at the MacGregor Mine. He lived in a house about 400 metres (440 yards) from where his body was found. Dr. C.S. Elliott, who examined the corpse, explained the absence of blood by saying that the man had died instantly and therefore his heart had stopped pumping. He could not say for sure whether the man had been killed there or murdered elsewhere and his body carried down.

A police officer was sent to the Marablito residence to inform Mrs. Carmello Marablito, forty-three, of her husband's death, but he found no one home. Some time later in the morning, he located her in the village in the company of two young men. One was Natali Neri, twenty-two, a friend of the family, and the other was Victor Pratti, a young Italian who worked in the mine and boarded at the Marablito home. All three appeared stunned and shocked when he informed them of the murder. Mrs. Marablito, whose face showed signs of previous weeping, broke out crying again and nearly collapsed. It was Victor Pratti, sometimes called Bracti, who gave the explanation for their presence in the village.

Pratti said he had worked his usual afternoon shift at the mines the previous day and had returned home around eleven-thirty at night to find Mrs. Marablito and Natali Neri in a state of concern. Mrs. Marablito had evidently been crying, but made him a cup of tea. She explained her tears by saying that her husband had gone out about eight-thirty to the village for some medicine but had not returned, and they were worried something had happened to him.

Victor Pratti had drunk his tea and retired for the night, but around two-thirty in the morning the other two had awakened him with the news that Peter had not yet returned home. At their request, he had accompanied them and they had spent several hours visiting various homes in the area in search of the missing man. From time to time, Carmello had broken out in new bursts of crying.

Natali Neri and Mrs. Marablito corroborated Victor Pratti's account.

The domestic situation at the Marablito home was simple, and quite characteristic of the district. Peter and Carmello, childless, lived in one-half of a single-storey company home about halfway between the mine and Evansville. Both were Italian. In 1914, Victor Pratti arrived from Italy and Peter got him a job in the MacGregor Mine. Some time later, Victor came to live with them as a boarder.

The other half of the company house was occupied by Alphonse and Eugenia Lemail, who kept several boarders. On being questioned, none of them recalled hearing any noise or unusual activity in the Marablito half of the building the previous evening. The Lemails reported that Peter and Carmello were excellent neighbours and that there was never any quarrelling or other disturbance. They had few visitors, except Natali Neri, who was almost like a boarder. Beyond the fact that Carmello and Natali referred to each other as brother and sister, there was no hint of a love triangle. On the contrary, Mrs. Marablito was in such poor health—people said it was her heart—that she was in no condition to "carry on."

. . .

Detective Carroll had very few options as he tried to fathom the murder. Peter Marablito might have been the victim of a robbery attempt, except that his wallet was intact and the trail where he was found was seldom used. When all reports indicated that he was a passive, friendly man whose only fault was an overfondness for wine, Carroll was inclined to rule out a revenge killing. That left only a family motive, and he thus concentrated on the Marablito home for further clues.

Like most families in the district, the Marablitos had the inevitable axe and hatchet. These were taken away for examination but showed no presence of blood. Likewise, there was no evidence of blood having been washed from the floor. The only suspicious find was a mat that had been thrown into a crawl space, or subcellar, beneath the kitchen floor. There were traces of blood on this, but not to the extent that might be expected considering the massive cuts on the victim's throat. And though all the clothing in the house was examined, none yielded any bloodstains.

Despite this lack of evidence, Carroll was convinced that Peter Marablito had been murdered in his own home. Because of the sickly condition of the wife, it was probable that either Natali Neri or Victor Pratti had killed him. Further, even though Peter Marablito weighed only 59 kilograms (130 pounds), it was unlikely that Mrs. Marablito had carried his body 400 metres down the trail. The corpse had undoubtedly been moved by Pratti and Neri. The motive? A love triangle between Natali and the woman? On the basis of this reasoning, he arrested all three and lodged them in prison that afternoon. Natali Neri was charged with murder, and the other two as accessories.

While awaiting preliminary hearing, all three gave statements and all three told the same story. Peter Marablito had left the house at eight-thirty to get some medicine in the village. He had not returned, and around two-thirty they had gone looking for him.

They knew nothing beyond this until informed by the police that his body had been found in the woods. The blood on the old mat in the cellar was from a small animal that had been killed.

Detective Carroll continued his digging, interviewing dozens of witnesses in an attempt to prove that Carmello and Natali were lovers, despite the age difference. The best he could come up with was one woman who remembered seeing the couple lying on a bed together, but even this had dubious value since Peter Marablito had also been present.

There were a great many rumours in the district about the murder and its motive, and one of these concerned a horse. In a biography of Detective Carroll, N. Carroll MacIntyre relates that after the murder, the killers were carrying the body down the trail to bury it when they heard a noise. It was from a grey horse, startled at their approach in the darkness, that had begun to run. Thinking that someone was nearby, the murderers dropped the body and fled. Such a story could only have arisen from a statement made by one of the participants, and MacIntyre leaves the impression that Carroll heard it from one of the accused. None of the defendants made any statements that were allowed into evidence, however, and the story smacks of folklore.*

Despite this total lack of evidence, the three appeared for a preliminary hearing and were committed for trial.

Believing that Victor Pratti knew more than he was revealing and that he might give damaging evidence if there was some hope of immunity, Crown Prosecutor Graham split the trio. Only Carmello Marablito and Natali Neri appeared before Mr. Justice Russell and jury in late October 1917. Pratti, though indicted, never stood trial, and all charges against him were later dropped.

Prosecutor Graham, assisted by Messrs. Dickson and Sinclair, made great efforts, but the evidence sounded weak and inconclusive. The only item even remotely associated with the case was the bloodstained mat, and there was no proof that the blood on it was human. All else was innuendo and circumstance. The star witness, Victor Pratti, took the stand but made no startling disclosures. He told the same story under direct and cross-examination that he gave the police the morning after the discovery of the body.

Apparently believing that the Crown's case was so flimsy that

---

* N. Carroll MacIntyre, *The Life and Adventures of Detective Peter Owen Carroll*, 1985.

there was no need to place his clients on the stand to reinforce Pratti's version, defence counsel William Macdonald did not advance a defence. He confined his attack to poking holes in the obviously weak Crown presentation.

To everyone's astonishment, the jury seemed to adopt the position that "if they did not do it, who else did?" On October 26, they returned a verdict of guilty against both Carmello Marablito and Natali Neri. Both prisoners were recommended to mercy but the jurors gave no reasons.

Shocked by the verdict, His Lordship had no recourse but to sentence both to be hanged at Pictou on January 15, 1918. He hurried from his bench and immediately composed letters to the Minister of Justice and the Secretary of State suggesting that there might have been a miscarriage of justice and recommending commutations.

The question of guilt in the instance of Carmello Marablito was solved without political intervention. Her health deteriorated rapidly in the death cell, and on December 24 she died of a heart attack.

Efforts continued to have Natali Neri's sentence commuted, and a huge petition went forward on his behalf. He maintained his innocence to the end. Along with the trial transcripts that were sent to the Department of Justice in Ottawa, however, someone included a damaging police communication providing material that was not permitted in evidence. Apparently on the basis of this secret report the decision was taken not to interfere with the sentence, and the death warrant was accordingly issued.

The last execution at Pictou had taken place in 1865, when a man named McPhair had been hanged in public at Hospital Point. An immense throng numbering in the thousands had attended from all parts of the colony. In contrast, the hanging of Natali Neri was a most private matter. A scaffold was erected inside the prison and on January 15, 1918, Arthur Ellis performed his deadly function swiftly and efficiently.

After that, the question of guilt or innocence was academic.

· · ·

Epilogue

*T*HE LAST WOMAN hanged in Canada was Mrs. Marguerite Pitre, executed at Bordeaux Jail on January 9, 1953. The last woman to be condemned was Lina Voisine in 1954. During the next fourteen years no woman was sentenced to death, and on December 29, 1967, the death penalty was abolished in all cases except for the murder of a prison guard or police officer. Again, no woman was convicted of a murder under these conditions. Finally, on July 26, 1976, capital punishment was replaced by incarceration for life.

Whatever one's personal convictions on the subject of capital punishment, history seems to indicate that the issue will continue to come before us with first one side and then the other victorious. Certain it is that if the death penalty returns, women will again stand within the shadow of the noose.

· · ·

References

Anderson, Frank. *Hanging in Canada: A Concise History of Capital Punishment.* Calgary, 1973.

Borthwick, Douglas. *History of Montreal Prisons.* Montreal, 1907.

Campbell, Lyall. *Sable Island.* Windsor, 1974.

Campbell, Marjorie Freeman. *A Mountain and a City.* Toronto, 1966.

——. *Torso.* Toronto, 1974.

Cell, Gillian T. *English Enterprises in Newfoundland, 1577 to 1660.* Toronto, 1969.

Couglan, D.W.F. "History and Function of Probation," *RCMP Quarterly,* January 1963.

Ellis, Arthur. *Memoirs.* Unpublished manuscript loaned to the author by Ellis's lawyer, the late Alex Edmison.

Fagan, Sgt. John, RCMP. "Early Prison Customs in Newfoundland," *RCMP Quarterly,* July 1962.

Firth, Edith G. *The Town of York, 1793 to 1815.* Toronto, 1962.

——. *The Town of York, 1815 to 1834.* Toronto, 1966.

Jenkins, Kathleen. *Montreal.* New York, 1966.

Kelley, Thomas P. *Famous Canadian Crimes.* Toronto, 1949.

Kidman, John. *The Canadian Prison.* Toronto, 1947.

Kirby, William. *The Golden Dog.* Toronto, 1863.

Leacock, Stephen. *Leacock's Montreal.* Toronto, 1963.

MacIntyre, N. Carroll. *The Life and Adventures of Detective Peter Owen Carroll.* Antigonish, 1985.

The Makers of Canada Series. Toronto, 1910.

O'Neill, Paul. The Oldest City. Don Mills, 1928.

——. *Seaport Legacy.* Don Mills, 1928.

Parole in Canada. Report of the Senate Standing Committee on Legal and Constitutional Affairs, Ottawa, 1974.

Randall, T.H. *Halifax, Warden of the North.* New York, 1965.

Roberts, Leslie. *Montreal.* Toronto, 1969.

Scadding, Henry. *Toronto of Old.* Lindsay, 1966.

Wade, Mason. *The French Canadians.* Toronto, 1955.

About the Author

*B*ORN IN BRANDON in 1919, Frank W. Anderson has been a prairie boy ever since. Graduating from the University of Saskatchewan in 1955 with a Bachelor of Arts, he went on to complete his Master of Social Work at Toronto in 1957. After serving as Executive Secretary of Calgary's John Howard Society and Senior Social Worker at the Provincial Guidance Clinic, he went into private practice as a consultant. In addition to his private work, he headed the Department of Social Welfare at Mount Royal Junior College, where the students later set up a scholarship in his honour. In 1974 he was appointed to the National Parole Board of Canada and served as Senior Member for the Prairie Division until his retirement.

In 1960, he and his wife, Edna, began Frontier Books, a series of thirty booklets on western history by authors such as Ken Liddell, Dr. Hugh Dempsey, Tom Primrose, and W.O. Mitchell. The series has earned two historical awards, and CFAC-TV in Calgary has produced twenty-six television programs based on the stories.

Frank and Edna currently reside in Saskatoon, where they continue to publish stories on crime and popular western history.